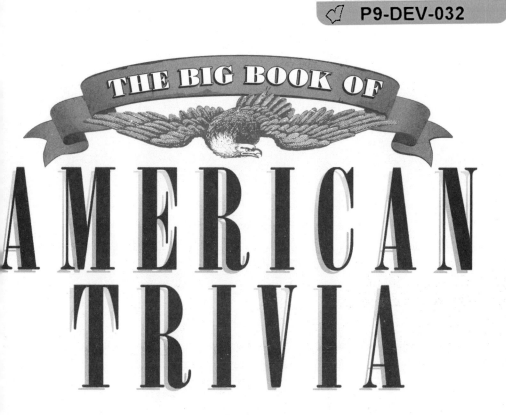

THE BIG BOOK OF

AMERICAN TRIVIA

★ ★ ★

J. STEPHEN LANG

Tyndale House Publishers, Inc.

CAROL STREAM, ILLINOIS

Visit Tyndale online at www.tyndale.com.

TYNDALE and Tyndale's quill logo are registered trademarks of Tyndale House Publishers, Inc.

The Big Book of American Trivia

Designed by Ron Kaufmann

Library of Congress Cataloging-in-Publication Data

Lang, J. Stephen.
 The big book of American trivia / J. Stephen Lang. — [Star-spangled ed.].
   p. cm.
 ISBN 978-1-4143-6454-4 (sc)
1. United States—Miscellanea. 2. Popular culture—United States—Miscellanea. I. Title.
 E156.L36 2011
 973—dc23   2011033958

Originally published in 1997 under ISBN 978-0-8423-8313-4.

Printed in the United States of America

17 16 15 14
 7   6   5   4

CONTENTS

★ ★

★ ★

PART THIRTEEN:

Things of the Spirit

PART FOURTEEN:

America Month by Month

★　★　★

PREFACE TO THE STAR-SPANGLED EDITION

★

IN HONOR OF THE TWO-HUNDREDTH ANNIVERSARY OF OUR NATIONAL ANTHEM, we present this updated edition of the original book, first published in 1997. The years between then and now have been exciting and eventful—perhaps, in cases such as September 11, 2001, *too* eventful. However, one positive result of the 9/11 attacks and their aftermath has been a deepening of Americans' patriotism. We may find much to complain about and we may find the news making us increasingly cynical, but when all is said and done, we are a deeply patriotic nation. And most people who stand to sing "The Star-Spangled Banner" put their hearts into it. Francis Scott Key would be pleased to know that the words he penned in 1814 on the back of an envelope are still being sung with gusto two centuries later.

The first edition of this book included a set of questions on flags ("Grand Old Flags") in part eleven. That set appears in this edition as well, but we've also added a new set of questions, "You're a Grand Old Anthem," about the song's history. Plus we've added more questions dealing with events of the still-in-progress twenty-first century.

INTRODUCTION

★

IS IT POSSIBLE THAT, with so many people fascinated with trivia and with such a great subject (America), no one has yet published a book of *American trivia*? It seems so. The book you are now holding is designed to fill that gap.

The problem is this: What to include? The possibilities seem endless.

Entertainment is a huge category and includes so much—music (pop, country, classical, and so on), television, movies, radio. Related is the whole category of **the arts**, with drama, museums, painting, sculpture. Also related is **literature**, including not only the classics but also newspapers and magazines. Likewise related is **leisure time**—clubs, holidays, parades, toys (and that Great American Toy, the automobile).

What about **places**? Geography need not be dull, not if you're curious about American place names, the great tourist attractions in states and cities, even things such as theme parks. (If your family is on a road trip, these questions are a great place to start.)

Knowing how most people love their home turf, I felt a section that included **state** questions was essential—ten questions about each state (and D.C., too), to be exact.

Then there is **history**. Of course, we all know more about our own century than any other, right? So there is a section on **the decades of the twentieth century**—a few questions on each decade, hitting the high points and bringing up a few oddities too.

Above all, there are **people**—from Pocahontas to Edgar Allan Poe to Abraham Lincoln to Mark Twain to Babe Ruth to Neil Armstrong to Oliver North. Our American family portrait includes millions of faces—not all pretty but always intriguing.

Under these broad categories are more than 150 topical sections. Included are "TV Record Holders," "Funny Names on the Map," "Beasts and Zoos and Such," "Grand Old Flags," "Great Americans on Film," "The Bible in America," "Halls of Fame," "Creating the American Song," and so on. I could not include *every* subject, but the range is wide—inventions; comic strips; famous women; rivers; advertising; quotations; word origins; and many, many others.

The topics are organized in fourteen parts. But despite the attempt at organization, the book is for browsing. It was made to fill up your family's time on a car trip, your daily commute on the train, the hour you spend waiting at the dentist's office, the times when you and the other people in your car pool are in the mood for a game of "quiz me." In other words, the book is designed to be read randomly, anywhere, and with no preparation of any kind. It is designed to entertain the person who unashamedly likes to be entertained—and challenged.

As the writing of this book progressed, it truly became a labor of love. After traveling abroad numerous times, I find that my home country is still the most fascinating, the one that lends itself most readily to the kind of book you are now holding.

If you find yourself able to answer every question in this book correctly, give yourself an A-plus in American studies. If not, then after reading this, you may consider yourself a little more knowledgeable, maybe even a little more appreciative, of this vast, enchanting land.

PART ONE

FOR THE RECORD

★ Biggest, Widest, Mostest: U.S. Records

1. With a thirty-five-foot-thick waist, she is probably the largest woman in America. Who is she? (Hint: statue)
2. The largest football stadium, seating 109,901, is found in what state?
3. What southern state (according to one study) has the highest percentage of obese adults?
4. In terms of revenue, what package delivery firm is the nation's largest transport company?
5. What Native American tribe, the largest in the U.S., also has the largest reservation?
6. The nation's tallest sand dunes are in what western state?
7. What is the distinction of the golf course at Cloudcroft, New Mexico? (Hint: clouds)
8. The world's largest aquarium opened in 2005 in what city?
9. The nation's largest maritime museum is Mystic Seaport in what New England state?
10. FedEx Field, the largest pro football stadium, is in what state?
11. What is the largest Protestant denomination in the U.S.? (Hint: south)
12. Quantico, Virginia, has the largest base for which military branch?
13. What landlocked state contains the largest saltwater body in the U.S.?
14. What is distinctive about the thirteen-thousand-acre South Mountain Preserve in Phoenix, Arizona?
15. What state capital is closest to the equator?
16. The smallest county in the U.S. has a huge population. What county is it?
17. What is the "anchorman" in each year's graduating class from the U.S. Naval Academy?
18. What southwestern state has the largest Native American population in the United States?
19. What state is home of the country's largest ranch?
20. The largest moose population in the forty-eight contiguous states is in which New England state?
21. Ribbon Falls, the U.S.'s highest waterfall, is in what western state?
22. The country's largest theology school, Southwestern Baptist Theological Seminary, is where?
23. What New England state has the lowest population east of the Mississippi?

QUESTIONS

Biggest, Widest, Mostest: U.S. Records // *Answers*

1. The Statue of Liberty
2. Michigan; it's Michigan Stadium in Ann Arbor.
3. Mississippi (Must be all that good southern cooking . . .)
4. UPS, United Parcel Service
5. The Navajo; the reservation covers more than twenty-five thousand square miles in three states.
6. Colorado; found in the Great Sand Dunes National Monument; some are seven hundred feet high.
7. It is the *highest* golf course in the country, at an elevation of over eight thousand feet.
8. Atlanta; it's called the Georgia Aquarium.
9. Connecticut
10. Maryland; it is home to the Washington Redskins.
11. The Southern Baptist, which has churches in all fifty states
12. The marines
13. Utah, with its Great Salt Lake
14. It's the largest city park in the U.S.
15. Honolulu, Hawaii
16. New York County, which is Manhattan Island, with twenty-two square miles (and a *lot* of people)
17. The graduate with the lowest grades
18. Oklahoma—not surprising, since it was originally called the Indian Territory
19. Texas, where else? It's the famous King ranch, near Kingsville.
20. Maine; Alaska has more, but then, Alaska is slightly larger than Maine.
21. California, in Yosemite National Park; Ribbon Falls drops 1,612 feet.
22. Fort Worth, Texas
23. Vermont

Biggest, Widest, Mostest: U.S. Records, continued . . .

24. According to *Time*, "He's preached in person to more people than any human being who ever lived." Who?
25. Whose record as the youngest international grand master in chess stood from 1958 to 1991?
26. The ten highest mountains in the U.S. are in what western state?
27. In what month have the most U.S. presidents' inaugurations occurred?
28. Pop Warner called whom "the greatest football player of all time"?
29. Which southern state is the largest state east of the Mississippi River?
30. The highest mountain east of the Mississippi is Mount Mitchell. What state is it in?
31. What western state has the highest percentage of Asians in the United States?
32. What painkiller is the most prescribed drug in America?

★ A World Record for . . .

America holds a lot of world records—ranging from tall buildings to enchiladas.

1. What San Francisco–based company is the world's largest apparel manufacturer? (Hint: denim)
2. The largest one-day sporting event in the world is held in Indiana. What is it?
3. America's tallest building, with 110 stories, is in Chicago. What department store chain was it originally named for?
4. What D.C. monument is the world's tallest obelisk?
5. The world's largest post office building is in what Illinois city?
6. The U.S. and Canada share the largest body of fresh water in the world. What lake is it?
7. What Seattle-based company is the largest airplane manufacturer in the world?
8. What Florida port handles more cruise ship passengers than any port in the world?

24. Billy Graham
25. Bobby Fischer
26. Alaska
27. March; having the inauguration in January is a fairly recent practice.
28. Jim Thorpe
29. Georgia
30. North Carolina
31. Hawaii—about 38 percent Asian in the 2010 census
32. Vicodin (generic name: hydrocodone)

A World Record for . . . // Answers

1. Levi Strauss, maker of Levi's, Dockers, etc.
2. The Indianapolis 500
3. Sears; the Sears Tower (now the Willis Tower) was the world's tallest building at the time it opened.
4. The Washington Monument
5. Chicago
6. Lake Superior
7. Boeing ("If it's not Boeing, I'm not going.")
8. Miami

QUESTIONS

9. Provo, Utah, has the world's largest Mormon university. What is it?
10. The world's largest stalagmite is found in Cathedral Caverns in what southern state?
11. What New York City museum calls itself the "World's Great" exhibition?
12. Louisville, Kentucky, contains the largest publishing house in the world for a particular group of people. Who?
13. Batavia, Illinois, is the home to the world's largest atom smasher, named for an Italian scientist. What is the name of the facility?
14. Kitt Peak National Observatory in Arizona has the world's largest collection of what type of instruments?
15. The largest living thing in the world is named for Civil War general William Sherman. What is it?
16. The world's largest natural rock bridge is in what western state?
17. Old Perpetual, the largest hot-water geyser in the world, is in what western state? (Hint: *not* Wyoming)
18. In what northern state could you see the world's largest loon?
19. What famous well did Edwin Drake drill in August 1859?
20. New York has "the world's largest store," which is what?
21. The world's longest mining tunnel is found in what mountain state?
22. You could see the world's largest enchilada at the Whole Enchilada Fiesta in what southwestern state?
23. Hibbing, Minnesota, calls itself the world capital of what important mineral ore?
24. The USS *Nautilus,* the world's first nuclear submarine, can be visited in what New England state?
25. The Gift of the Waters Pageant in Wyoming celebrates a land exchange from the Native Americans to the people of Wyoming. What land did the people receive?
26. The largest piece of granite in the world is what tourist attraction near Atlanta, Georgia?
27. What Native American athlete was the king of Sweden speaking to in 1912 when he said, "You, sir, are the greatest athlete in the world"?
28. Boston, Massachusetts, has the oldest commissioned navy ship in the world. What is it?
29. The World's Largest Garage Sale is held each October in Warrensburg. What northeastern state is it in?

9. Brigham Young University, with more than twenty-seven thousand students; it is Provo's largest employer.
10. Alabama
11. The Guinness World of Records Exhibition, naturally
12. The blind
13. Fermi National Accelerator Laboratory—better known as Fermilab, named for Enrico Fermi
14. Telescopes
15. A giant sequoia tree in California, over 275 feet tall
16. Utah; it is Rainbow Bridge, spanning over 275 feet.
17. Oregon; it spouts every ninety seconds, sometimes as high as seventy feet.
18. Minnesota; it's twenty feet long, ten feet high, made of fiberglass, and swimming in Silver Lake in the town of Virginia.
19. The world's first oil well, in Titusville, Pennsylvania
20. Macy's
21. Colorado; it is five miles long.
22. New Mexico, in the city of Las Cruces
23. Iron ore; Hibbing has the world's largest open-pit iron mine.
24. Connecticut; it's at Groton, a major submarine base.
25. The world's largest mineral hot springs, now in the town of Thermopolis
26. Stone Mountain, carved with images of Confederate heroes Robert E. Lee, Jefferson Davis, and "Stonewall" Jackson
27. Jim Thorpe, who had won several medals at the 1912 Olympics (in Sweden, which is why the king was addressing him)
28. The USS *Constitution*, also called "Old Ironsides"; it was built in 1797.
29. New York

30. The oldest living thing on earth, a tree, is in what western state?
31. Manhattan's eighty-story building was the world's tallest building when it opened in 1913. What five-and-dime chain owned it?

★ The Oldest . . .

We don't want to be old, but we're certainly fascinated by old things. We're especially fascinated by knowing that something is the oldest of its kind, aren't we?

1. The oldest city in the U.S. is in what state?
2. The oldest state capital has a Spanish name. What is it?
3. Which New England state's constitution is the oldest written constitution still in effect?
4. The oldest band in the U.S., nicknamed the President's Own, is what?
5. America's oldest English colony, found in Virginia, has nothing remaining but a church tower. What was the colony?
6. The nation's oldest seaside resort is in New Jersey, but it isn't Atlantic City. What is it?
7. America's oldest amusement park is in Bristol in which New England state?
8. Voorlezer's House, the nation's oldest elementary school, was built in 1695 on what famous New York island?
9. The oldest and largest national military park in the U.S. commemorates Civil War fighting in which two southern states?
10. The oldest state capitol in continuous use is where?
11. The oldest inhabited town in the U.S. is probably the Acoma Pueblo, a Native American community in which southwestern state?
12. The nation's oldest house (in Santa Fe, New Mexico) was built by what group of European settlers?
13. The Wayside Inn, founded in 1702, is America's oldest inn still in operation. What New England state is it in?

QUESTIONS

30. California; the bristlecone pine is said to be 4,600 years old.
31. Woolworth's; it is still the Woolworth Building.

The Oldest . . . // Answers

1. Florida; it is St. Augustine, founded by the Spanish in 1565.
2. Santa Fe, capital of New Mexico
3. Massachusetts's
4. The Marine Band
5. Jamestown, settled in 1607
6. Cape May
7. Connecticut; it's Lake Compounce Festival Park.
8. Staten Island
9. Tennessee and Georgia; it is Chickamauga and Chattanooga National Military Park, with over eight thousand acres.
10. Annapolis, Maryland; the State House was begun in 1772.
11. New Mexico; it has been inhabited continuously since 1100.
12. None; the eight-hundred-year-old house was built by Native Americans before the Spanish settled Santa Fe.
13. Massachusetts

14. San Francisco is noted for its cable cars, but what Deep South city has the oldest continuously operating streetcars in the country?
15. The country's oldest public building in continuous use is the Palace of the Governors in what southwestern capital?

☆ The One and Only . . .

There are many examples of uniqueness in America. Maybe it's because we're fascinated by the unusual, the offbeat.

1. What is the only state with a one-syllable name?
2. Who was the only Catholic president?
3. What large state is the only one that can choose to divide itself into five states?
4. What's the only state with an area of less than two thousand square miles?
5. What is the only state named for another country?
6. Where would you find the nation's only monument to an insect?
7. Canada lies *south* of the U.S. at only one point, near a famous Michigan city. Which one?
8. Who is the only president to have a national park named for him?
9. What is the only state capital with a one-syllable name?
10. What breed of dog, with a city in its name, is the only breed of dog developed in the U.S.?
11. What conservative and pro-family politician was the only divorced man to serve as president?
12. New Jersey has the only state university that was begun in the colonial period. What is the name?
13. What state has the only American diamond field open to the public?
14. What two men are the only appointees to the office of vice president?
15. What is the only state that borders only one state?
16. What southern state is the only state with laws not based on British law?

14. New Orleans, whose streetcar line has been operating since 1835
15. Santa Fe, New Mexico

The One and Only . . . // Answers

1. Maine
2. John F. Kennedy
3. Texas; considering how much Texans love *bigness*, this will never happen.
4. Rhode Island; many states have *counties* bigger than Rhode Island.
5. New Mexico, of course
6. Enterprise, Alabama, which has a very dignified Greek-style monument to . . . the boll weevil, a cotton-crop-destroying bug from Mexico
7. Detroit
8. Theodore Roosevelt; the park, in North Dakota, is a scenic "badlands" area containing part of Roosevelt's ranch.
9. Pierre, South Dakota; Pierre is pronounced as only one syllable (PEER), as any South Dakota native will quickly tell you.
10. The Boston terrier
11. Ronald Reagan
12. Rutgers
13. Arkansas, which has the Craters of Diamonds State Park
14. Gerald Ford and Nelson Rockefeller; Ford was appointed by Nixon; Rockefeller was appointed by Ford.
15. Maine, which borders only New Hampshire; Alaska and Hawaii border *no* states.
16. Louisiana, which (being French in heritage) has laws based on the Code Napoleon

17. What is the only U.S. city to have its coliseum and arts complex named for a German rocket scientist?
18. Who was the only U.S. president who admitted to having an illegitimate child?
19. John Sevier was the only governor of what state?
20. Venice, Florida, has the world's only training school for what type of comical entertainers?
21. What is the only U.S. state that formed as a result of popular vote to separate from another state?
22. *Cabbages and Kings* was the only novel by America's most famous short-story writer. Who?
23. John Witherspoon was the only clergyman to sign which noted American document?
24. Who is the only president buried in Washington's National Cathedral? (Hint: World War I)
25. What is the only underwater monument to a Civil War battle?
26. The only national park dedicated to the performing arts is in Vienna, Virginia. What is its name?
27. The only national park in the northeastern U.S. is the nation's second most visited. What is it?
28. What New England state was the only colony not invaded by the British during the Revolutionary War?
29. The only museum in the world devoted to uranium mining is in what southwestern state?
30. Pennsylvania has the only U.S. town named for a Native American athlete. Who?
31. Carville, Louisiana, has the only American hospital for the treatment of a disease that was well known in ancient times. What is it?

QUESTIONS

17. Huntsville, Alabama; its Von Braun Civic Center is named for NASA scientist Wernher von Braun.

18. Grover Cleveland; this fact was used against him by political opponents.

19. The state of Franklin—the name taken by Tennessee before it formally became a state in 1796

20. Clowns; the town is the winter quarters of the Ringling Brothers and Barnum & Bailey Circus.

21. West Virginia, made up of the twenty-six Virginia counties that voted to leave Virginia when Virginia joined the Confederacy

22. O. Henry; the novel was published in 1899.

23. The Declaration of Independence

24. Woodrow Wilson

25. The Monitor-Merrimack Memorial Bridge-Tunnel at Newport News, Virginia; it is named for the naval battle between the Confederacy's *Merrimack* and the Union's *Monitor.*

26. Wolf Trap Farm, which offers opera, symphony, folk, jazz, and many other performances

27. Acadia, in Maine

28. New Hampshire

29. New Mexico, the U.S.'s chief supplier of uranium

30. Jim Thorpe, the 1912 Olympic medalist

31. Leprosy, also known as Hansen's disease

PART TWO

LET US ENTERTAIN YOU

★ The Tube: TV in America

Was there life before TV? There was, but it's hard to imagine, isn't it? Americans think they watch too much—then go on watching. But it isn't all bad. Most of us have pleasant memories of some favorite shows. And whether it's bad or good, it's here to stay, a fixture on the American scene.

There's one problem with TV trivia questions: where to stop? The following are just a sampling. Someone could do a whole book of TV trivia (and probably already has).

1. What cable channel has its headquarters in, appropriately, downtown Nashville?
2. What sitcom (a spinoff from another sitcom) holds the record number of Emmys for a comedy series?
3. What comedienne ended her weekly shows by tugging on her left earlobe?
4. What beloved children's show had such characters as Mr. Moose, Bunny Rabbit, Miss Worm, and Mr. Green Jeans?
5. What fitness guru with a long-running daily workout show died in 2011 at age ninety-six?
6. AMOMI is in a former movie studio in Queens, New York. What is it?
7. Charles Ginsburg led the team that invented what once-omnipresent entertainment device?
8. What plump comic's show featured the June Taylor Dancers?
9. What TV puppeteer gave the world Lamb Chop, Charlie Horse, and Hush Puppy?
10. What handsome and hirsute actor lost out (twice!) as a contestant on *The Dating Game*? (Hint: Hawaii)
11. Who was the host of the original *Jeopardy* (pre–Alex Trebek)?
12. What type of commercial aired for the last time on December 31, 1970?
13. What popular game show of the 1970s (revived in the 1990s) featured nine celebrities in an enormous tic-tac-toe board?
14. The Clio awards are given annually for what?
15. Earl Hammer Jr. created what beloved family drama of the 1970s?
16. Who wrote the newspaper column "Little Old New York" before his variety show became a fixture of Sunday night TV?

The Tube: TV in America // Answers

1. CMT (Country Music Television)
2. _Frasier_, a spinoff of _Cheers_
3. Carol Burnett
4. _Captain Kangaroo_
5. Jack LaLanne
6. The American Museum of the Moving Image, devoted to film, TV, and video
7. The VCR
8. Jackie Gleason's
9. Shari Lewis
10. Tom Selleck, also known as Magnum
11. Art Fleming, who died in 1995
12. Cigarette ads
13. _Hollywood Squares_
14. TV commercials
15. _The Waltons_
16. Ed Sullivan

The Tube: TV in America, continued . . .

17. Archie and Edith sang "Those Were the Days" as the opening of what popular sitcom?
18. The goofy Griffin household is the subject of what popular animated series?
19. "Goodbye, Farewell, and Amen" was the popular final episode of what long-running sitcom (that ended in 1983)?
20. Paul Henning, who died in 2005, created what "down home" sitcom?
21. What man, the first host of *The Tonight Show,* emceed *Meeting of Minds* for PBS in 1977?
22. Of the country's thousands of fan clubs, what TV series has the most clubs? (Hint: space)
23. What word is used for a long TV ad bought by a company to promote its product?
24. What famous news channel has its headquarters in Atlanta, Georgia?
25. In 1957 what theater duo created the musical *Cinderella* expressly for TV?
26. What TV comic was so popular that in 1951 NBC signed him to a thirty-year contract?
27. Country music stars Roy Clark and Buck Owens hosted what long-running variety show?
28. What information and communication item did Russian-born Vladimir Zworykin introduce to the world?
29. What brassy sitcom star had turned down the role of Peg Bundy in *Married . . . with Children?*
30. What TV teacher is the only person to have won an Emmy for a religious program? (Hint: Catholic)
31. What religious broadcaster hosts *The 700 Club?*
32. The first televised presidential debates, in 1960, featured which two men?
33. What respected NBC anchorman died in 2003?

QUESTIONS

17. *All in the Family*
18. *Family Guy*
19. *M*A*S*H*
20. *The Beverly Hillbillies*—as well as *Green Acres* and *Petticoat Junction;* Henning also composed the *Hillbillies* theme song, "The Ballad of Jed Clampett."
21. Steve Allen
22. *Star Trek,* with more than six hundred chapters
23. Infomercial (mixing *information* and *commercial*)
24. CNN, the Cable News Network
25. Rodgers and Hammerstein, famous for *Oklahoma! The King and I,* and other classic musicals
26. Milton Berle; he was *not* on the air for thirty years.
27. *Hee Haw*
28. The TV picture tube
29. Roseanne Barr, who had plenty of success with *Roseanne*
30. Bishop Fulton Sheen
31. Pat Robertson
32. Richard Nixon and John F. Kennedy
33. David Brinkley, of Huntley-Brinkley fame

★ Great Americans on Film

*Many great American movies are about . . . great Americans—
or at least famous ones.*

1. What Republican president was the subject of a controversial 2008 film directed by Oliver Stone?
2. Philip Seymour Hoffman won an Oscar playing what colorful author?
3. In the 2004 movie *The Aviator,* Leonardo DiCaprio played what eccentric millionaire?
4. What World War II general was the subject of a 1970 film that won actor George C. Scott an Oscar?
5. In *Walk the Line,* Joaquin Phoenix and Reese Witherspoon played what country music couple?
6. Jamie Foxx won an Oscar for playing what soulful blind singer?
7. *Wild Bill* was a 1995 movie about western gunslinger Wild Bill Hickok. What actor (and son of a famous actor) played him?
8. What two outlaws were portrayed in a 1967 movie with Warren Beatty and Faye Dunaway?
9. *Man of a Thousand Faces* starred James Cagney as the best-known star of silent films. Who?
10. *JFK* was, obviously, about John F. Kennedy. Who starred in the film?
11. *Jefferson in Paris* (1995) starred what tall blond actor as tall red-haired President Thomas Jefferson?
12. James Cagney won an Oscar playing songwriter and performer George M. Cohan. What patriotic movie was it?
13. Anne Bancroft played devoted teacher Annie Sullivan in a film about a courageous blind woman. Who?
14. *The Untouchables* (1987) was the story of what noted federal crime fighter?
15. The 2003 Civil War epic *Gods and Generals* featured Stephen Lang playing what honored Confederate general?
16. *Bugsy* was a 1991 film about gangster Benjamin "Bugsy" Siegel. What handsome leading man played Siegel?
17. Meryl Streep played what famous chef in a 2009 film?
18. Sally Field won an Oscar playing a real-life labor union organizer in what 1979 movie?

Great Americans on Film // Answers

1. George W. Bush; the title was *W.*
2. Truman Capote, in the movie *Truman*
3. Howard Hughes
4. George S. Patton; Scott was Patton.
5. Johnny Cash and June Carter Cash
6. Ray Charles, in the movie *Ray*
7. Jeff Bridges (son of Lloyd)
8. Bonnie Parker and Clyde Barrow in *Bonnie and Clyde*
9. Lon Chaney, who died in 1930 after making one sound movie
10. Kevin Costner, who did not play Kennedy himself
11. Nick Nolte
12. *Yankee Doodle Dandy* (1942)
13. Helen Keller; the movie was *The Miracle Worker.*
14. Eliot Ness, played by Kevin Costner
15. "Stonewall" Jackson
16. Warren Beatty
17. Julia Child, in the movie *Julie and Julia*
18. *Norma Rae*

Great Americans on Film, continued . . .

19. *Coal Miner's Daughter* had Sissy Spacek playing what country music queen?

20. William Powell played the lead in the 1936 Oscar winner about America's greatest stage producer. Who was he?

21. *The Cross and the Switchblade* told the tale of ghetto evangelist David Wilkerson. What former pop singer played the lead?

22. George Hamilton starred in a 1971 film about a famous motorcycle stuntman. Who?

23. *Bound for Glory* (1976) was the tale of folksinger Woody Guthrie. Who played him?

24. Robert De Niro played brutal boxer Jake LaMotta in what 1980 film?

25. *Boys Town* was about the boys' home and its founder, Father Flanagan. What down-to-earth actor won an Oscar for playing Flanagan?

26. What famed baseball slugger did portly actor John Goodman portray?

27. *Baby Face Nelson* (1957) was played by what baby-faced (and short) actor?

28. *Knute Rockne, All American* (1940) starred Pat O'Brien as the legendary football coach. What future president also starred in the film?

29. Dean Jones played a convicted Watergate burglar who becomes a devout Christian. What was the film?

30. What two outlaws did Robert Redford and Paul Newman portray in a very popular 1969 film?

31. Doris Day sang her way through a role as what western sharpshooter?

32. What great Italian explorer did Frederic March play in a 1949 film?

33. Fess Parker played what famous frontiersman in a 1955 Disney film?

34. Dan Emmett, who wrote "Dixie," was the subject of the 1943 film *Dixie*. What popular crooner played Emmett?

19. Loretta Lynn
20. Florenz Ziegfeld; the movie was *The Great Ziegfeld.*
21. Pat Boone
22. Evel Knievel
23. David Carradine
24. *Raging Bull*
25. Spencer Tracy
26. Babe Ruth, in *The Babe*
27. Mickey Rooney
28. Ronald Reagan, who played George Gipp
29. *Born Again* (1978), the story of Charles Colson
30. Butch Cassidy and the Sundance Kid
31. Calamity Jane
32. Christopher Columbus; his wife, Florence Eldridge, played Queen Isabella.
33. Davy Crockett; later, on TV, he played Daniel Boone.
34. Bing Crosby

☆ Leading Men (On Screen, That Is)

How well do you know Hollywood's leading men, past and present? If you saw the names of three films an actor had starred in, would his name come to mind? Find out.

1. *Raiders of the Lost Ark, Patriot Games, The Fugitive*
2. *Forrest Gump, Apollo 13, Bonfire of the Vanities*
3. *Casablanca, The Maltese Falcon, The Petrified Forest*
4. *The Mask, Batman Forever, Dumb and Dumber*
5. *Some Like It Hot, The Defiant Ones, Spartacus*
6. *Top Hat, Easter Parade, Shall We Dance?*
7. *The Conversation, The French Connection, Unforgiven*
8. *Planet of the Apes, The Ten Commandments, Ben-Hur*
9. *Rain Man, The Graduate, Kramer vs. Kramer*
10. *Judge Dredd, Oscar, Rocky*
11. *The Lost Weekend, The Uninvited, Bugles in the Afternoon*
12. *Cape Fear, Ryan's Daughter, The Night of the Hunter*
13. *Tumblin' Tumbleweeds, Back in the Saddle, Carolina Moon*
14. *Cool Hand Luke, The Sting, The Hustler*
15. *Wolf, One Flew Over the Cuckoo's Nest, The Shining*
16. *Singin' in the Rain, Francis the Talking Mule, Call Me Madam*
17. *The Fisher King, Hook, Jumanji*
18. *Spellbound, Moby Dick, To Kill a Mockingbird*
19. *Bugsy, Reds, Bonnie and Clyde*
20. *The Champ, Grand Hotel, Min and Bill*
21. *The Wild Bunch, Marty, Barabbas*
22. *A Streetcar Named Desire, The Godfather, Julius Caesar*
23. *The Ten Commandments, The King and I, The Magnificent Seven*
24. *White Heat, Public Enemy, Yankee Doodle Dandy*
25. *You Can't Take It with You, Grand Hotel, Key Largo*
26. *The Prince of Tides, Lorenzo's Oil, Jefferson in Paris*
27. *The Story of Louis Pasteur, The Good Earth, The Life of Emile Zola*
28. *The Thin Man, Life with Father, My Man Godfrey*
29. *The Mark of Zorro, The Razor's Edge, In Old Chicago*
30. *Love Me Tender, Jailhouse Rock, Blue Hawaii*
31. *The Phantom of the Opera, The Hunchback of Notre Dame, The Unholy Three*

QUESTIONS

Leading Men (On Screen, That Is) // *Answers*

1. Harrison Ford
2. Tom Hanks
3. Humphrey Bogart
4. Jim Carrey
5. Tony Curtis
6. Fred Astaire
7. Gene Hackman
8. Charlton Heston
9. Dustin Hoffman
10. Sylvester Stallone
11. Ray Milland
12. Robert Mitchum
13. Gene Autry
14. Paul Newman
15. Jack Nicholson
16. Donald O'Connor
17. Robin Williams
18. Gregory Peck
19. Warren Beatty
20. Wallace Beery
21. Ernest Borgnine
22. Marlon Brando
23. Yul Brynner
24. James Cagney
25. Lionel Barrymore
26. Nick Nolte
27. Paul Muni
28. William Powell
29. Tyrone Power
30. Elvis Presley
31. Lon Chaney

32. *The Gold Rush, The Great Dictator, The Kid*
33. *From Here to Eternity, A Place in the Sun, The Misfits*
34. *Sergeant York, Mr. Deeds Goes to Town, High Noon*
35. *Raising Arizona, Moonstruck, Honeymoon in Vegas*
36. *Going My Way, Holiday Inn, The Road to Utopia*
37. *Spartacus, Lust for Life, Gunfight at the OK Corral*
38. *The Bridges of Madison County, Play Misty for Me, Unforgiven*
39. *Rose Marie, Naughty Marietta, Sweethearts*
40. *My Little Chickadee, You Can't Cheat an Honest Man, David Copperfield*

★ Cartoons, Moving and Nonmoving

Obviously the comic strip (an American invention) preceded the animated cartoon (another American invention). The two have become cultural institutions, making us laugh and holding a mirror up to us (particularly in the political cartoon).

1. "Good grief!" was often said by characters in what long-running comic strip?
2. What 2003 film told the story of a clown fish searching for his son?
3. What strip did Jim Davis launch in 1978 because he thought the world needed a comic strip about cats?
4. The world's first movie-length cartoon was what 1937 fairy-tale classic from Walt Disney?
5. What TV cartoon rodent's continuing nemesis was Oil Can Harry?
6. The Okefenokee Swamp was the setting for what long-running comic strip about a possum and his friends?
7. In the comic strip "Doonesbury," what president was represented by a waffle?
8. In comic books, whose secret identity was Dr. Bruce Banner?
9. What comic strip with a biblical title has the characters Rat, Pig, Zebra, and Goat?
10. Cartoonist Robert Ripley became popular with what syndicated feature?

32. Charlie Chaplin
33. Montgomery Clift
34. Gary Cooper
35. Nicholas Cage
36. Bing Crosby
37. Kirk Douglas
38. Clint Eastwood
39. Nelson Eddy
40. W. C. Fields

Cartoons, Moving and Nonmoving // Answers

1. "Peanuts"
2. *Finding Nemo*
3. "Garfield"
4. *Snow White and the Seven Dwarfs,* released on videotape in 1993
5. Mighty Mouse
6. "Pogo," by Walt Kelly
7. Bill Clinton
8. The Incredible Hulk (In the TV series he was *David* Banner.)
9. "Pearls Before Swine," by Stephan Pastis
10. "Ripley's Believe It or Not"

Cartoons, Moving and Nonmoving, continued . . .

11. Walt Disney himself provided the voice for which animated character?
12. What mop-haired comic-strip girl's favorite expression was "Leapin' lizards!"?
13. What visual contribution did cartoonist Thomas Nast make to American politics?
14. The Museum of Cartoon Art is at White Plains in what northeastern state?
15. What "Man of a Thousand Voices" provided many of the voices for the Looney Tunes characters?
16. The National Cartoonists Society gives what annual awards for the best cartoons?
17. What popular feature did zany cartoonist Gary Larson terminate in 1994, claiming he didn't want the humor to become stale?
18. What giddy animated bird's archenemy was another bird, Buzz Buzzard?
19. "The Web Slinger" is a nickname for what Marvel Comics superhero?
20. What satirical strip featuring the hillbillies of Dogpatch ran from 1943 to 1977?
21. The long-running strip "Hi and Lois" was spun off from what earlier strip set on an army base?
22. What family comic by Bil Keane always appears drawn in a circle?
23. What blond, mischievous little boy was featured on a set of 2010 postage stamps?
24. Comedian Wally Cox provided the voice for what meek but powerful animated TV dog hero?
25. America's first daily comic strip, "A. Mutt," began in 1907. What strip, with two men in the title, did it become?
26. The comic strip "Thimble Theater" had the Oyl family as characters, plus a pipe-smoking sailor. What was his name?

QUESTIONS

11. Mickey Mouse; Walt pinched his nose when doing the Mickey voice.
12. Little Orphan Annie's
13. The elephant and donkey symbols for the Republicans and Democrats
14. New York
15. Mel Blanc, who did the voices for Bugs Bunny, Daffy Duck, and many others
16. The Reuben Awards, named for cartoonist Reuben "Rube" Goldberg
17. "The Far Side"
18. Woody Woodpecker
19. Spider-Man
20. "L'il Abner," by Al Capp
21. "Beetle Bailey"; Beetle's sister was Lois Flagston of "Hi and Lois."
22. "The Family Circus," which Keane had wanted to name "Family Circle," until the magazine of that name protested
23. Dennis the Menace; the set also included Archie, Beetle Bailey, Garfield, and Calvin and Hobbes.
24. Underdog
25. "Mutt and Jeff"
26. Popeye, who eventually dominated the strip and became an animated cartoon character

★ Out Here in Radio Land

Radio is as pervasive as air. For years it was practically the property of teen listeners (and those country music fans out there, too). Then in the 1990s, adults decided they liked radio again—maybe because of that great revival of social analysis, the call-in show. Radio is alive and well in America, folks.

1. What raspy-voiced DJ, born Robert Smith, died of a heart attack in 1995? (Hint: howl)
2. What clever name did disc jockey George D. Hay bestow on his "Barn Dance" country music show?
3. What often-controversial political commentator was barred from entering the United Kingdom in 2009?
4. What letter do radio stations west of the Mississippi River begin with?
5. What new form of radio was launched by Sirius Satellite in 2008?
6. What foul-mouthed New York call-in host became the "Shock Jock" of the 1990s?
7. The Museum of Television and Radio is, appropriately, in what north-eastern metropolis?
8. What ever-young "American Bandstand" host was still doing Top 40 radio countdowns in the 1990s?
9. What former *Saturday Night Live* cast member began hosting a daily radio show in 2007?
10. WLS was for years an institution in Chicago radio. What Chicago-based department store chain owned the station?
11. What radio host claims to work "with half my brain tied behind me"?
12. What communication and entertainment medium did Edwin Armstrong invent in 1939?
13. Conservative host Laura Ingraham served for a time as an aide to what Supreme Court justice?
14. What name was given to the sixteen-inch records formerly played only by radio stations?
15. What name does weird disc jockey Barry Hansen broadcast under?
16. Fanny Brice played what hilarious (and obnoxious) little girl on radio?
17. Who, after thirty-nine years on the air, retired from hosting "American Top 40" in 2009?

Out Here in Radio Land // Answers

1. Wolfman Jack
2. Grand Ole Opry; Hay was spoofing the preceding program, a broadcast of grand opera.
3. Michael Savage, host of *The Savage Nation*
4. K, usually
5. Internet radio
6. Howard Stern
7. New York
8. Dick Clark, of course
9. Dennis Miller
10. Sears; the WLS stood for "World's Largest Store."
11. Rush Limbaugh
12. FM radio
13. Clarence Thomas
14. Transcriptions; as CDs came into vogue, transcriptions became a thing of the past.
15. Dr. Demento, famous for playing novelty songs
16. Baby Snooks
17. Kasey Kasem, who also provided voices for cartoon characters such as Shaggy in *Scooby-Doo, Where Are You!*

Out Here in Radio Land, continued . . .

18. What two fictional taxi drivers of radio fame worked for the Fresh Air Cab Company?

★ More Great Americans on Film

1. *All the President's Men* was concerned with the downfall of what twentieth-century president?
2. John Dunbar, a soldier who begins a new life with a Native American tribe, is the subject of what 1991 Oscar-winning film?
3. *Pride of the Yankees* (1942) had Gary Cooper playing one of baseball's greats, who dies at the height of his fame. Who?
4. What 1991 movie starred Val Kilmer as Jim Morrison, the controversial lead singer of a 1960s rock group with the same name?
5. *Pat Garrett and Billy the Kid* (1973) starred what two pop music idols?
6. Gary Cooper starred in *The Plainsman* (1936) as what Old West gunslinger?
7. *American Hot Wax* (1978) was about *the* great disc jockey of early rock and roll. Who was he?
8. William "Bull" Halsey, the World War II naval hero, was the subject of *The Gallant Hours* (1959). What spunky redheaded actor played him?
9. What 1995 film told of an ill-fated space mission of 1970?
10. *The Long Riders* (1980) used real-life brother actors to portray two sets of Old West outlaw brothers. Who were the outlaw brothers?
11. What flamboyant general of World War II and the Korean War was played by Gregory Peck in a 1977 film?
12. What short and boyish actor played *Young Tom Edison* in a 1940 film?
13. *Reds* (1981) told the story of American communist John Reed, the only American buried in the Kremlin. Who served as both star and director?
14. *My Darling Clementine* (1946) has Henry Fonda playing an Old West sheriff who wipes out the Dalton gang. Who was he?
15. *Beau James* (1957) told the story of New York mayor Jimmy Walker, a world celebrity of the 1920s. What noted stand-up comic and actor played the role? (Hint: Christmas specials)

18. Amos and Andy, two supposedly black men played (on radio) by two whites

More Great Americans on Film // Answers

1. Richard Nixon
2. *Dances with Wolves*
3. Lou Gehrig
4. *The Doors*
5. Kris Kristofferson and Bob Dylan
6. Wild Bill Hickok; the movie also featured the characters Calamity Jane and Buffalo Bill.
7. Alan Freed, who coined (or at least popularized) the term *rock and roll*
8. James Cagney
9. *Apollo 13*
10. The James brothers and the Younger brothers
11. Douglas MacArthur
12. Mickey Rooney
13. Warren Beatty
14. Wyatt Earp
15. Bob Hope

QUESTIONS

16. *Night and Day* (1946) had Cary Grant playing one of America's most popular and sophisticated songwriters. Who?

17. *Mommie Dearest* (1981) told the tale of a popular (and supposedly sadistic) film queen. Who?

18. Robert Taylor played Col. Paul Tibbetts in the World War II film *Above and Beyond* (1952). What world-changing event was Tibbetts famous for?

19. *Man of Conquest* (1939) told of the man who served as governor of Tennessee, president of Texas, and a longtime friend of the Native Americans. Who?

20. *The Spirit of St. Louis* (1957) had Jimmy Stewart playing one of America's greatest aviators, famed for flying solo across the Atlantic. Who was he?

21. What tall, lean actor played Lincoln in *Abe Lincoln in Illinois* (1940)?

22. NASA's *Mercury* astronauts were the subject of what popular 1983 movie?

23. Singer Nat King Cole played blues composer W. C. Handy in what 1958 movie named for one of Handy's classics?

24. *The Scarface Mob* (1958) focused on Al Capone's gang and starred Robert Stack as a federal agent he would later play on TV. Who?

25. Controversial comedian Lenny Bruce was the subject of *Lenny* (1974). What Oscar-winning actor played him?

26. What world-famous inventor was played by Spencer Tracy in a 1940 film? (Hint: light)

27. A popular 1955 film starred Richard Todd as a Scottish preacher who becomes U.S. Senate chaplain. What was the film?

28. *The Adventures of Mark Twain* (1944) starred what solid actor as Twain?

29. What 1972 movie was a musical celebration of the Founding Fathers and the Declaration of Independence?

30. *Stars and Stripes Forever* (1952) was the story of what bandmaster and march composer?

31. What beloved cowboy comedian was portrayed by his own son in a 1950 biopic?

32. *Beloved Infidel* starred Gregory Peck as one of the great twentieth-century novelists (and an alcoholic). Who?

33. Tyrone Power and Henry Fonda played two notorious outlaw brothers in what 1938 Western?

34. *The Unsinkable Molly Brown* (1964) was a musical about a real Denver socialite who survived the sinking of the *Titanic*. What perky star played Molly?

16. Cole Porter
17. Joan Crawford, played in the movie by Faye Dunaway
18. Dropping the A-bomb on Japan
19. Sam Houston
20. Charles Lindbergh
21. Raymond Massey
22. *The Right Stuff*
23. *St. Louis Blues*
24. Eliot Ness
25. Dustin Hoffman
26. Thomas Edison; the film is *Edison the Man.*
27. *A Man Called Peter,* the story of Peter Marshall
28. Frederic March
29. *1776*
30. John Philip Sousa
31. Will Rogers; Will Jr. played him in *The Story of Will Rogers.*
32. F. Scott Fitzgerald
33. *Jesse James;* the two actors played brothers Jesse and Frank James.
34. Debbie Reynolds

★ America on Stage

Americans love a good play. Mark Twain's **Huckleberry Finn** *tells of two con artists staging* **The Royal Nonesuch,** *which involved an actor scampering on the stage wearing nothing but body paint. Fortunately, most American theater has been of much higher quality. And much of it is concerned with the American experience itself.*

1. What ever popular musical (named for a state) was originally titled *Away We Go*?
2. Theatre West Virginia has an outdoor musical about the country's most famous two-family feud. Who were the two families?
3. What famous New York City section runs from 41st to 53rd Streets and 6th to 9th Avenues?
4. The outdoor drama *The Lost Colony* tells of a famous English colony that disappeared without a trace in 1590. What state was it in?
5. *The Stephen Foster Story,* an outdoor drama on the life of the great songwriter, is held in what state?
6. What musical play about the Founding Fathers has a numerical title?
7. *Unto These Hills* is an outdoor drama telling of a Native American tribe's removal from North Carolina to Oklahoma. What tribe?
8. The popular Mesa Arizona Easter Pageant is staged by what religious group?
9. The musical *Jersey Boys* features songs made popular by what singing group?
10. Arthur Miller's drama *The Crucible* is about what episode in colonial history?
11. *Baby It's You,* which opened on Broadway in 2011, is billed as a "jukebox musical" about what singing group of the 1960s?
12. The popular musical *Gypsy* tells of the girlhood of what colorful woman?
13. New London, Connecticut's theater center, is named for America's most famous playwright. Who?
14. Antoinette Perry, an actress and theatre producer, lent her name to what annual awards?
15. The North Carolina outdoor drama *Strike at the Wind* concerns the Lumbee people and their sorrows. What sort of people were they?

1. *Oklahoma!*
2. The Hatfields and the McCoys
3. Broadway, the theater district
4. North Carolina, on Roanoke Island, site of the Lost Colony
5. Kentucky, near the spot where Foster wrote the song "My Old Kentucky Home"
6. *1776*
7. The Cherokee; the drama is staged near Great Smoky Mountains National Park.
8. The Mormons; the pageant takes place on the grounds of the Mesa Temple.
9. Frankie Valli and the Four Seasons
10. The Salem witch trials
11. The Shirelles
12. Gypsy Rose Lee
13. Eugene O'Neill, the first American playwright to win the Nobel Prize for Literature, author of *Anna Christie, Strange Interlude,* and other classic dramas
14. The Tonys, awarded for Broadway plays
15. Native Americans

America on Stage, continued . . .

16. Chillicothe, Ohio, has an outdoor drama on the life of one of the country's most famous Native American leaders. Who?

17. What Stephen Sondheim musical's cast includes John Wilkes Booth, Lee Harvey Oswald, and John Hinckley?

18. In what state would you find the Andy Griffith Playhouse?

19. What drama concerns blind-and-deaf Helen Keller and her teacher?

20. Who is the main character in an outdoor drama seen by millions in Eureka Springs, Arkansas?

21. The musical *Big River* is a bouncy adaptation of what great American novel?

22. *Knickerbocker Holiday* is a musical about Peter Stuyvesant, the tyrannical Dutch governor of which colony?

23. A 1938 play by Robert Sherwood concerns what beloved president?

24. *The Gentleman from the Cane* is staged at a Tennessee state park named for the play's hero, a famous frontiersman who died at the Alamo. Who?

25. *Trumpet in the Land,* an outdoor drama, tells the tale of sixty Native American Christians who were massacred in the 1700s. Where is the play held?

26. What musical that opened on Broadway in 1997 concerns a ship disaster in 1912?

27. Which southeastern state is the "Outdoor Theatre Capital of America"?

28. What all-American musical is set in River City, Iowa?

29. The musical *All Shook Up* features songs made famous by what pop star?

30. In what state could you see the Mormon Miracle Pageant, with a cast of six hundred?

31. The delightful musical *The Unsinkable Molly Brown* concerns a woman who survived what disaster?

★ TV Record Holders

1. What annual sports program is (as if you couldn't guess) always one of the year's top-rated TV shows?

2. What sitcom's final episode in February 1983 was the highest-rated TV show of all time? (Hint: army)

16. Tecumseh
17. *Assassins*
18. North Carolina; it's in Griffith's hometown, Mount Airy.
19. *The Miracle Worker*
20. Jesus; the drama is *The Great Passion Play.*
21. *The Adventures of Huckleberry Finn*
22. New York, back when it was called New Amsterdam; oddly, the play makes Stuyvesant a sympathetic character.
23. Lincoln; the play is the perennially popular *Abe Lincoln in Illinois.*
24. Davy Crockett; the play is at Davy Crockett State Park. "Gentleman from the Cane" was Crockett's nickname when he served in Congress. "Cane" meant "the backwoods."
25. Ohio, in the town of New Philadelphia, near the play's setting
26. *Titanic*
27. North Carolina, which has numerous productions every summer, including *The Lost Colony, Horn in the West, The Sword of Peace, Worthy Is the Lamb, Unto These Hills,* and several others
28. *The Music Man*
29. Elvis Presley; oddly, the play's plot is based (loosely) on Shakespeare's comedy *Twelfth Night.*
30. Utah; it is held in the town of Salina.
31. The sinking of the *Titanic*

TV Record Holders // Answers

1. The Super Bowl
2. *M*A*S*H*

3. What classic 1939 film, shown in two parts, was the top-rated movie on TV?

4. What chase show's final episode in January 1967 was one of the top-rated TV shows of all time? (Hint: a one-armed man)

5. What Sunday-night show, running from 1948 to 1971, was the top-rated TV variety show ever?

6. What Sunday-night Western charmed TV audiences for twenty years, from 1955 to 1975? (Hint: Hoss)

7. What was TV's longest-running animal series, running 1954–71?

8. TV's longest-running comedy show (1951–71) was hosted by what rubber-faced comic?

9. The top sitcoms of the 1980s were *The Cosby Show* and what show set in a Boston tavern?

10. What show (with a redheaded star) was the top sitcom of the 1950s?

11. The top sitcom of the 1960s starred a southern comic as a southern sheriff. What was the show?

12. What evening soap's November 21, 1980, episode was one of the top-rated TV shows of all time? (Hint: Who shot . . . ?)

13. What "champagne music-maker's" TV show ran from 1955 to 1971 (and is still popular in reruns)?

14. What Jack Webb series was the top-rated cop drama of the 1950s? (Hint: Just the facts, ma'am.)

☆ The Fabulous Funnies

Comic strips are an American invention, and their characters become almost as real as real people. In fact, if you heard the names of some characters, you could probably identify the strip they're a part of.

1. Sarge, Otto, Plato, Miss Blips, Gen. Halftrack

2. Helga, Lucky Eddie, Honi, Snert, Dr. Zook

3. Dagwood, Herb, Tootsie, Cookie, Daisy, Mr. Dithers

4. Dolly, Billy, Jeffy, P. J., Barfy

3. *Gone with the Wind*
4. *The Fugitive*
5. *The Ed Sullivan Show*
6. *Bonanza*
7. *Lassie*
8. Red Skelton
9. *Cheers*
10. *I Love Lucy,* naturally
11. *The Andy Griffith Show*
12. *Dallas;* this was the episode when America learned who shot J. R. Ewing.
13. Lawrence Welk's
14. *Dragnet*

The Fabulous Funnies // Answers

1. "Beetle Bailey"
2. "Hagar the Horrible"
3. "Blondie"
4. "The Family Circus"

5. Jughaid, Tater, Loweezy, Silas, Elviney
6. Joey, Mr. Wilson, Ruff, Margaret, Gina
7. The Asp, Daddy Warbucks, Sandy, Punjab
8. Daisy Mae, Marryin' Sam, Mammy Yokum, Moonbeam McSwine
9. Sir Rodney, the King, Spook, the Wizard
10. Marcie, Lucy, Woodstock, Spike, Rerun, Linus
11. April, Ellie, Edgar, Elizabeth, Mike
12. Hobbes, Susie, Dad, Mom
13. The Fox family: Paige, Jason, Peter, Mom, and Dad
14. Jon, Odie, Liz, the spider, Nermal
15. Green Gills, Pajamas, Hildegarde Hamhocker, the Sheriff
16. Opus, Bill the Cat, Steve Dallas
17. Junior, Moon Maid, Mumbles, B. O. Plenty, Gravel Gertie, Luscious Mahoney
18. Howland Owl, Churchy Lafemme, Miss Mamselle
19. Grimmy, Sumo, Attila
20. Dot, Ditto, Dawg, Thurston
21. Sluggo, Aunt Fritzi, Irma
22. Mom, Dad, Electra, Andrea
23. Skyler, Loon, Roz, Cosmo, the Senator
24. Peter Parker, M. J.
25. Sally, Ted, Hilary

⋆ Make Me Laugh

Americans love to laugh. Our humorous streak goes all the way back to the colonial period, when Benjamin Franklin made people chuckle. Even the Puritans had their jocular side. Nowadays an entire cable channel is devoted to nothing but comedy. Well, why not? Making people laugh is serious business.

1. What comic and quiz show host gained fame with "You might be a redneck if . . ."?
2. What manic comic often ad-libbed his routines on the TV sitcom *Mork and Mindy*?

5. "Snuffy Smith"
6. "Dennis the Menace"
7. "Little Orphan Annie"
8. "Li'l Abner"
9. "The Wizard of Id"
10. "Peanuts"
11. "For Better or for Worse"
12. "Calvin and Hobbes"
13. "Foxtrot"
14. "Garfield"
15. "Tumbleweeds"
16. "Bloom County"
17. "Dick Tracy"
18. "Pogo"
19. "Mother Goose and Grimm"
20. "Hi and Lois"
21. "Nancy"
22. "Cathy"
23. "Shoe"
24. "The Amazing Spider-Man"
25. "Sally Forth"

Make Me Laugh // Answers

1. Jeff Foxworthy
2. Robin Williams

3. What long-lived comic received the Congressional Medal of Honor for his USO work?

4. What red-haired TV comedienne had the good fortune of always having her name in her series' titles?

5. The famous Second City comedy troupe is, thanks to changes in the census, now centered in the *Third* City, which is what?

6. What rope-swinging cowboy humorist first used the stage name "the Cherokee Kid"?

7. What puffy-faced stand-up comic always complained he "got no respect"?

8. What stingy comic always claimed to be thirty-nine years old?

9. What wild-haired comedienne always complained about her husband, Fang?

10. What two animal characters, a cockroach and a cat, were the subjects of columns by humorist Don Marquis?

11. What author's books include *Republican Party Reptile, Give War a Chance,* and *Eat the Rich*?

12. What ventriloquist gave the world Charlie McCarthy and Mortimer Snerd?

13. What popular cartoonist illustrated Art Linkletter's humorous book *Kids Say the Darndest Things*?

14. What American humor author was born in 1835, the year Halley's Comet appeared, and claimed he would die seventy-six years later when the comet reappeared?

15. What hillbilly couple, starring in several films, first appeared in the movie *The Egg and I*?

16. What "blue-collar" comedian's nickname is "Tater Salad"?

17. What syndicated columnist, writing from Miami, is famous for the phrase "I'm not making this up"?

18. What impish comic often played the characters Geraldine Jones and Reverend Leroy?

19. Humor writer James Thurber wrote affectionately of his hometown, an Ohio metropolis. What was it?

20. What female humor columnist wrote the best-selling nonfiction books of 1978 and 1979?

QUESTIONS

3. Bob Hope ("Thanks for the memories . . .")
4. Lucille Ball, star of *I Love Lucy, The Lucy Show,* and *Here's Lucy*
5. Chicago; Los Angeles overtook Chicago as number two in the 1990 census.
6. Will Rogers
7. Rodney Dangerfield, who died in 2004
8. Jack Benny, who died in 1974—several years older than thirty-nine
9. Phyllis Diller
10. archy (the cockroach) and mehitabel (the cat) the columns were always written without capitals and punctuation
11. P. J. O'Rourke
12. Edgar Bergen
13. Charles Schulz, creator of "Peanuts"
14. Mark Twain; it happened as he predicted.
15. Ma and Pa Kettle, played by Marjorie Main and Percy Kilbride
16. Ron White, of Blue Collar Comedy fame
17. Dave Barry
18. Flip Wilson
19. Columbus
20. Erma Bombeck; the books were *If Life Is a Bowl of Cherries, What Am I Doing in the Pits?* and *Aunt Erma's Cope Book.*

★ Still More Great Americans on Film

1. What Native American princess was the subject of a 1995 Walt Disney animated movie?
2. *The Greatest* (1977) had boxer Muhammad Ali playing what character?
3. What frontier hero did John Wayne play in *The Alamo*?
4. Gary Busey played a rock-and-roll pioneer in what 1978 film? (Hint: "Peggy Sue")
5. *Swanee River* (1939) had Don Ameche playing America's favorite songwriter of the 1800s. Who?
6. *The Jolson Story* (1946) starred Larry Parks as legendary singer Al Jolson. Who provided Jolson's singing voice?
7. Wallace Beery played in a 1934 movie about the greatest showman of the nineteenth century, famed as a circus mogul. Who was he?
8. *The Pride of St. Louis* (1952) starred Dan Dailey as a baseball star and commentator. Who? (Hint: His initials are the same as Dailey's.)
9. Gary Cooper played a World War I army hero in a film that won him an Oscar. What was the title?
10. Rod Steiger played Chicago's most famous gangster in what 1959 movie?
11. Steve Allen played the world's most famous clarinetist in what 1955 film?
12. *Annie Oakley* (1935) starred what vivacious actress in the title role?
13. *Rhapsody in Blue* (1945) was the story of what renowned jazz and classical composer?
14. What handsome leading man played the title role in *Billy the Kid* (1941)?
15. What Wild West showman did Joel McCrea portray in a 1944 film?
16. *Sunrise at Campobello* (1960) had the lovely Greer Garson playing a very *un*lovely First Lady. Who?
17. Paul Newman played an Old West outlaw judge in what 1972 movie?
18. *W. C. Fields and Me* (1976) told the tale of hard-drinking comic Fields. What chubby actor played the chubby comic?
19. *Pony Express* (1953) had Charlton Heston and Forrest Tucker playing two notorious western gunslingers. Who?
20. *The Paleface* (1948) was an Old West comedy starring Bob Hope as a timid dentist. What historical western gunwoman did Jane Russell play?
21. Spencer Tracy starred in *Plymouth Adventure* (1952). What group of colonists was the movie about?
22. What actor played the title role in *The Story of Alexander Graham Bell* (1939)?

QUESTIONS

Still More Great Americans on Film // Answers

1. Pocahontas
2. Muhammad Ali
3. Davy Crockett; it was one of the few movies in which Wayne's character died.
4. *The Buddy Holly Story*
5. Stephen Foster
6. Al Jolson
7. P. T. Barnum; the movie was *The Mighty Barnum*.
8. Dizzy Dean
9. *Sergeant York*, concerning Alvin York
10. *Al Capone*
11. *The Benny Goodman Story*
12. Barbara Stanwyck
13. George Gershwin, played by actor Robert Alda (father of Alan Alda)
14. Robert Taylor
15. Buffalo Bill
16. Eleanor Roosevelt, wife of Franklin
17. *The Life and Times of Judge Roy Bean*
18. Rod Steiger
19. Wild Bill Hickok and Buffalo Bill
20. Calamity Jane
21. The Pilgrims, who landed in 1620 at Plymouth Rock in Massachusetts
22. Don Ameche; the movie was such a hit that for a while *ameche* was slang for telephone.

23. *The Story of G.I. Joe* (1945) starred Burgess Meredith as what famous World War II correspondent?
24. *Red Mountain* (1951) starred Alan Ladd in a brutal tale of Quantrill's Raiders. What war were they a part of?
25. *The Buccaneer* (1937) had Frederic March playing America's most famous pirate, a Frenchman in Louisiana. Who was he?
26. Blonde beauty Carroll Baker played a blonde movie queen of the 1930s. Who?
27. A 1940 film starred Dean Jagger as the Mormon leader who blazed the path to Utah. Who was he?
28. Dr. Samuel Mudd's story was told in *The Prisoner of Shark Island* (1936). What famous assassin was Mudd involved with?
29. *Words and Music* (1948) told the tale of songwriting partners Richard Rodgers and Lorenz Hart. What diminutive actor played the even more diminutive Hart?
30. Abraham Lincoln's early career as a lawyer was featured in *Young Mr. Lincoln* (1939). What laid-back actor played Lincoln?
31. *Citizen Kane* (1941), Orson Welles's masterpiece, was based on the life of what famous newspaper magnate?
32. The Howard in the film *Melvin and Howard* was what reclusive multimillionaire?

★ Kid Stuff: Theme Parks and Such

Who are we kidding? Theme parks aren't just for kids, are they? Adults like to pretend they're "taking the kids to the park," but we enjoy it as much as—probably more than—the kids.

One thing's for sure: America leads the world in theme parks. It's one of our unique contributions to civilization—maybe not the greatest contribution, but one of the most fun, anyway.

1. What two world-famous parks are entered through Main Street, U.S.A.?
2. What gigantic shopping center is home to the Nickelodeon Universe theme park and its SpongeBob SquarePants ride?

23. Ernie Pyle, who died before the war's end
24. The Civil War; "Bloody Bill" Quantrill's gang was a notorious band of Confederate guerrillas.
25. Jean Lafitte
26. Jean Harlow, in *Harlow* (1965)
27. Brigham Young
28. John Wilkes Booth, who shot Lincoln; poor Dr. Mudd had the misfortune to treat Booth's wounded leg and help him (temporarily) escape.
29. Mickey Rooney
30. Henry Fonda
31. William Randolph Hearst
32. Howard Hughes

Kid Stuff: Theme Parks and Such // Answers

1. Disney World (in Florida) and Disneyland (in California)
2. The Mall of America, in Minnesota

Kid Stuff: Theme Parks and Such, continued . . .

3. What Smoky Mountain theme park is owned by a country music star and was originally named Rebel Railroad?

4. Disney's Epcot Center is a popular attraction. What does Epcot stand for?

5. Where does the Carowinds Park get its name?

6. At what popular Pennsylvania park could you ride Big Bird's Rambling River and Ernie's Waterworks?

7. In what southern capital could you ride Goliath, Dare Devil Dive, and the Wile E. Coyote Canyon Blaster?

8. In what park (one of the oldies but goodies) could you find the Finding Nemo Adventure Submarine Voyage, Toontown, and Peter Pan's Flight?

9. What New Jersey park has Nitro, the third-highest roller coaster in the world?

10. What legendary lumberman is the center of a theme park in Brainerd, Minnesota?

11. The entrance to Universal Studio's Islands of Adventure has a replica of one of the Seven Wonders of the World. Which one?

12. The Tree of Life is found in the book of Genesis but also in what Florida park?

13. Hollywood's largest and busiest studio is also a popular theme park. What film studio is it?

14. The first theme park built around a country music theme was what?

15. If you are riding the Loch Ness Monster, Apollo's Chariot, and Griffon, what Virginia theme park are you experiencing?

16. What Pennsylvania park is owned by a candy company?

17. Frontier City is a family theme park in what western capital?

18. LEGOLAND Florida, which opened in 2011, is on the site of what earlier tourist attraction, famed for its water ski shows?

19. What Orlando park has replicas of many of the sites in the Gospels?

20. In what theme park could you visit Morocco, China, Japan, and Italy without ever leaving the United States?

21. Magic Springs Family Theme Park is in what southern state?

22. Arlington, Texas, has what famous park?

23. If you are dining at Cinderella's Castle, where are you?

24. If you are having fun in Crackaxle Canyon, Rockville, or Kidzopolis, what Texas theme park are you in?

3. Dollywood, named for Dolly Parton
4. Experimental Prototype Community of Tomorrow (You can see why they prefer to call it EPCOT.)
5. From the Carolinas; the park is in North Carolina and very near the South Carolina border. It celebrates the two states' past and present.
6. Sesame Place, named for TV's *Sesame Street*
7. Atlanta, at Six Flags over Georgia
8. Disneyland
9. Six Flags Great Adventure
10. Paul Bunyan; the Paul Bunyan Amusement Center has a twenty-six-foot animated Paul and a fifteen-foot Babe, his blue ox.
11. The Pharos (lighthouse) of ancient Alexandria
12. Disney's Animal Kingdom, in Orlando
13. Universal
14. Opryland, in (of course) Nashville, Tennessee
15. Busch Gardens Europe, near Williamsburg
16. Hersheypark, owned by (what else?) the Hershey chocolate company
17. Oklahoma City
18. Cypress Gardens, which closed in 2009
19. The Holy Land Experience
20. Epcot
21. Arkansas
22. Six Flags over Texas, first of the Six Flags parks to open
23. Florida's Walt Disney World
24. Six Flags Fiesta Texas, near San Antonio

Kid Stuff: Theme Parks and Such, continued . . .

25. The Raging Bull roller coaster, with a track almost a mile long, is the big attraction at what midwestern park?
26. If you are riding the Dominator (a floorless coaster) or Shockwave (a stand-up coaster), what Virginia park are you in?
27. The starred hat worn by Mickey Mouse as the sorcerer's apprentice is the symbol of which Disney park?
28. If you are visiting France, Germany, Italy, and England while you are near colonial Williamsburg, where are you?
29. Pandemonium and the SkyScreamer are rides at what mid-America park?
30. Which Florida park has the floorless Kraken roller coaster and the inverted Manta coaster?
31. If you are riding the wooden Apocalypse coaster and the in-reverse Déjà Vu coaster, what Six Flags park are you visiting?
32. If you are riding the roller coasters at Worlds of Fun, where are you?
33. If you are riding the terrifying SheiKra, the first drop coaster in America, where are you?
34. What California park bills itself as America's first theme park? (Hint: jellies)
35. The Amity section of Universal Studios Florida is built around what scary movie of the 1970s?

★ Leading Men (Again)

Given the names of three of an actor's major films, would you know the actor's name?

1. *Far and Away; Days of Thunder; Born on the Fourth of July*
2. *The War of the Roses; Disclosure; Wall Street*
3. *On Golden Pond; The Grapes of Wrath; My Darling Clementine*
4. *Mutiny on the Bounty; Red Dust; Gone with the Wind*
5. *Arsenic and Old Lace; North by Northwest; The Philadelphia Story*
6. *Sabrina; The Wild Bunch; Sunset Boulevard*
7. *The Road to Morocco; The Paleface; Fancy Pants*
8. *Grumpy Old Men; The Odd Couple; The Sunshine Boys*

25. Six Flags Great America, in Gurnee, Illinois, near Chicago

26. King's Dominion, a few miles north of Richmond

27. Disney's Hollywood Studios

28. Busch Gardens Williamsburg

29. Six Flags St. Louis (formerly Six Flags Mid-America)

30. Sea World Orlando

31. Six Flags Magic Mountain in Valencia, California

32. Kansas City, Missouri

33. Busch Gardens Tampa Bay

34. Knott's Berry Farm, which began as a roadside jelly stand

35. *Jaws*

Leading Men (Again) // Answers

1. Tom Cruise

2. Michael Douglas

3. Henry Fonda

4. Clark Gable

5. Cary Grant

6. William Holden

7. Bob Hope

8. Jack Lemmon

ANSWERS

9. *The Nutty Professor; The Patsy; The Bellboy*

10. *Bullitt; The Great Escape; The Magnificent Seven*

11. *The Best Years of Our Lives; Dr. Jekyll and Mr. Hyde; Anna Karenina*

12. *Cat Ballou; Point Blank; The Man Who Shot Liberty Valance*

13. *Wonder Bar; The Jazz Singer; Mammy*

14. *Hans Christian Andersen; The Secret Life of Walter Mitty; Up in Arms*

15. *All of Me; The Jerk; Father of the Bride*

16. *Scent of a Woman; The Godfather; And Justice for All*

17. *Tender Mercies; The Godfather; The Great Santini*

18. *The General; Sherlock Jr.; The Navigator*

19. *Kings Row; Bedtime for Bonzo; Knute Rockne, All American*

20. *The Sting; Butch Cassidy and the Sundance Kid; The Way We Were*

21. *The Sea Wolf; Little Caesar; Scarlet Street*

22. *The Hospital; Patton; Dr. Strangelove*

23. *Seven Brides for Seven Brothers; Calamity Jane; Kiss Me Kate*

24. *Pal Joey; The Man with the Golden Arm; From Here to Eternity*

25. *Singin' in the Rain; Brigadoon; An American in Paris*

26. *This Gun for Hire; The Glass Key; The Great Gatsby*

27. *Kiss of Death; Samson and Delilah; My Darling Clementine*

28. *Rear Window; You Can't Take It with You; It's a Wonderful Life*

29. *Quo Vadis; Ivanhoe; Billy the Kid*

30. *Father of the Bride; Judgment at Nuremberg; Boys Town*

31. *Doc Hollywood; Back to the Future; Bright Lights, Big City*

32. *Casino; The Godfather Part II; Raging Bull*

33. *Broadway Danny Rose; Love and Death; Hannah and Her Sisters*

34. *The Sheik; The Four Horsemen of the Apocalypse; Blood and Sand*

35. *Deliverance; Coming Home; Catch Twenty-two*

36. *The Cannonball Run; Smokey and the Bandit; The Longest Yard*

37. *The Alamo; True Grit; Rio Lobo*

38. *Groundhog Day; Ghostbusters; What about Bob?*

39. *Young Frankenstein; Stir Crazy; Willy Wonka and the Chocolate Factory*

40. *Jane Eyre; Othello; Citizen Kane*

41. *The Story of Alexander Graham Bell; Heaven Can Wait; Cocoon*

9. Jerry Lewis
10. Steve McQueen
11. Frederic March
12. Lee Marvin
13. Al Jolson
14. Danny Kaye
15. Steve Martin
16. Al Pacino
17. Robert Duvall
18. Buster Keaton
19. Ronald Reagan
20. Robert Redford
21. Edward G. Robinson
22. George C. Scott
23. Howard Keel
24. Frank Sinatra
25. Gene Kelly
26. Alan Ladd
27. Victor Mature
28. James Stewart
29. Robert Taylor
30. Spencer Tracy
31. Michael J. Fox
32. Robert De Niro
33. Woody Allen
34. Rudolph Valentino
35. Jon Voight
36. Burt Reynolds
37. John Wayne
38. Bill Murray
39. Gene Wilder
40. Orson Welles
41. Don Ameche

ANSWERS

★ Toys and Games and Other Playful Things

1. What ever popular blonde doll did Jack Ryan create in 1958?
2. Pong, introduced by Atari in 1975, was what new type of game?
3. What popular board game features Chance and Community Chest cards?
4. What Milton Bradley game was marketed as a "Sweet Little Game for Sweet Little Folks"?
5. What popular "course" game did Garnet Carter introduce in 1927? (Hint: windmills)
6. What bouncy, rideable toy was introduced by inventor George Hansburg in 1919?
7. What type of doll was such a hot item in 1983 that some stores sold them for a hundred dollars each?
8. What California company introduced the Frisbee in 1957 and the Hula Hoop in 1958?
9. What huggable and ever popular toy was named for a U.S. president?
10. What perennially popular items for kids have been produced for years by the Binney & Smith Company?
11. What pliable substance, sold as a toy, was introduced by inventor Peter Hodgson?
12. What type of hat did TV's Davy Crockett popularize for kids in the 1950s?
13. What word game played on a board was invented by Alfred Mosher Butts in 1932?
14. What very popular question-and-answer game was introduced in 1983?
15. What type of word puzzle was introduced in the *New York World* in 1913?
16. The toy logs that have amused generations of American kids are named for what president?
17. What familiar plastic toy is the focus of a September festival on the National Mall in Washington, D.C.?
18. What movable toys are the center of a museum in Strasburg, Pennsylvania?
19. What type of cuddly toy is displayed at Frannie's Museum in Naples, Florida?
20. In the 1930s, what game was played in movie theaters on "Bank Nights"?
21. Faro, once called America's National Card Game, took its name from what?
22. Using letters from their names, Harold Matson and Elliot Handler named their toy company what?

Toys and Games and Other Playful Things // Answers

1. Barbie
2. Video
3. Monopoly
4. Candyland
5. Miniature golf
6. The pogo stick
7. Cabbage Patch Kids
8. Wham-O
9. The teddy bear, named for Theodore Roosevelt
10. Crayola Crayons
11. Silly Putty
12. Coonskin
13. Scrabble
14. Trivial Pursuit
15. The crossword
16. Lincoln
17. The Frisbee
18. Toy trains, electric and nonelectric
19. Teddy bears
20. Bingo
21. A picture of an Egyptian pharaoh was on one of the king face cards.
22. Mattel

Toys and Games and Other Playful Things, continued . . .

23. In 1860 what lithographer devised "The Checkered Game of Life" for people to play?
24. The Ideal Company marketed dolls named for what popular child star of the 1930s?
25. The two-person game called draughts in England is called what in the U.S.?

☆ Queens of the Screen

Could you guess the name of a Hollywood leading lady if given the name of three of her films? Find out.

1. *The Other Boleyn Girl, Black Swan, Thor*
2. *Chicago, The Rebound, The Legend of Zorro*
3. *The Iron Lady, The Bridges of Madison County, Sophie's Choice*
4. *Bridget Jones's Diary, Cold Mountain, Chicago*
5. *Moonstruck, Silkwood, Mermaids*
6. *Places in the Heart, Norma Rae, Steel Magnolias*
7. *Cabaret; The Sterile Cuckoo; New York, New York*
8. *The Fabulous Baker Boys, Wolf, The Age of Innocence*
9. *Coal Miner's Daughter, The River, Crimes of the Heart*
10. *The Big Sleep, Key Largo, To Have and to Have Not*
11. *Fancy Pants; Mame; The Long, Long Trailer*
12. *The Graduate, The Miracle Worker, The Pumpkin Eater*
13. *On Golden Pond, The Lion in Winter, Bringing Up Baby*
14. *Rear Window, To Catch a Thief, High Society*
15. *Whatever Happened to Baby Jane?, Mildred Pierce, Grand Hotel*
16. *Come to the Stable, The Farmer's Daughter, Man's Castle*
17. *You Can't Take It with You, Mr. Deeds Goes to Town, Shane*
18. *Father of the Bride, Annie Hall, Reds*
19. *Private Benjamin, Death Becomes Her, The Sugarland Express*
20. *All about Eve, Dark Victory, The Little Foxes*
21. *Calamity Jane, Pillow Talk, Send Me No Flowers*
22. *The Heiress, The Snake Pit, Anthony Adverse*

QUESTIONS

23. Milton Bradley
24. Shirley Temple
25. Checkers

Queens of the Screen // Answers

1. Natalie Portman
2. Catherine Zeta-Jones
3. Meryl Streep
4. Renee Zellweger
5. Cher
6. Sally Field
7. Liza Minnelli
8. Michelle Pfeiffer
9. Sissy Spacek
10. Lauren Bacall
11. Lucille Ball
12. Anne Bancroft
13. Katharine Hepburn
14. Grace Kelly
15. Joan Crawford
16. Loretta Young
17. Jean Arthur
18. Diane Keaton
19. Goldie Hawn
20. Bette Davis
21. Doris Day
22. Olivia De Havilland

Queens of the Screen, continued . . .

QUESTIONS

23. *Bonnie and Clyde, Network, Supergirl*
24. *Cold Mountain, Moulin Rouge, The Rabbit Hole*
25. *The Wizard of Oz, Meet Me in St. Louis, A Star Is Born*
26. *Maytime, Rose Marie, San Francisco*
27. *Terms of Endearment, The Apartment, Steel Magnolias*
28. *Boomtown, It Happened One Night, The Egg and I*
29. *David and Bathsheba, I Want to Live, My Foolish Heart*
30. *Stepmom, Dead Man Walking, The Rocky Horror Picture Show*
31. *Miss Congeniality, The Proposal, The Blind Side*
32. *My Man Godfrey, Nothing Sacred, To Be or Not to Be*
33. *The Thin Man, The Best Years of Our Lives, Cheaper by the Dozen*
34. *Running with Scissors, Bugsy, Regarding Henry*
35. *Some Like It Hot, The Seven Year Itch, Gentlemen Prefer Blondes*
36. *Singin' in the Rain, The Unsinkable Molly Brown, The Singing Nun*
37. *Top Hat, Swing Time, Kitty Foyle*
38. *Double Indemnity, Meet John Doe, The Lady Eve*
39. *Cleopatra, Cat on a Hot Tin Roof, National Velvet*
40. *The Little Colonel, Bright Eyes, Curly Top*
41. *Peyton Place, Imitation of Life, The Postman Always Rings Twice*
42. *Klondike Annie, Belle of the Nineties, My Little Chickadee*
43. *West Side Story, Gypsy, Miracle on 34th Street*

23. Faye Dunaway
24. Nicole Kidman
25. Judy Garland
26. Jeanette MacDonald
27. Shirley MacLaine
28. Claudette Colbert
29. Susan Hayward
30. Susan Sarandon
31. Sandra Bullock
32. Carole Lombard
33. Myrna Loy
34. Annette Bening
35. Marilyn Monroe
36. Debbie Reynolds
37. Ginger Rogers
38. Barbara Stanwyck
39. Elizabeth Taylor
40. Shirley Temple
41. Lana Turner
42. Mae West
43. Natalie Wood

PART THREE

OUR LOVE AFFAIR WITH MUSIC

✭ "They're Playing My Song"

Some performers become so identified with a particular song that it is forever **their** *song. For instance, "Bridge Over Troubled Water" will always be identified with Simon and Garfunkel. Try your hand at matching the song with its key performer. These range from early crooners to contemporary artists—from Al Jolson to Aerosmith and beyond. By the way, we had to leave out the Beatles, ABBA, etc., since this is* **American** *trivia.*

1. "Friends in Low Places"
2. "Hound Dog"
3. "Chattahoochee"
4. "Margaritaville"
5. "Me and Bobby McGee"
6. "Puff the Magic Dragon"
7. "By the Time I Get to Phoenix"
8. "California Girls"
9. "Courtesy of the Red, White, and Blue"
10. "Mrs. Robinson"
11. "Daddy Sang Bass"
12. "Your Cheatin' Heart"
13. "Mona Lisa"
14. "Flowers on the Wall"
15. "Hold Tight"
16. "Cheek to Cheek"
17. "White Christmas"
18. "The Devil Went Down to Georgia"
19. "Blue Suede Shoes"
20. "The Little Old Lady from Pasadena"
21. "Wabash Cannonball"
22. "Stand by Your Man"
23. "Dream On"
24. "Rock around the Clock"
25. "Feels So Right"
26. "Light My Fire"

"They're Playing My Song" // Answers

1. Garth Brooks
2. Elvis Presley
3. Alan Jackson
4. Jimmy Buffett
5. Janis Joplin
6. Peter, Paul, and Mary
7. Glen Campbell
8. The Beach Boys
9. Toby Keith
10. Simon and Garfunkel
11. Johnny Cash
12. Hank Williams
13. Nat King Cole
14. The Statler Brothers
15. The Andrews Sisters
16. Fred Astaire
17. Bing Crosby
18. Charlie Daniels
19. Carl Perkins
20. Jan and Dean
21. Roy Acuff
22. Tammy Wynette
23. Aerosmith
24. Bill Haley and the Comets
25. Alabama
26. The Doors

"They're Playing My Song," continued . . .

27. "Stormy Weather"
28. "You've Got a Friend"
29. "Joy to the World"
30. "Mack the Knife"
31. "Rocky Mountain High"
32. "Venus"
33. "Stop! In the Name of Love"
34. "Tip-Toe Thru' the Tulips with Me"
35. "The Night They Drove Old Dixie Down"
36. "Bye Bye Love"
37. "Up-Up and Away"
38. "Sixteen Tons"
39. "Song Sung Blue"
40. "American Pie"
41. "California Dreamin' "
42. "Everybody Loves Somebody"
43. "Banana Boat (Day-O)"
44. "Call Me Irresponsible"

★ Singers, Crooners, and So Forth

1. What tragedy prompted Alan Jackson's song "Where Were You When the World Stopped Turning"?
2. Of the many fan clubs for singers, what deceased rocker has the most clubs?
3. What sultry-voiced songstress was born Norma Deloris Egstrom?
4. What crooner and former movie partner of Jerry Lewis died on Christmas Day 1995?
5. What beloved jazz singer performed with the Billy Graham crusades in her later years?
6. An eighty-eight-acre theme park is Pigeon Forge, Tennessee's most popular attraction. What bigger-than-life country singer is it named for?
7. What late black singer was the Queen of Gospel Singers?

27. Lena Horne
28. James Taylor
29. Three Dog Night
30. Bobby Darin
31. John Denver
32. Frankie Avalon
33. The Supremes
34. Tiny Tim
35. Joan Baez
36. The Everly Brothers
37. 5th Dimension
38. Tennessee Ernie Ford
39. Neil Diamond
40. Don McLean
41. The Mamas and the Papas
42. Dean Martin
43. Harry Belafonte
44. Jack Jones

Singers, Crooners, and So Forth // Answers

1. The terrorist attacks on September 11, 2001
2. Elvis Presley, with more than 450 registered clubs
3. Peggy Lee, who died in 2002
4. Dean Martin
5. Ethel Waters
6. Dolly Parton; the park is Dollywood.
7. Mahalia Jackson

Singers, Crooners, and So Forth, continued . . .

8. What musical satirist founded the Mothers of Invention in 1964?
9. What sometimes controversial TV preacher (and singer) is a cousin of country singers Jerry Lee Lewis and Mickey Gilley?
10. What belting Broadway singer titled her 1956 autobiography *Who Can Ask for Anything More?*
11. When they recorded, what "brothers" did Bill Medley and Bobby Hatfield become?
12. What country singer has a parkway named for him in his residence of Hendersonville, Tennessee? (Hint: wears black)
13. What Mormon family group started out singing at Disneyland?
14. What two instruments did the two Smothers Brothers play (and who played which instrument)?
15. The Jordanaires and the Blue Moon Boys were backup singers for what pop idol?
16. What patriotic singer was at one time named the "First Lady of Radio"?
17. What laid-back crooner, who died in 2001, worked as a barber in his younger days?
18. Michael, Jackie, Jermaine, Marlon, Randy, and Tito were what brother act in pop music?
19. What much loved pop singer and movie actress started her career as one of the singing Gumm Sisters? (Hint: Toto)
20. Patty, Maxene, and LaVerne were what close-harmony sister group?
21. What country singer was enshrined in the Country Music Hall of Fame *and* the Cowboy Hall of Fame (and was also the father of a sitcom actor)?
22. What rock singer who sang with the First Edition later became a country star?
23. What Christian/pop singer married country singer Vince Gill in 2000?
24. What four singing sisters made their reputation on *The Lawrence Welk Show* on TV?
25. Who was for many, many years the singing host of the Miss America pageant?
26. What pioneering pop singer died in a plane crash on February 3, 1959? (Hint: glasses)
27. What Western movie star also sang with the Sons of the Pioneers?
28. What baritone star of MGM movie musicals died in 2004?
29. What U.S. military band features the Singing Sergeants?

8. Frank Zappa
9. Jimmy Swaggart
10. Ethel Merman
11. The Righteous Brothers
12. Johnny Cash
13. The Osmonds
14. Guitar (Tom) and stand-up bass (Dick); both were singers as well.
15. Elvis Presley
16. Kate Smith
17. Perry Como
18. The Jacksons (or, in their original form, the Jackson 5)
19. Judy Garland, who was born Frances Gumm
20. The Andrews Sisters
21. Tex Ritter, father of John Ritter
22. Kenny Rogers
23. Amy Grant
24. The Lennon Sisters
25. Bert Parks ("There she is, Miss America . . .")
26. Buddy Holly
27. Roy Rogers
28. Howard Keel
29. The Air Force Band

Singers, Crooners, and So Forth, continued . . .

30. What singer-pianist won Clio Awards for his commercial jingles?
31. What pop idol was launched by the small Sun Record Company of Memphis?
32. What popular singer spoke the words, "Wait a minute, you ain't heard nothing yet" in the 1927 movie, *The Jazz Singer?*
33. What long-lived pop group has counted Peter Cetera and Robert Lamm among its vocalists? (Hint: "numerical" albums)
34. What future country music star was in prison at San Quentin when Johnny Cash gave his 1960 concert there?
35. What singer-fiddler-guitarist launched the Volunteer Jam concerts in Nashville?
36. What music legend who died in 2004 was backed up by the Raelettes?
37. What "redheaded stranger," a country superstar, was born in Abbott, Texas, in 1933?
38. Wide-mouthed Steven Tyler, who kicked his destructive drug habit, is lead singer for what hard rock group?
39. What popular crooner had been part of a trio called the Rhythm Boys?

★ Creating the American Song

1. What famous patriotic song was written on the back of an envelope during the bombing of a fort?
2. What New England state's state song is "Yankee Doodle"?
3. What is the only state with its state song coming from a Broadway musical?
4. What popular wedding song did Irving Berlin compose to win the hand of Ellin Mackay?
5. What patriotic song did teacher Katherine Lee Bates pen in 1893 after viewing Pike's Peak?
6. What great songwriter's first song, written when he was eighteen, was "Open Thy Lattice, Love"? (Hint: "Swanee River")
7. What state's official song was a favorite Confederate marching song in the Civil War (even though the state itself was *not* in the Confederacy)?

30. Barry Manilow, who wrote (among other jingles) "I Am Stuck on Band-Aid"

31. Elvis Presley; Sun also helped launch Johnny Cash, Carl Perkins, and Jerry Lee Lewis.

32. Al Jolson; the movie is credited with being the first talkie.

33. Chicago

34. Merle Haggard

35. Charlie Daniels

36. Ray Charles

37. Willie Nelson

38. Aerosmith; Tyler's nickname is "Demon of Screamin'."

39. Bing Crosby

Creating the American Song // Answers

1. "The Star-Spangled Banner," written during the bombing of Baltimore's Fort McHenry in 1814

2. Connecticut

3. Oklahoma; the song "Oklahoma!" is from (what else?) the play *Oklahoma!*

4. "Always"

5. "America the Beautiful"

6. Stephen Foster, more famous for "Camptown Races," "Beautiful Dreamer," and "My Old Kentucky Home"

7. Maryland's; the song is "Maryland, My Maryland," sung to the same tune as "O Christmas Tree."

Creating the American Song, continued . . .

8. Liliuokalani, Hawaii's last queen, wrote what popular song?

9. What 1893 song, one of the most-sung songs in America, was originally titled "Good Morning to You"?

10. In Bobbie Gentry's 1967 song, what boy jumped off the Tallahatchee Bridge?

11. What was the significance of Glenn Miller's recording of the song "Chattanooga Choo-Choo"?

12. Samuel Francis Smith wrote what great patriotic song (which is almost a second national anthem)?

13. What beloved Christmas song by Irving Berlin was introduced by Bing Crosby in the 1942 movie *Holiday Inn*?

14. What name is Stephen Foster's plantation song "Old Folks at Home" better known by?

15. "High Hopes" was the campaign song of what Democratic presidential candidate of the 1960s?

16. What famed poet of the Midwest collected folk songs in *The American Songbag*?

17. "I Don't Want to Walk without You, Jesus" was written for evangelist Aimee Semple McPherson. With a (slightly) new title and lyrics, what pop song did it become?

18. Henry Mancini's song "Red River" became better known by what title? (Hint: Audrey Hepburn sang it.)

19. The song "Let's Dance" was the theme song for what noted band leader and clarinetist?

20. What patriotic poem (later set to music) first appeared in the *Baltimore American* on September 20, 1814?

21. Utah's multicolored Big Rock Candy Mountain was made famous in a song by what folksinger?

22. What country singer made Muskogee, Oklahoma, world famous with his song "Okie from Muskogee"?

23. What much loved song—practically an anthem of the western U.S.—was written by Dr. Brewster Higley? (Hint: buffalo)

24. What state has (appropriately) a country music standard as its state song?

25. What president of the late 1800s found his opponent using the campaign song "Ma, Ma, Where's My Pa? Gone to the White House! Ha! Ha! Ha!"?

8. "Aloha Oe"
9. "Happy Birthday to You"
10. Billie Joe, in the "Ode to Billie Joe"
11. It was the first gold (million-selling) single.
12. "My Country 'Tis of Thee," written in 1831; curiously, Smith didn't realize the tune he selected was the tune used for the British national anthem, "God Save the King."
13. "White Christmas"
14. "Swanee River"
15. John F. Kennedy
16. Carl Sandburg
17. "I Don't Want to Walk without You, Baby"
18. "Moon River"
19. Benny Goodman
20. "The Star-Spangled Banner"
21. Burl Ives
22. Merle Haggard
23. "Home on the Range"
24. Tennessee, with "The Tennessee Waltz"
25. Grover Cleveland, who bore the stigma of having fathered an illegitimate child

QUESTIONS

26. What southern state's state song came under fire in the 1990s because it supposedly contained racist elements?

27. "Happy Trails" was the familiar theme song of what movie cowboy?

28. Composer Irving Berlin wrote the campaign song "I Like Ike" for what presidential candidate?

29. What composer has two of his songs used as state songs?

30. The British drinking song "Battle of the Kegs" became what song of the Revolutionary War?

31. What two talented brothers wrote such classics as "I Got Rhythm," "Summertime," and "I Got Plenty of Nothin' "?

32. If you are singing "On the Banks of the Wabash," what state song are you singing?

33. What Plains state has "Home on the Range" as its state song?

34. The English drinking song "To Anacreon in Heaven" lent its tune to what familiar patriotic song?

⋆ Composers and Songwriters and Such

1. What military band composer was "the March King"?

2. What composer, who conducted the Boston Pops Orchestra, is famous for film music, including *Star Wars, E.T.,* and *Raiders of the Lost Ark*?

3. What patriotic songwriter, known as the Yankee Doodle Dandy, wrote over five hundred songs?

4. Leonard Bernstein wrote the music for a famous play about New York street gangs. What was it?

5. What beloved writer of songs about the South hardly ever visited the region?

6. What musical theater duo gave the world such classics as *The Sound of Music, The King and I, South Pacific,* and *Oklahoma*?

7. Charleston, South Carolina's Spoleto Festival is a world-famous celebration of art and music. What noted composer introduced the festival?

8. Decorah, Iowa, has a huge monument to what Czech composer?

26. Virginia's; the song is "Carry Me Back to Old Virginny."
27. Roy Rogers
28. Dwight Eisenhower
29. Stephen Foster, who wrote "Swanee River" (Florida) and "My Old Kentucky Home" (Kentucky, of course)
30. "Yankee Doodle"
31. George and Ira Gershwin
32. Indiana's
33. Kansas
34. "The Star-Spangled Banner"

Composers and Songwriters and Such // Answers

1. John Philip Sousa, who wrote "Stars and Stripes Forever" and other band classics
2. John Williams
3. George M. Cohan, the subject of the movie *Yankee Doodle Dandy*
4. *West Side Story*
5. Stephen Foster, a Pennsylvanian who spent almost no time in the South
6. Richard Rodgers and Oscar Hammerstein
7. Gian Carlo Menotti, famous especially for his Christmas opera *Amahl and the Night Visitors*
8. Antonin Dvorak, famous for his *New World Symphony*

Composers and Songwriters and Such, continued . . .

9. Sedalia, Missouri, hosts a ragtime music festival named for what noted composer? (Hint: *The Sting*)
10. Lehigh University in Pennsylvania has one of America's oldest festivals celebrating a great baroque composer. Who?
11. What blind hymn writer wrote more songs than anyone who ever lived?
12. Composer Ferde Grofé wrote the famous *Grand Canyon Suite* and also a suite about what great river?
13. Songwriter Johnny Mercer donated an award he'd won to his hometown of Savannah, Georgia. What was it?
14. Aaron Copland wrote a suite called *Appalachian Spring* and also music for a ballet on a legendary gunslinger. Who?
15. Near the Okefenokee Swamp is a park named for which world-famous American composer?

9. Scott Joplin, who wrote "The Entertainer," "Maple Leaf Rag," and many other popular songs
10. J. S. Bach; the Bach Festival each May is a major event.
11. Fanny Crosby, famous for "Blessed Assurance" and many other songs
12. The Mississippi; it's the *Mississippi Suite.*
13. An Academy Award—that is, the Oscar—which he won for a song he'd written for a movie
14. Billy the Kid
15. Stephen Foster; the Swanee River, made famous by Foster's song, is not far away.

PART FOUR

LEISURE TIME, AMERICAN STYLE

✮ Holidays, Holy Days, and Other Special Days

QUESTIONS

1. What holiday, the unofficial end of summer, was first observed in 1894?
2. National Whiners Day, which first began in 1986, falls on the day after what holiday?
3. What U.S. autumn holiday is also celebrated in Spain, Italy, and Latin America?
4. What Confederate general's birthday, January 19, was a holiday in some southern states?
5. In 1915 President Wilson designated what holiday as the second Sunday in May?
6. What holiday is the number-one day for sales of fresh-cut flowers?
7. What spring holiday was originally called Decoration Day?
8. What assassinated president's February 12 birthday became a federal holiday in 1892?
9. What was the meaning of wearing a red carnation on Mother's Day?
10. On what patriotic holiday did presidents John Adams, Thomas Jefferson, and James Monroe die?
11. Technically, how many national holidays are there?
12. President's Day combines the birthdays of which two presidents born in February?
13. On what Christian holiday was Abraham Lincoln shot?
14. Punxsutawney, Pennsylvania, has the nation's "official" animal connected with what winter holiday? (Hint: rodent)
15. What historic New England capital celebrates Bunker Hill Day each June?
16. By 1966 presidential proclamation, what holiday was fixed as the third Sunday in June?
17. In 1789 what fall holiday became the first U.S. holiday designated by presidential proclamation?
18. Armistice Day, made a legal holiday in 1938, now goes by what name?
19. The last Friday in April is what nature-centered holiday?
20. What fall holiday was first celebrated in 1792?
21. What patriotic day was proclaimed by Woodrow Wilson in 1916?
22. What federal holiday began in 1880 as a holiday for government workers in Washington, D.C.?

1. Labor Day
2. Christmas; presumably the day after Christmas is a good day to whine.
3. Columbus Day; Columbus was an Italian working for Spain, and his voyages led to the settlement of Latin America.
4. Robert E. Lee's
5. Mother's Day
6. Valentine's Day
7. Memorial Day; it was Decoration Day because graves were tended and decorated with flowers.
8. Abraham Lincoln's
9. It meant the wearer's mother was still living. A white carnation meant she had died.
10. Independence Day
11. Technically, none. The U.S. can declare certain days to be holidays for federal employees, but the states themselves have to designate holidays.
12. George Washington (Feb. 22) and Abraham Lincoln (Feb. 12)
13. Good Friday
14. Groundhog Day; Punxsutawney Phil is the unofficial rodent weather forecaster of the U.S.
15. Boston, Massachusetts
16. Father's Day
17. Thanksgiving
18. Veterans Day
19. Arbor Day, dedicated to trees and their preservation
20. Columbus Day; the 1792 fest was the tricentennial celebration of Columbus's 1492 voyage.
21. Flag Day (June 14)
22. George Washington's birthday (February 22)

★ Four-Wheeled Friend: The Automobile

We Americans have a love affair with our cars, don't we? And why not, since they started here?

1. What automaker was called the "Father of Mass Production"?
2. What tiny two-seat car went on sale in 2008?
3. What make of car was named for a chief of the Ottawa tribe?
4. What radical change did automaker Henry Ford make in his employees' workday in 1914?
5. In 1907 what cars for hire appeared in New York with meters and gas-powered engines?
6. Before cars were advertised with the slogan "It starts from the seat!" how were they started?
7. What sporty car did Ford introduce in April 1964 for the price of $2,368?
8. What Japanese automaker built a plant in Smyrna, Tennessee?
9. Manny, Moe, and Jack, who retail automotive parts, are better known by what name?
10. What small item developed by Henry F. Phillips transformed assembly line production?
11. What make of car is the oldest active American make?
12. What fuel-inefficient (and *cramped*) model did Chevrolet introduce in September 1975?
13. What was the first Japanese company to sell more than one hundred thousand cars in the United States in one year?
14. Hydromatic, Fordomatic, and Dynaflow were what type of automobile feature?
15. The P'up, which went on sale in 1981 in the United States, was made by what Japanese company?
16. What auto executive's autobiography was the best-selling nonfiction book of 1984 and 1985?
17. What popular Toyota model went on sale in 1982?
18. What luxury make of car had the longtime slogan "Standard of the World"?
19. What product became durable when heated with sulfur, as discovered accidentally by Charles Goodyear?
20. The U.S.'s highest auto road climbs up what Colorado mountain?
21. What maker of hulking, tanklike cars went out of business in 2010?

Four-Wheeled Friend: The Automobile // Answers

1. Henry Ford
2. Smart Fortwo
3. Pontiac; the make was discontinued in 2010.
4. He shortened it to eight hours.
5. Taxicabs
6. Cranking, of course; the starter was introduced in 1914.
7. The Mustang
8. Nissan
9. The Pep Boys
10. The Phillips screw; in 1937 Cadillac became the first maker to use Phillips screws and drivers on assembly lines.
11. Buick; it got its start in 1899.
12. The Chevette
13. Toyota
14. Early names for the automatic transmission
15. Isuzu; it was its first model in the United States.
16. Lee Iacocca of Chrysler
17. The Camry
18. Cadillac
19. Rubber; this made durable, all-weather tires a possibility—a major breakthrough for automobiles.
20. Pike's Peak, near Denver
21. Hummer

Four-Wheeled Friend: The Automobile, continued...

22. What Korean-made cars hit the U.S. market in 1986?
23. The rearview mirror on cars had its beginning at what famous auto race?
24. What crucial auto part did William Champion begin manufacturing in 1908?
25. In 1897, Ransom E. Olds began the automobile industry in what capital city?

★ Join the Club

Americans are a sociable people, and we look for something to bring us together—churches, sports teams, Tupperware parties, whatever. Some of the clubs and associations in the U.S. do wonderful works for charity. And some are strictly for fun.

1. What Beverly Hills club was famous for its comical "roasts" of celebrities?
2. What organization registers purebred pooches?
3. What service club's name indicates that it is the "least pessimistic" club in America?
4. The LOOM is what fraternal organization for men? (Hint: antlers)
5. What organization that was originally founded for urban evangelism is now noted for teaching swimming and lifesaving?
6. What club for high school students has a seal featuring a plow, an eagle, and an owl?
7. Caroline Harrison, wife of President Benjamin Harrison, was head of what prestigious social organization for women?
8. The NRA is dedicated to protecting Second Amendment rights. What is the NRA?
9. What lickable items are collected by people in the American Philatelic Society?
10. What is the more common one-word name for members of the Imperial Council of the Ancient Arabic Order of the Nobles of the Mystic Shrine?

22. Hyundais

23. The Indianapolis 500

24. Spark plugs (Remember Champion spark plugs?)

25. Lansing, Michigan

Join the Club // Answers

1. The Friars Club

2. American Kennel Club

3. The Optimists

4. The Moose Lodges—Loyal Order of the Moose

5. The YMCA, which was (as people often forget) the Young Men's *Christian* Association

6. National FFA Organization (formerly Future Farmers of America)

7. The DAR, Daughters of the American Revolution

8. The National Rifle Association, which opposes gun control

9. Stamps; philately is the fancy name for stamp collecting.

10. Shriners, of course

Join the Club, continued . . .

11. What grassroots conservative political organization was founded by religious broadcaster Pat Robertson?
12. What noted civic businessmen's organization is headquartered in Evanston, Illinois? (Hint: wheels)
13. What conservative political organization operates the American Opinion Bookstores?
14. What coin-collecting association exhibits a dazzling coin collection in Colorado Springs?
15. What college sports organization awards the Bobby Bowden Awards?
16. What noted fraternal organization (named for an animal) has its headquarters in Chicago?
17. Washington, D.C.'s House of the Temple is owned by what famous men's fraternity?
18. The SCV, organized in Richmond, Virginia, in 1896, represents what group?
19. What veterans' fraternity, formed after World War I, is organized into "posts"?
20. What conservative political organization was founded by TV preacher Jerry Falwell?
21. What famous twelve-step organization was founded by Dr. Bob and Bill W.?
22. What sort of activity is promoted by the National Forensic League?
23. The GAR, Grand Army of the Republic, was composed of which war's veterans?
24. The Society of Mayflower Descendants, founded in 1897, requires what of its members?
25. "Men of Integrity" is the tagline of what Christian men's group founded in 1990?
26. Political activist Phyllis Schlafly founded what organization in 1972?

✷ Christmas, American Style

1. What popular Christmas flower was named for an American ambassador to Mexico?
2. The names of Santa Claus's eight reindeer are from what famous 1823 poem by Clement Moore?

11. The Christian Coalition
12. The Rotary Club
13. The John Birch Society
14. The American Numismatic Association
15. The Fellowship of Christian Athletes
16. The Elks
17. The Masons
18. The Sons of Confederate Veterans
19. The American Legion
20. The Moral Majority, later renamed Liberty Federation
21. Alcoholics Anonymous (noted for not using its members' last names)
22. Public speaking, particularly among high school students
23. The Civil War; the GAR was composed of *Union* veterans, not Confederates.
24. Descent from a signer of the Mayflower Compact of 1620
25. Promise Keepers
26. The Eagle Forum

Christmas, American Style // Answers

1. The poinsettia, named for Joel Poinsett; the flower is native to Mexico, and Poinsett liked it so much he brought some back with him.
2. "The Night before Christmas," originally titled "A Visit from St. Nicholas"

3. Cowboy singer Gene Autry introduced what luminous animal to American Christmas?

4. What beloved song begins, "The sun is shining, the grass is green"?

5. What Russian ballet is often performed at Christmastime?

6. What Christian denomination is noted for its Christmas season bell-ringing fund-raisers?

7. Las Posadas, a Christmas tradition in San Antonio, Texas, celebrates what event?

8. What ever-popular TV special first aired on December 9, 1965?

9. If you see "putzes" while visiting Bethlehem, Pennsylvania, at Christmas, what are you seeing?

10. What northern "rust belt" state leads the nation in the growing of Christmas trees?

11. What historic resort town in Virginia restricts its Christmas decorations to items that colonial people would have used?

12. "A Country Christmas" is the annual display at what large Nashville hotel?

13. The Temple Square Christmas celebration is held in what western capital?

14. What choral work, first performed in 1742, is often performed at Christmastime?

15. Every Christmas at Trenton, New Jersey, you could see the reenactment of a famous Revolutionary War general crossing the Delaware River. Who?

16. In the 1960s, Christmas trees lit by a rotating color wheel were made of what substance?

17. In Galveston, Texas, you could see Dickens on the Strand, with yuletide representations of characters from what famous Christmas book?

18. What northwestern metropolis has a stunning Christmas Ships Parade on the Willamette and Columbia Rivers?

19. How did "America's Christmas city," Bethlehem, Pennsylvania, get its name?

20. Phillips Brooks's statue stands beside his church, historic Trinity Church in Boston. What famous Christmas carol is Brooks known for?

21. What appropriately named Florida town receives thousands of pieces of mail every Christmas sent by people wanting the town's postmark?

3. Rudolph the red-nosed reindeer, of course

4. "White Christmas," by Irving Berlin—widely considered the most popular pop song of all time

5. *The Nutcracker,* with music by Tchaikovsky

6. The Salvation Army

7. Mary and Joseph's search for an inn (see Luke 2:7); *posada* is Spanish for "inn."

8. *A Charlie Brown Christmas*

9. A type of Nativity scene; "putz" was the name used by the early Moravian Christian settlers.

10. Michigan

11. Williamsburg

12. The Opryland Hotel

13. Salt Lake City, Utah

14. George Frideric Handel's *Messiah*

15. George Washington, of course; his famous crossing took place on Christmas Day, 1776.

16. Aluminum

17. *A Christmas Carol,* Charles Dickens's great contribution to the world's celebration of Christmas

18. Portland, Oregon

19. Its Moravian settlers had sung a Christmas hymn praising the town of Jesus' birth; they liked the name, so they used it.

20. "O Little Town of Bethlehem"

21. Christmas, naturally

★ I Love a Parade

1. New York City's biggest parade is on what holiday? (Hint: green)
2. What Florida attraction has the daily Main Street Electrical Parade?
3. San Francisco's annual Golden Dragon Parade takes place in what ethnic community?
4. On what holiday does Detroit hold its famous Santa Claus Parade?
5. What parade, held on January 1, 1954, became the first nationwide TV broadcast in color?
6. What port city holds its Gasparilla Parade of Pirates each January?
7. What feathered farm animal is celebrated in an annual parade in Wayne, Nebraska?
8. In what northwestern capital could you join in the annual Vigilante Parade each May?
9. What historic masked parade takes place in Philadelphia on New Year's Day?
10. What evangelist was once the Grand Marshall in Pasadena's grand Tournament of Roses Parade?
11. What world-famous part of New Orleans culture first began in 1857?
12. Where would you see a parade in which all the floats tell a story from the Bible?
13. What city has the nation's biggest Thanksgiving Day parade?

★ For Kids' Sake

1. What popular children's book (also a movie) was originally titled *The Emerald City*?
2. Larry Harmon, who died in 2008, was famous for portraying what big-footed, red-haired character?
3. What two familiar characters in children's readers were created by Zerna Sharp?
4. What world-famous children's hospital is in Memphis, Tennessee?
5. What boys' organization was founded by Daniel Carter Beard?
6. In E. B. White's popular children's book *Charlotte's Web,* Charlotte is a spider. What type of animal is the title character in White's *Stuart Little*?

I Love a Parade // Answers

1. St. Patrick's Day
2. Walt Disney World
3. Chinatown
4. Thanksgiving Day
5. The Tournament of Roses parade
6. Tampa, Florida
7. Chickens; the Chicken Show each July includes omelet cook-offs, egg games, a chicken art show, and a chicken parade.
8. Helena, Montana
9. The Mummers Parade
10. Billy Graham
11. The Mardi Gras parade
12. In Humboldt, Kansas, with its annual Biblesta Parade; the name is a combination of *Bible* and *fiesta*. All people on the floats must wear biblical costumes.
13. New York, naturally

For Kids' Sake // Answers

1. *The Wonderful Wizard of Oz*
2. Bozo the Clown; Harmon not only portrayed Bozo but also owned the Bozo franchise, meaning he licensed (and sometimes trained) other actors who portrayed Bozo in the United States and abroad.
3. Dick and Jane ("See Dick read the trivia book.")
4. St. Jude Children's Research Hospital
5. The Boy Scouts of America
6. A mouse

For Kids' Sake, continued . . .

7. What popular childhood sports organization had its birthplace in Williamsport, Pennsylvania?
8. What construction toy had its origin when its inventor saw children playing with pencils and spools of thread?
9. Miami University has a museum devoted to an educator famed for his "readers" for children. Who was he?
10. What famous home for undisciplined children was founded in Omaha, Nebraska, by Father Flanagan?
11. Launched in 1986, American Girl is a popular line of what?
12. What popular children's book by Ernest Thompson Seton features Lobo the wolf, Bingo the dog, and Redruff the partridge?
13. The world's oldest children's museum is in what New York City borough?
14. What two fictional boy detectives lived in the town of Bayport?
15. What organization began as the American Girl Guides in 1912?
16. What popular toy, launched in 1960, was a plastic box filled with aluminum powder?
17. What federal official is honorary head of the Camp Fire Girls?
18. Orchard House was the home where Louisa May Alcott wrote what classic book for girls?
19. What fictional girl detective lived in River Heights with her lawyer father?
20. What toy company was founded in 1945 by Harold Matson and Elliot Handler?
21. What "contorting" game by Milton Bradley went on sale in 1966?
22. What animated TV series on Nickelodeon featured eight toddlers?
23. What medal is awarded annually to the best American book for children?

★ Festivals of Food

All festivals involve food in some way, but some festivals in these fifty states are about some particular food.

1. Since 1930, Plant City, Florida, has drawn thousands to its May festival of what fruit? (Hint: freckles)

7. Little League baseball, which has a museum and its international headquarters there
8. Tinkertoys
9. William Holmes McGuffey; the famous McGuffey's Readers were used in schools for many years.
10. Boys Town, formerly for boys only
11. Dolls and their accompanying books
12. *Wild Animals I Have Known*
13. Brooklyn
14. The Hardy Boys
15. The Girl Scouts
16. Etch A Sketch, one of the best-loved toys of all time
17. The U.S. president
18. *Little Women*
19. Nancy Drew
20. Mattel, a name formed from Matson and Elliot
21. Twister
22. *Rugrats*
23. The Newberry Medal, which has been awarded since 1922

Festivals of Food // Answers

1. Strawberries; the Florida Strawberry Festival is one of the biggest food festivals in the nation.

Festivals of Food, continued...

2. Oyster Bay, New York, has an annual festival named for what edible sea creatures?

3. Shreveport, Louisiana, hosts Mudbug Madness. What are mudbugs?

4. In what Gulf Coast state could you join in the National Shrimp Festival in early October?

5. The Peanut Valley Festival does not take place in the South but in a fairly dry southwestern state. Which one?

6. Rockland, Maine, hosts the annual festival for what clawed creature?

7. With more than half its population being of German ancestry, Cincinnati makes a big fuss over what autumn German festival?

8. Beef Empire Days take place in what notable beef-producing state?

9. What fruit, much used in baking, is celebrated with a festival in Indio, California?

10. What fruit is the center of an annual festival in Georgia each June?

11. Emporia, Virginia, hosts a festival for what type of meat? (Hint: not kosher)

12. Oakdale, California, hosts an annual festival celebrating what popular sweet?

13. World Veg Day, promoting vegetarian food, is held in what state?

14. What green vegetable (not everyone's favorite) is the center of a spring festival in Stockton, California?

15. What fruit industry centers around Medford, Oregon? (Hint: Bartlett)

16. Belzoni, Mississippi, holds the World Festival for what scaleless fish?

17. Morgan City, Louisiana, stages an annual festival celebrating its two major products. One is a type of food, the other a mineral product. What are they?

18. What does Springfield, Massachusetts, feature at its annual pancake breakfast?

19. What state hosts the annual Hatch Chile Festival each September?

20. The town of Houlton's annual Potato Fest is not in Idaho but in what eastern state?

2. Oysters, what else?

3. Crawfish

4. Alabama; the festival is held at Gulf Shores.

5. New Mexico; the area around Portales grows many peanuts—thanks to irrigation.

6. Lobster, at the Maine Lobster Festival

7. Oktoberfest, with a real feast of German food

8. Kansas

9. The date; about 95 percent of American dates are grown in this area.

10. Peaches, since Georgia is the "Peach State"; in fact, the festival is held in Peach County.

11. Pork

12. Chocolate. The town was once home to a Hershey plant; the festival continues though the plant is gone.

13. California

14. Asparagus

15. Pears; the city has a Pear Blossom Festival every April.

16. Catfish

17. Shrimp and oil; the Shrimp and Petroleum Festival is held each Labor Day weekend.

18. A four-block-long table, in the attempt to serve "the world's largest breakfast"

19. New Mexico; Hatch bills itself as the Chile Capital of the World.

20. Maine, almost as famous for potatoes as Idaho is

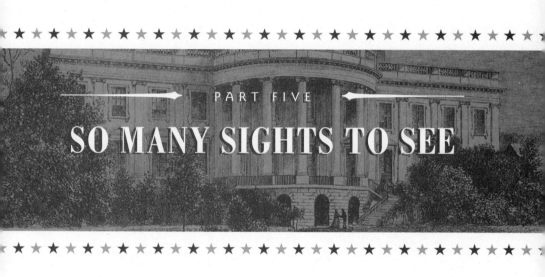

PART FIVE

SO MANY SIGHTS TO SEE

★ Capitols: Those State-ly Buildings

Note: If you're irked at not finding your own state mentioned in these questions, take heart. Scattered throughout the book are references to every state's capitol.

1. What famous capitol building sits on Jenkins Hill?
2. What state maintains its old state capitol as a museum because of its Abraham Lincoln connections?
3. In what capitol did Jefferson Davis take office as president of the Confederacy?
4. What president's imposing life-size statue stands under the dome in Virginia's capitol?
5. What western state capitol has a stunning Gold Room, adorned with gold from the state's mines?
6. The capitol in Santa Fe, New Mexico, is modeled after a Native American *kiva*. What is a *kiva*?
7. What northeastern state's capitol was designed as a $25 million granite French chateau?
8. What president, famous for masterminding the Mexican War, is buried on the capitol grounds in Nashville, Tennessee?
9. What small capital of a small state has a capitol building dating from 1792?
10. Missouri has had three state capitols. Why?
11. The capitol in Harrisburg, Pennsylvania, was modeled after one of the world's most famous cathedrals. Which?
12. The capitol in Springfield, Illinois, has statues of what opposing debaters on the grounds?
13. If you are looking at the capitol on Goat Hill, what southern capital are you in?
14. What state capitol building served as the U.S. capital in 1783–84?
15. What part of the D.C. Capitol has statues of each state's favorite sons and daughters?
16. The State House, built in 1795, is the capitol in what New England state?
17. What product was pumped from the ground under Oklahoma's capitol?
18. Virginia's capitol has a life-size bronze statue of the man who accepted command of the Confederate armies. Who was he?
19. What state's capitol dome is larger than that of any other state?

QUESTIONS

1. The U.S. Capitol in Washington
2. Illinois; the old capitol in Springfield served as capitol till 1876.
3. Montgomery, Alabama
4. George Washington's, a Virginia native
5. Utah's capitol in Salt Lake City
6. An underground ceremonial chamber
7. New York's, in Albany
8. James K. Polk, the eleventh president
9. Delaware; the capitol, in Dover, is called the State House.
10. The first two burned.
11. St. Peter's, in the Vatican in Rome
12. Stephen Douglas and Abraham Lincoln
13. Montgomery, Alabama; for the sake of dignity, Goat Hill is now usually called Capitol Hill.
14. The State House in Annapolis, Maryland
15. Statuary Hall; these statues are also seen in the Rotunda.
16. Massachusetts
17. Oil; the capitol grounds' oil pump operated from 1941 to 1986.
18. Robert E. Lee; the statue stands on the spot where he accepted the command.
19. Texas's, of course

Capitols: Those State-ly Buildings, continued . . .

20. What causes the flame in the "flaming fountain" at South Dakota's capitol?
21. What New England state's pretty capitol sits by the Kennebec River?
22. What state capitol has a Confederate monument on its grounds?
23. What southern capitol has a monument to Confederate spy Sam Davis?

QUESTIONS

★ Statues, Stadiums, and Such: City Landmarks

Think of New York City, and you think of the Statue of Liberty. Think of Seattle, and you think of the Space Needle. Think of . . . well, you get the idea. Try to identify the cities connected with these landmarks. (Note: If you're from a smaller town and don't find your town's landmarks listed here, don't feel bad. It just means they're a well-kept secret—for now.)

1. The Jefferson Memorial, the Smithsonian Institution, Ford's Theatre
2. Ryman Auditorium, Country Music Hall of Fame, the Hermitage
3. Graceland, Mud Island, Mississippi River Museum
4. Metrodome, Minnehaha Park, American Swedish Institute
5. Stone Mountain, CNN Studios, the World of Coca-Cola
6. Declaration House, Norman Rockwell Museum, Congress Hall
7. Grant Park, the John Hancock Center, the Adler Planetarium
8. Fort McHenry, the National Aquarium, Harborplace
9. The Vieux Carré, Jackson Square, St. Louis Cathedral
10. USS *Constitution,* Paul Revere House, Park Street Church
11. Monument Avenue, Hollywood Cemetery, White House of the Confederacy
12. Wells Fargo Center, KOIN Center, Washington Park Zoo
13. The Battery, St. Michael's Church, the Citadel
14. Boblo Island, Belle Isle, Renaissance Center
15. Mitchell Park, Joan of Arc Chapel, Marquette University

20. Sulfur; the fountain's water has so much sulfur that it can be burned.
21. Maine's, in Augusta
22. Montgomery, Alabama, which was also the first capitol of the Confederacy
23. Nashville, Tennessee's

Statues, Stadiums, and Such: City Landmarks // Answers

1. Washington, D.C.
2. Nashville, Tennessee
3. Memphis, Tennessee
4. Minneapolis, Minnesota
5. Atlanta, Georgia
6. Philadelphia, Pennsylvania
7. Chicago, Illinois
8. Baltimore, Maryland
9. New Orleans, Louisiana
10. Boston, Massachusetts
11. Richmond, Virginia
12. Portland, Oregon
13. Charleston, South Carolina
14. Detroit, Michigan
15. Milwaukee, Wisconsin

ANSWERS

Statues, Stadiums, and Such: City Landmarks, continued ...

16. The Billy Graham Parkway, Discovery Place, Carowinds
17. RCA Dome, Chase Tower, Eagle Creek Park
18. Rock and Roll Hall of Fame, Key Tower, Dunham Tavern
19. Churchill Downs, Colonel Harlan Sanders Museum, Riverfront Plaza
20. Balboa Park, Coronado Island, Cabrillo National Monument
21. Sea World, Universal Studios, Disney World
22. Cathedral of St. John the Divine, Bloomingdale's, Whitney Museum of American Art
23. The Space Needle, Elliott Bay, the Kingdome
24. Caesar's Palace, Luxor, Bellagio, the Stratosphere
25. Southeast Financial Center, Parrot Jungle, Crandon Park
26. Biltmore Estate, Thomas Wolfe Memorial, Folk Art Center
27. Governor's Palace, College of William and Mary, Busch Gardens
28. Vulcan Park, Lane Park, Legion Field
29. Gerald Ford birthplace, St. Cecilia Cathedral, USS *Hazard*
30. Florida Aquarium, Ybor City, Busch Gardens
31. Rock Creek Park, Folger Shakespeare Library, Vietnam Veterans Memorial
32. Old Salem, Bethabara Park, Wake Forest University
33. The Naval Base, the Douglas MacArthur Memorial, the Waterside, Nauticus
34. Fort Pulaski, Forsyth Park, Factor's Walk
35. Fountain Square, Carew Tower, Great American Ball Park

QUESTIONS

16. Charlotte, North Carolina
17. Indianapolis, Indiana
18. Cleveland, Ohio
19. Louisville, Kentucky
20. San Diego, California
21. Orlando, Florida
22. New York, New York
23. Seattle, Washington
24. Las Vegas, Nevada
25. Miami, Florida
26. Asheville, North Carolina
27. Williamsburg, Virginia
28. Birmingham, Alabama
29. Omaha, Nebraska
30. Tampa, Florida
31. Washington, D.C.
32. Winston-Salem, North Carolina
33. Norfolk, Virginia
34. Savannah, Georgia
35. Cincinnati, Ohio

ANSWERS

✰ Ivy and Ivory Towers: Colleges and Universities

Colleges do more than teach. They provide art, culture, and sports for the surrounding communities, not to mention great job-training facilities. And some of them are just downright historic.

1. What famous military college was established by Congress in 1802?
2. What state university has campuses at Tuscaloosa, Huntsville, and Birmingham?
3. What Ivy League school awards the Pulitzer Prizes?
4. What Atlantic Coast town in Florida is the favorite destination for college students on spring break?
5. The University of South Carolina, the South Carolina State Museum, and the State House are all in what city?
6. The nation's oldest medical school is at what Philadelphia college?
7. What two televangelists have colleges named after themselves?
8. What enormous state college in the South has a much visited Rural Life Museum? (Hint: Fighting Tigers)
9. Lexington, Virginia, is home to what all-male military college? (Hint: Keydets)
10. What noted New Jersey college began in the city of Elizabeth but later moved to the town that shares its name?
11. Macon, Georgia's Wesleyan College was chartered in 1836 specifically to grant degrees to a certain type of person. What type?
12. If you are in Gainesville, Florida, what large university are you near? (Hint: Gators)
13. What is distinctive about the tuition payments at Berea College in Kentucky?
14. What city on Lake Michigan has DePaul, Loyola, Roosevelt, and fifty-five other colleges and universities?
15. The lovely Gustavus Adolphus College in St. Peter, Minnesota, is named for a king of what nation?
16. At what New York university did Dwight Eisenhower serve as president before entering politics?

1. The U.S. Military Academy at West Point, New York
2. The University of Alabama
3. Columbia University in New York
4. Daytona Beach
5. Columbia, the state capital
6. The University of Pennsylvania
7. Oral Roberts and Jimmy Swaggart
8. Louisiana State University (LSU)
9. VMI, the Virginia Military Institute
10. Princeton, which originally was called the College of New Jersey
11. Women; it was the first American college founded for this purpose.
12. The University of Florida
13. There is no tuition. All students perform some kind of work on the campus.
14. Chicago
15. Sweden; he was a great Protestant hero in the religious wars of the 1600s. He was also Lutheran, which is the college's denominational affiliation.
16. Columbia

Ivy and Ivory Towers: Colleges and Universities, continued . . .

17. If you were in the southern town of Oxford, what large state university would you be near? (Hint: Rebels)
18. What city is home to the University of Minnesota's College of Agriculture?
19. What large university in Alabama was originally established as a Methodist men's college, primarily to train ministers? (Hint: War Eagle)
20. What energy source can be found on the campus of the University of Missouri at Rolla?
21. Manhattan's Yeshiva University is the nation's oldest and largest school run by what religious group?
22. What state university is located in the Nittany Valley?
23. Bloomington, Indiana, is home to what enormous college?
24. You'd find the Lyndon Baines Johnson School of Public Affairs on the main campus of what university? (Hint: Longhorns)
25. What Ivy League college is in Ithaca, New York?
26. What two famous black leaders are associated with Tuskegee University in Alabama?

★ Famous Forts

1. Fort Dearborn became what Illinois metropolis?
2. The settlement of Fort Nashborough later became what state capital?
3. Famous as the site where Francis Scott Key wrote "The Star-Spangled Banner," Fort McHenry was built to protect what city?
4. What ill-fated cavalryman left Fort Abraham Lincoln on May 17, 1876?
5. Fort Lee, near Petersburg, Virginia, is named for what famous soldier?
6. What improperly named Texas metropolis has *never* been a fort?
7. Fort Clatsop in Oregon reproduces the living quarters of what famous explorer duo?
8. How did historic Fort Nonsense in New Jersey gets its name?
9. Fort Pitt, named for British statesman William Pitt, became what industrial city of Pennsylvania?
10. In February 1909 what great Apache leader died at Fort Sill, Oklahoma?

17. The University of Mississippi, "Ole Miss"
18. St. Paul, which is not exactly a rural place
19. Auburn, now a state school
20. A nuclear reactor
21. Judaism
22. Pennsylvania State University, home of the Nittany Lions
23. Indiana University's main campus
24. University of Texas
25. Cornell
26. Educator Booker T. Washington and scientist George Washington Carver (The school was known until recently as Tuskegee Institute.)

Famous Forts // Answers

1. Chicago
2. Nashville, Tennessee, naturally
3. Baltimore, Maryland
4. Gen. George Custer; he never returned.
5. Confederate general Robert E. Lee, naturally
6. Fort Worth; it has had military encampments but never an actual fort structure.
7. Lewis and Clark, who left Fort Clatsop in 1806 to return east
8. Long after its construction in 1777, local residents had forgotten its purpose, so they called it "nonsense."
9. Pittsburgh, of course
10. Geronimo

Famous Forts, continued . . .

11. Fort Christina, built in Delaware in 1638, was named for a queen of what country?

12. What Florida metropolis on the Gulf grew out of the army post of Fort Brooke?

13. Fort Donelson in Tennessee was the site of a Union general's demand for "unconditional and immediate surrender." What future president issued this ultimatum?

14. Fort Necessity in Pennsylvania was the site of the opening battle of what great war of the colonial era?

15. New York's capital, Albany, began as a trading post, Fort Nassau, in 1614. What nation established this?

16. In 1565 the Spanish destroyed the French Fort Caroline and built what settlement in what is now Florida?

17. In what state would you find Fort King George, a colonial historic site?

18. What was notable about the Civil War Battle of Fort Tyler in Georgia?

19. An important Florida fort was constructed on December 25, 1837, as a defense during the Seminole War. What appropriate name was given to the fort?

20. What historic Florida fort has a name referring to the Spanish slaughter of French Protestants?

21. If you are in Fort Eustis, Virginia, viewing helicopters, trains, and marine craft, what museum are you touring?

22. Historic Fort Ticonderoga, used in the French and Indian War and the Revolution, is in what northeastern state?

23. Fort Putnam from the Revolutionary War overlooks what U.S. service academy?

QUESTIONS

11. Sweden; the original settlers of Delaware were Swedish.

12. Tampa

13. U. S. Grant, the eighteenth president; people said "U. S." stood for "Unconditional Surrender."

14. The French and Indian War

15. The Netherlands

16. St. Augustine

17. Georgia, naturally; the state and the fort were both named for England's King George II.

18. It was fought after the Confederate surrender—due to the slowness of communication in those days.

19. Fort Christmas

20. Fort Matanzas, near St. Augustine; the name Matanzas means "slaughters." (Apparently the Spanish were not ashamed of what they'd done.)

21. The U.S. Army Transportation Museum

22. New York

23. The U.S. Military Academy at West Point

☆ Parks, Caverns, and So Forth: State Landmarks

You might visit a state to see friends and relatives. Or you might be there to see the sights, whatever those might be. Given a list of a state's "sights worth seeing," could you guess the name of the state?

1. The Grand Canyon, Painted Desert, Petrified Forest
2. Waikiki Beach, Haleakala National Park, Wailua River State Park
3. Shenandoah National Park, Busch Gardens, Luray Caverns
4. Space and Rocket Center, Gulf Shores, Bellingrath Gardens
5. Mystic Seaport, P. T. Barnum Museum, USS *Nautilus*
6. Yosemite National Park, Universal Studios, Lake Tahoe
7. Salvador Dali Museum, the Everglades, Busch Gardens
8. Circus World Museum, the Dells, Lake Winnebago
9. Vicksburg National Military Park, Natchez Trace, Beauvoir
10. Rocky Mountain National Park, Garden of the Gods, Pike's Peak
11. Padre Island National Seashore, the Alamo, Six Flags
12. Carlsbad Caverns, White Sands National Monument, Chaco Canyon
13. Chickamauga Battlefield, Six Flags, CNN Studios
14. Independence Hall, Valley Forge, Gettysburg National Military Park
15. Wyandotte Cave, Benjamin Harrison's home, New Harmony
16. Acadia National Park, Sugarloaf ski area, Bath Iron Works
17. Henry Ford Museum, Pictured Rocks, Isle Royale
18. Great Smoky Mountains, Rock City, the Grand Ole Opry
19. Minnehaha Falls, Guthrie Theatre, Voyageurs National Park
20. Glacier National Park, Little Bighorn Battlefield, Lewis and Clark Caverns
21. Mount Rainier, San Juan Islands, the Space Needle
22. Glacier Bay National Park, Denali National Park, Katmai National Park
23. Sequoia National Park, Disneyland, HMS *Queen Mary*
24. Yellowstone National Park, Grand Teton National Park, Buffalo Bill Museum
25. The Field Museum, Nauvoo Mormon settlement, Abraham Lincoln's home
26. Plymouth Rock, Walden Pond, Basketball Hall of Fame

1. Arizona
2. Hawaii
3. Virginia
4. Alabama
5. Connecticut
6. California
7. Florida
8. Wisconsin
9. Mississippi
10. Colorado
11. Texas
12. New Mexico
13. Georgia
14. Pennsylvania
15. Indiana
16. Maine
17. Michigan
18. Tennessee
19. Minnesota
20. Montana
21. Washington
22. Alaska
23. California
24. Wyoming
25. Illinois
26. Massachusetts

ANSWERS

Q
U
E
S
T
I
O
N
S

27. Harrah's, Circus Circus, Lake Mead, Death Valley
28. First White House of the Confederacy, Helen Keller's birthplace, the Vulcan statue
29. Pro Football Hall of Fame, Schoenbrunn Village, Mill Creek Park
30. Cape Hatteras, Biltmore mansion, Fort Raleigh
31. Mammoth Cave, Shaker Village, Cumberland Gap National Historical Park
32. Nottoway Plantation, Rosedown Plantation, Jean Lafitte Park
33. Zion National Park, Temple Square, Lake Powell
34. Newport cottages, Gilbert Stuart birthplace, Touro Synagogue
35. Fort Sumter, Magnolia plantation, Patriots Point
36. Cowboy Hall of Fame, Cherokee Cultural Center, Fort Gibson
37. Multnomah Falls, Newberry Volcano, Columbia River Gorge
38. Eisenhower Museum, Old Cowtown, Fort Leavenworth
39. London Bridge, Meteor Crater, Canyon Diablo
40. Universal Studios, Ringling Museum of Art, Walt Disney World
41. Hot Springs, Crater of Diamonds, Ozark Folk Center
42. The Corn Palace, Badlands, Mount Rushmore
43. Craters of the Moon, Sun Valley, River of No Return
44. U.S. Naval Academy, Fort McHenry, Antietam National Battlefield
45. Thomas Edison Museum, Prudential Center, Six Flags Great Adventure

★ Colors on the Map

The American map is a colorful thing—all sorts of towns, mountains, rivers, etc., named after Blue, White, Green, etc. There is no Turquoise Town or Lavender Valley, but there are a lot of other colorfully named places.

1. What Wyoming national park is known for its geysers, particularly Old Faithful?
2. The thousand-mile-long river separating Texas and Oklahoma has what colorful name?

27. Nevada
28. Alabama
29. Ohio
30. North Carolina
31. Kentucky
32. Louisiana
33. Utah
34. Rhode Island
35. South Carolina
36. Oklahoma
37. Oregon
38. Kansas
39. Arizona
40. Florida
41. Arkansas
42. South Dakota
43. Idaho
44. Maryland
45. New Jersey

Colors on the Map // Answers

1. Yellowstone, which Wyoming shares with Idaho and Montana
2. Red River

ANSWERS

Colors on the Map, continued . . .

QUESTIONS

3. What scenic parkway connects the Shenandoah and Great Smoky Mountain National Parks?

4. The Great White Way is what famous New York street?

5. In what famous D.C. home could you visit the Blue, Red, and Green Rooms?

6. What colorful lawn grass gives Kentucky its nickname?

7. In what two cities could you tour the White House of the Confederacy?

8. What southern state has a Black Belt?

9. "Red Stick," translated into French, is the name of what Louisiana city?

10. In Blue Mounds, Wisconsin, what type of ethnic village could you visit?

11. What Wisconsin football town has a colorful name?

12. Why is the White House white?

13. What appropriate botanical name is given to the Florida county that contains Orlando?

14. What 730-mile river in Utah and Wyoming flows into the Colorado River?

15. What color are the mice and lizards that live in the White Sands National Monument of New Mexico?

16. What colorful vegetable company logo can you see (fifty-five feet high) in Blue Earth, Minnesota?

17. It's called the Green Mountain State and its name means "green mountain." What is it?

18. White Plains is a posh suburb of what eastern metropolis?

19. The Black Mountains in the eastern U.S. are part of what colorfully named mountain chain?

20. Black Warrior and the Native American word *tuscaloosa* have the same meaning. In what state is the city of Tuscaloosa *and* the Black Warrior River?

21. The Black Hills are in what two western states?

22. Mount Washington, New Hampshire's tallest peak, is in what mountain chain?

23. If you wish to see the famous Pink Cliffs, what national park in Utah will you visit?

24. Garden Grove, Santa Ana, and Anaheim are suburbs in what wealthy California county? (Hint: trees)

25. What river, flowing out of Canada, forms the border between North Dakota and Minnesota?

3. The Blue Ridge Parkway
4. Broadway
5. The White House
6. Bluegrass
7. Montgomery, Alabama, and Richmond, Virginia; both cities were Confederate capitals, and both have the residences of Confederate president Jefferson Davis.
8. Alabama; the Belt is actually a wide band of rich, black soil crossing the state's center.
9. Baton Rouge, the state capital
10. Norwegian; Little Norway is a popular tourist site and includes a lovely wooden stave church.
11. Green Bay, of course
12. It was painted white after the fires of the War of 1812 had blackened the original gray walls.
13. Orange
14. The Green River
15. White, like the sand, as protective coloration; they are almost the sole inhabitants of this barren area.
16. The Jolly Green Giant, standing in Green Giant Park
17. Vermont, from the French *vert mont*
18. New York City
19. The Blue Ridge
20. Alabama
21. South Dakota and Wyoming
22. The White Mountains
23. Bryce Canyon
24. Orange
25. The Red River (not the same as the one in question 2)

★ Funny Names on the Map

"Funny" is in the ear of the beholder. If you grew up in Hackensack or Schenectady, you probably don't find the names funny, although others might. Anyway, the American map has more than its share of offbeat names. The ones here are only the tip of the iceberg.

QUESTIONS

1. Molokai, Lanai, Kauai, Kahoolawe, and Niihau are islands in what state?
2. If you scurry to Scurry County, what western state are you in?
3. What New Mexico town is named for a radio program of the 1940s?
4. What famous 435,000-acre swamp sits astride the border of Georgia and Florida?
5. If you want to go to Kingdom Come, where do you go?
6. If you wanted to see Jupiter, Mars, Venus, and Neptune, what southern state would you visit?
7. Where was the short-lived state of Nickajack?
8. What historic city was founded in 1718 and given the name Nouvelle-Orleans?
9. What Florida lake is both extremely large (750 square miles) and extremely shallow (twenty-two-feet deep)?
10. If you're a tourist in the South visiting Chick-Chatt, where are you?
11. What simple-living Christians founded the village of Bird-in-Hand in Pennsylvania?
12. What noted fraternal organization (named for an animal) has its head-quarters in Mooseheart, Illinois?
13. If you ride the hill-climbing trolleys of the Monongahela Incline and Duquesne Incline, what Pennsylvania city are you in?
14. Jockey's Ridge State Park on the North Carolina coast has some amazing objects more than a hundred feet high. What are they?
15. If you are at the Sleeping Bear Dunes National Lakeshore, what state are you in?
16. Port Tobacco is a town in what noted tobacco-growing state?
17. What small Alabama town on the Tennessee River is noted as a recording center?
18. The French-settled town of Natchitoches, founded in 1714, is the oldest town in what southern state?

Funny Names on the Map // Answers

1. Hawaii
2. Texas; Scurry is a top oil-producing county.
3. Truth or Consequences, named for a show hosted by Ralph Edwards; the town was originally named Hot Springs.
4. The Okefenokee
5. Kentucky; it's a state park in the southwestern part of the state.
6. Florida; they are towns on the Atlantic Coast.
7. In northern Alabama; the residents of Winston County voted to secede from Alabama after the state seceded from the Union and joined the Confederacy. Winston County became (never officially) the state of Nickajack.
8. New Orleans, of course
9. Lake Okeechobee
10. On a Civil War battlefield; Chick-Chatt is the short name for Chickamauga and Chattanooga National Military Park in Tennessee and Georgia.
11. The Amish
12. The Moose (Did anyone miss this?)
13. Pittsburgh; both give excellent views of the city.
14. Sand dunes, which many people use for hang gliding
15. Michigan; some of the large dunes supposedly resemble sleeping bears.
16. Maryland
17. Muscle Shoals
18. Louisiana, noted for its French connections

Funny Names on the Map, continued . . .

19. The charming town of Bishop Hill in Illinois, formerly known as Bishopskuna, was settled by people from what country?

★ On the Road Again

1. All interstate highways that run coast to coast end in what number?
2. The scenic Blue Ridge Parkway connects what two much-visited national parks?
3. If you are walking the Street of the Golden Palace in Los Angeles, what ethnic neighborhood are you in?
4. The colonial sites of Jamestown, Yorktown, and Williamsburg are connected by what (appropriately named) highway?
5. What name is given to U.S. Highway 101 on its 380-mile run through California's sequoia country?
6. What street runs past Graceland in Memphis?
7. What novel highway phenomenon was introduced at Woodbridge, New Jersey, in 1929?
8. If you are at Mile Zero on U.S. Highway 1, what famous Florida island are you on?
9. The New Jersey Turnpike was actually built to connect two cities *not* in New Jersey. One was New York. What was the other?
10. What famous street, much loved by New Orleans tourists, is now a pedestrians-only zone?
11. Montgomery Street, the "Wall Street of the West," is in what California metropolis?
12. The tree named Wawona, which has a road passing through it, is in what Wyoming national park?
13. The first of the nation's superhighways was the 470-mile turnpike in what northeastern state? (Hint: Quakers)
14. What western capital limits street names to eight letters?
15. What notable (and long) highway connects Key West, Florida, with Fort Kent, Maine?

QUESTIONS

19. Sweden; it was settled by a Swedish religious sect. Bishopskuna means "Bishop Hill."

On the Road Again // Answers

1. 0
2. Shenandoah (in Virginia) and Great Smoky Mountains (in Tennessee and North Carolina)
3. Chinatown
4. The Colonial Parkway
5. The Redwood Highway
6. Elvis Presley Boulevard, which runs past Presley's home, Graceland
7. The cloverleaf interchange
8. Key West, the "end of the road" (or the beginning) for the eastern U.S.
9. Philadelphia, Pennsylvania
10. The famous (and infamous) Bourbon Street
11. San Francisco
12. Yellowstone
13. Pennsylvania
14. Salt Lake City, Utah
15. U.S. Highway 1

On the Road Again, continued...

16. What type of highway is only 4 percent of the nation's total road system but carries 40 percent of all the traffic?
17. Charlotte, North Carolina, has a highway named for a famous preacher. Who?
18. If you are driving the Going-to-the-Sun Road in Glacier National Park, what state are you in?
19. What was the interstate highway speed limit imposed in 1974 as an energy-saving measure?
20. If you are riding on the Overseas Highway, U.S. 1, what scenic part of Florida are you in?
21. The blues and Beale Street are associated with what major Tennessee city?
22. If you are "inside the Beltway," where are you?
23. The Old Pecan Street Arts Festival is held in which western state capital?
24. The Rim of the World Highway is in what scenic western state?

★ Beantown, Barb City, and Other City Nicknames

New York is the Big Apple, and most big cities—and a few small ones—have notable nicknames.

1. What city on Lake Michigan is the Windy City?
2. Beantown is what New England capital?
3. What southern capital, with a thriving recording industry, is Music City USA?
4. Motown is what Michigan metropolis?
5. What Rocky Mountain capital is the Mile High City?
6. What North Carolina college town was formerly known as Tobacco Town?
7. The Crawfish Capital of the World is the town of Breaux Bridge in what state?
8. What large Kentucky city is known as Heart of the Bluegrass?

On the Road Again // Answers // continued . . .

16. Interstates
17. Billy Graham, a native of the area
18. Montana
19. It was 55 mph. This was changed in 1995.
20. The Keys
21. Memphis
22. Washington, D.C., or near it; the Capital Beltway is the heavily traveled freeway encircling the city.
23. Austin, Texas; Pecan Street is Austin's version of New Orleans's Bourbon Street.
24. California; it's a forty-five-mile mountain road near San Bernardino.

Beantown, Barb City, and Other City Nicknames // Answers

1. Chicago, Illinois, of course
2. Boston (as in "Boston baked beans")
3. Nashville, Tennessee
4. Detroit, the "Motor Town"
5. Denver, Colorado, whose elevation is (surprise!) about 5,280 feet
6. Durham, home of Duke University; the Duke family, wealthy tobacco farmers, gave millions of dollars to the college.
7. Louisiana, noted for its use of crawfish in cooking
8. Lexington; the Bluegrass refers to the region of north central Kentucky.

Beantown, Barb City, and Other City Nicknames, continued . . .

9. What Missouri resort town is often called Nashville West?
10. America's foremost desert resort was named *Agua Caliente* ("hot water") by the Spanish. What is it now called?
11. DeKalb, Illinois, is nicknamed Barb City. Why?
12. Steamboat Springs, considered Ski Town U.S.A., is in what state?
13. Valdosta, Georgia, is known as "the Gateway to" which popular vacation state?
14. What humid southern city calls itself the City That Care Forgot?
15. What northern Alabama city is Rocket City?
16. Who founded Philadelphia, the City of Brotherly Love, in 1682?
17. What huge city is called City of Brotherly Shove on account of its supposed rudeness?
18. America's Smoky City is now bright and clean. What Pennsylvania industrial city is now "non-smoky"?
19. What southern capital is sometimes called the Protestant Vatican?
20. What major California city is the Capital of Silicon Valley?
21. The town of Stowe calls itself the Ski Capital of the East. What New England state is it in?
22. Decatur, Illinois, proudly calls itself the "_____ Capital of the World." (Fill in the blank with the name of a common food crop.)
23. What city was the Gateway to the Goldfields of California?
24. It was called Second City for many years, but Los Angeles passed it in the 1990 census. What was it?
25. Rockland is the Schooner Capital in what rock-bound New England state?
26. The Big Easy is what laid-back Louisiana city?
27. What Oklahoma metropolis was for years the Oil Capital of the World?

★ Notable Purchases

1. What island did Dutchman Peter Minuit purchase from the Man-a-hat-a tribe in 1626?
2. During what president's administration was the Louisiana Territory purchased?

9. Branson, noted for its many country music concert halls
10. Palm Springs, California
11. The nation's first barbed-wire manufacturing company was there.
12. Colorado
13. Florida; Valdosta is near the heavily traveled I-75.
14. New Orleans
15. Huntsville, home of the NASA Space Flight Center
16. William Penn
17. New York; whether the rudeness is real or imaginary is a matter of opinion.
18. Pittsburgh
19. Nashville, Tennessee, which has the national offices of several Protestant denominations
20. San Jose, center of the state's computer industry
21. Vermont
22. Soybean
23. The capital, Sacramento
24. Chicago, formerly second in population to New York, is now third.
25. Maine
26. New Orleans (or, if you prefer, N'awlins)
27. Tulsa

Notable Purchases // Answers

1. Manhattan Island, bought from Native Americans for twenty-four dollars' worth of beads and trinkets
2. Thomas Jefferson's

Notable Purchases, continued . . .

3. What future vacation state did the U.S. purchase from Spain in 1819?
4. What historic Virginia port was purchased in 1682 for ten thousand pounds of tobacco?
5. With what 1853 purchase did the territory of the forty-eight U.S. states become complete?
6. The site for what 840-acre New York City park was purchased by the city in 1856?
7. What president claimed that the Louisiana Purchase was his greatest achievement, although he wasn't president when it occurred?
8. Philadelphia businessman Henry Disston paid twenty-five cents per acre for 4 million acres in what southern state?
9. What southern capital's site was purchased in 1609 by John Smith and named None Such?
10. Who turned twenty-seven thousand acres of Florida swampland into one of the largest entertainment complexes in the world?
11. On October 20, 1803, the Senate ratified the treaty for what major land acquisition?
12. What state, purchased from Russia in 1867, was called "Seward's Icebox"?

★ Little Egypt, Big Muddy, and Other Place Nicknames

Great cities, states, and other locales are sometimes as well known by nicknames as by their proper names.

1. "The Old North State" is actually in the South. What state is it?
2. What famous baseball stadium is "the House That Ruth Built"?
3. What humid southern state calls itself the "Sportsman's paradise"? (Hint: crawdads)
4. What state's unofficial nickname is "Little Rhody"?
5. "America's Most Historic Square Mile" is the Independence National Historical Park in what city?

3. Florida
4. Norfolk
5. The Gadsden Purchase
6. Central Park
7. James Monroe, who negotiated the purchase as Thomas Jefferson's diplomat to France
8. Florida; after Disston's purchase, the development of southern Florida proceeded rapidly.
9. Richmond, Virginia
10. Walt Disney, who purchased the land for Disney World in 1965
11. The Louisiana Purchase
12. Alaska, purchased at the urging of Secretary of State William Seward; people thought he was a fool to want the chilly wilderness. It was also called "Seward's Folly."

Little Egypt, Big Muddy, and Other Place Nicknames // Answers

1. North Carolina; its other nickname, "Tar Heel State," is equally puzzling.
2. Yankee Stadium—or, to be precise, the *old* Yankee Stadium, which was demolished in 2009 (the new Yankee opened that same year). Ruth was, of course, "the Babe," the Yankee legend.
3. Louisiana, which excels in both fishing and hunting
4. Rhode Island, naturally
5. Philadelphia

Little Egypt, Big Muddy, and Other Place Nicknames, continued . . .

6. Idaho's "River of No Return" is actually named for an edible fish. What?
7. If you are in the "Buckeye State," where are you?
8. Which southern state is the "Peach State"?
9. If you are visiting a downtown area called the Loop, what metropolis are you in?
10. One southern state was known as the "Land of the Four Cs," referring to its four Native American tribes (Cherokee, Creek, Chickasaw, and Choctaw). Which state?
11. Which highly urbanized eastern state is the "Garden State"?
12. What southern state is home to a farming area known as the "Sugar Bowl of America"?
13. What southern state earned the nickname "Volunteer State" by sending so many soldiers to fight in the War of 1812?
14. What midwestern state's southern tip is known as Little Egypt?
15. What state's nickname comes from the early lead miners who lived in their mining holes?
16. What state calls itself the "Land of Opportunity" (a name that supposedly should apply to the whole U.S.)?
17. What state, site of a famous gold rush, is the "Golden State"?
18. What famous southern highway was called the "Devil's Backbone"?
19. Which southern state is the "Old Dominion"?
20. The five-mile Mackinac Bridge connecting Michigan's Upper and Lower Peninsulas has what nickname?
21. What picturesque southwestern state is the "Land of Enchantment"?
22. "Old Ab," the Absecon Lighthouse, is a landmark at what New Jersey resort town?
23. What, appropriately enough, is the nickname of the flat-landed state of Illinois?
24. What major river is called the "Big Muddy"? (Hint: *not* the Mississippi)
25. What Pacific Northwest state is the "Evergreen State"?
26. Pennsylvania's "Land between the Mountains" is what popular resort area?
27. What New York canal, finished in 1825, was called the "Gateway to the West"?
28. Faneuil Hall, built in 1742, has been called the "Cradle of Liberty." What historic city is it in?

6. Salmon
7. Ohio
8. Georgia; if you'd noticed all the streets named "Peachtree" in Atlanta, you'd know this.
9. Chicago
10. Alabama
11. New Jersey
12. Louisiana; the name refers to a wide area of sugarcane plantations.
13. Tennessee
14. Illinois's; several town names are Cairo, Thebes, and Karnak, all places in Egypt. The farmland supposedly reminded settlers of the fertile Nile River plains.
15. Wisconsin's; for their resemblance to ground-dwelling badgers, the miners were called "badgers," thus Wisconsin is the "Badger State."
16. Arkansas
17. California, naturally
18. The five-hundred-mile-long Natchez Trace, running from Nashville to the Mississippi River
19. Virginia
20. "Mighty Mac"
21. New Mexico
22. Atlantic City
23. "The Prairie State," besides being called "Land of Lincoln"
24. The Missouri
25. Washington
26. The Pocono Mountains
27. The Erie Canal, which connected the Hudson River with Lake Erie, opening up the western lands of the U.S.
28. Boston, Massachusetts

Little Egypt, Big Muddy, and Other Place Nicknames, continued . . .

29. What name was given to New England's forty-foot granite likeness of a man's face, formed by nature?
30. Its state flower is red clover, but it's known as the "Green Mountain State." What is it?
31. America's "Fourth Coast" is the Great Lakes, connected by the St. Lawrence Seaway. What nation shared this project with the U.S.?
32. What Deep South state is the "Heart of Dixie"?
33. What southern state is the "Pelican State"?

★ Scraping the Sky: Tall Buildings

As much as we love small towns and the country, we have to go to big cities to see really tall buildings. The world has changed a lot since the day when a ten-story building was called a "skyscraper."

1. Little Rock, Arkansas's tallest building was named for what yogurt company?
2. You couldn't "copy" the tallest building in Rochester, New York. What company owns it?
3. What northeastern university has twenty-two "nationality classrooms," each furnished by local ethnic communities, in its forty-two-story Cathedral of Learning?
4. The tallest building in Salt Lake City, Utah, belongs (not surprisingly) to what large religious group?
5. The forty-eight-story TransAmerica Pyramid is a landmark (and the tallest building) in what Pacific metropolis?
6. According to D.C. law, what is the maximum height of a building?
7. The Nauru Tower, the Ala Moana Hotel, and the Royal Iolani are tall buildings in what city?
8. The tallest building in Richmond, Virginia, is named for the country's fifth president. Who was he?
9. The sixty-story John Hancock Tower is, appropriately, in what New England state?

29. "The Old Man of the Mountain," sometimes called the "Great Stone Face"; sadly, the granite formation suffered breakage in 2003, so the Old Man no longer exists.
30. Vermont, whose name in French, *vert mont*, means "green mountain"
31. Canada
32. Alabama, so called because of its central location in the South
33. Louisiana

Scraping the Sky: Tall Buildings // Answers

1. TCBY (The Country's Best Yogurt); the forty-story TCBY Tower is now the Metropolitan Tower.
2. Xerox; the Xerox Tower is thirty stories.
3. The University of Pittsburgh; the Cathedral is one of the tallest college buildings in the world.
4. The Mormons; it's the LDS (Latter-Day Saints) Church Office Building.
5. San Francisco, California
6. Thirteen stories (Can you guess the significance of thirteen?)
7. Honolulu, of course
8. A Virginian (naturally), James Monroe
9. Massachusetts; it's in Boston.

Scraping the Sky: Tall Buildings, continued . . .

10. One Liberty Place, at sixty-one stories, is the tallest building in what historic metropolis?
11. What Manhattan skyscraper was scaled by King Kong (in a movie, that is)?
12. Pittsburgh's tallest building, the sixty-four-story USX Tower, is owned by what metals company?
13. What name is given to the 630-foot stainless steel arc on the riverfront at St. Louis?
14. The highest point in Washington, D.C., is in what famous church?
15. What company's Pittsburgh headquarters is a thirty-story skyscraper draped in aluminum waffle?
16. What 1,454-foot Manhattan building, built in 1931, is at 350 Fifth Avenue?
17. The sixty-three-story Peachtree Center is in what southern capital (with a lot of "Peachtree" addresses)?
18. Sacramento, California's tallest building is the thirty-story center of a famous cargo and armored car company. What?
19. The tallest buildings in Las Vegas are (as you might assume) what type of building?
20. What famous New York statue is 152 feet high and covered with copper?

★ More Funny Names on the Map

1. The town of Jackpot is in what appropriate western state?
2. If you are on Bathhouse Row, what national park are you visiting?
3. "Rat's Mouth" is the name of a Florida town, but the name is usually given in its Spanish form. What is it?
4. Mexico is in what state?
5. If you are in Shark Valley, what popular Florida region are you in?
6. What Washington town is named for the hero of a Shakespearian tragedy?
7. Possum Kingdom State Park is in what southwestern state?
8. What resort town got its name as the California equivalent of Saratoga?
9. Manitou Springs, Colorado, is named for whom?

10. Philadelphia, Pennsylvania; the second-tallest building is *Two* Liberty Place.
11. The Empire State Building
12. U.S. Steel
13. The Gateway Arch, symbol of the westward expansion of the U.S.
14. The National Cathedral, in its central bell tower
15. The aluminum company Alcoa's
16. The Empire State Building
17. Atlanta, Georgia
18. Wells Fargo
19. Hotels—or, to be specific, hotel-casinos
20. The Statue of Liberty

More Funny Names on the Map // Answers

1. Nevada, of course, notorious for its gambling
2. Hot Springs, in Arkansas
3. Boca Raton; the name refers to pointed rocks near the entrance of the site's inlet.
4. Missouri; there are several amusing theories about how the town got its name.
5. The Everglades
6. Othello
7. Texas
8. Calistoga (Get it? California + Saratoga = Calistoga.)
9. God—to be specific, the "Great Spirit," which is what the Native American word *Manitou* means

10. If you visit the Superstition Mountains, what southwestern state are you in?
11. Rolla, Missouri, was named for what southern capital?
12. Goblin Valley State Park, with fantastic sandstone formations, is in what western state?
13. What California city's original name was El Pueblo de Nuestra Señora La Reina de Los Angeles de Porciuncula?
14. Bottineau, North Dakota, has the Four Chaplains Monument, a memorial to four men whose ship was torpedoed in 1943. What did the four men do to be so honored?
15. What northeastern state capital originally had the Dutch name Beverwyck?
16. What oddly named New Jersey city was originally called New Barbados?
17. What Pennsylvania town was named for a European king?
18. Taum Sauk is the highest mountain in what state? (Hint: Mark Twain)
19. Passengers aboard the Tweetsie Railroad can experience mock robberies and Native American attacks. Where could you ride the Tweetsie?

★ Replicas: When You Can't Have the Real Thing ...

1. What Las Vegas hotel has replicas of the Statue of Liberty and the Empire State Building?
2. What famous temple of ancient Greece would you find in Nashville, Tennessee?
3. The Arkansas capitol in Little Rock is a replica of what famous government building?
4. "The Holy Land of America," with replicas of famous sites in the Holy Land, is in what major city?
5. If you are touring the tiny ships *Discovery, Godspeed,* and *Susan Constant,* where are you?
6. In what state would you see replicas of the Wright brothers' work shed and living quarters?

10. Arizona
11. Raleigh, North Carolina; the town was named by a Raleigh native who apparently spelled the name as he pronounced it.
12. Utah
13. Los Angeles; the old Spanish name means "The town of our Lady the Queen of the angels of Porciuncula."
14. They gave up their life jackets so other passengers could have them.
15. Albany, New York, held by the Dutch until 1664
16. Hackensack
17. King of Prussia—which was actually named not for the king but for the sign on a local inn
18. Missouri
19. North Carolina

Replicas: When You Can't Have the Real Thing . . . // Answers

1. The appropriately named New York-New York
2. The Parthenon—or, at least, a full-size replica of it; it is in much better condition than the one in Athens, Greece.
3. The U.S. Capitol; Little Rock's is smaller.
4. Washington, D.C.; it is found at the city's Franciscan Monastery.
5. Jamestown, Virginia; they are replicas of the ships that brought the first English colonists to Jamestown in 1607.
6. North Carolina; the replicas are at the Wright Brothers National Memorial at Kill Devil Hills.

Replicas: When You Can't Have the Real Thing . . . , continued . . .

7. The Biblical Art Center, with a replica of Christ's tomb, is in what Texas metropolis?

8. Brackettville, Texas, has a replica of what ill-fated battle site?

9. In Concord, Massachusetts, you can see a replica of Henry David Thoreau's house on what famous pond?

10. You could see a replica of a Gutenberg printing press at what religious group's New York headquarters?

11. Odessa, Texas, has a replica of what famous Shakespearian theatre of England?

12. What three tiny ships were sent by the government of Spain on a tour of U.S. ports in 1992?

13. In Lima, Ohio, you could see a ten-by-fifteen-foot scale model of what famous presidential home?

14. Where in the U.S. are the walls of Jerusalem?

QUESTIONS

★ Happy Trails to You

1. What two-thousand-mile hiking trail extends from Mount Katahdin in Maine to Mount Oglethorpe in Georgia?

2. What name was given to the relocation of southern Native American tribes to lands beyond the Mississippi River?

3. Who were the chief travelers on the old Chisholm Trail from the Mexican border to Abilene?

4. What historic five-hundred-mile road connected the Mississippi River with Nashville, Tennessee?

5. What famous pioneer trail took its name from a southwestern state capital?

6. The Oregon Trail ended in what state?

7. And began in what state?

8. What wagon trail led many immigrants from Pennsylvania to the South?

9. The Mormon Trail led to what state?

10. The Old Spanish Trail ran from Los Angeles to what historic city in New Mexico?

7. Dallas; the center also has a painting of Pentecost that is 20 feet wide and 124 feet long.
8. The Alamo, part of the leftover set from the 1959 John Wayne movie
9. Walden Pond; Thoreau's time there led him to write the classic book *Walden.*
10. The American Bible Society's; the significance is, of course, that a Gutenberg press produced the first printed Bible.
11. The Globe, home to Shakespeare's plays; the city hosts an annual Shakespeare Festival.
12. The *Pinta*, the *Niña*, and the *Santa Maria*, replicas of Columbus's three ships; they were sent out in honor of the five hundredth anniversary of Columbus's first voyage.
13. George Washington's home, Mount Vernon
14. Eureka Springs, Arkansas; the late Gerald L. K. Smith pioneered the project of building replicas of Old Jerusalem sites in Arkansas. The walls, at present, are all that have been completed.

Happy Trails to You // Answers

1. The Appalachian Trail (known as the AT to seasoned hikers)
2. The Trail of Tears
3. Cattle (plus human beings, of course)
4. The Natchez Trace, a Native-American trail that is now administered by the National Park Service
5. The Santa Fe Trail, named for the town that eventually became the capital of New Mexico
6. Oregon (naturally), which didn't actually become a state until 1859
7. Missouri, in the town of Independence
8. The Great Wagon Road, particularly used by Scotch-Irish and German settlers moving to Virginia and North Carolina
9. Utah, naturally
10. Santa Fe

PART SIX

CALL OF THE WILD

★ Big Waters: America's Rivers

1. What big river's name means "big river"?
2. What midwestern metropolis has a river that flows backward?
3. What mighty river begins at Point Park in Pittsburgh?
4. What famous river is seen in New York's Whirlpool State Park?
5. What eastern metropolis is situated on the Anacostia and Potomac Rivers?
6. What name is given to the dikes that keep the Mississippi from flooding the streets of New Orleans?
7. Yonkers, New York, has a museum devoted to what historic river?
8. Riverfest is the chief festival of what riverside Ohio city?
9. What river (appropriately named) flows through Rockford, Illinois?
10. What river, famous in a Stephen Foster song, originates in the Okefenokee Swamp?
11. What metropolis would you enter if you crossed the Delaware River via the Benjamin Franklin Bridge?
12. The "Grand Canyon of the East" is the Genesee River Gorge in what northeastern state?
13. John Wesley Powell, who explored the Colorado River and the Grand Canyon in the 1860s, had what notable handicap?
14. What federal organization was formed to control the flood-prone Tennessee River?
15. In the 1960s the U.S. and Mexico built an artificial riverbed to prevent what river from shifting course?
16. What appropriately named river flows through the capital of Kentucky?
17. What river becomes very scenic as it passes through Great Falls Park in Virginia?
18. What name is given to the imaginary line that separates the Atlantic coastal plain from the Appalachian Mountains?
19. The Murderkill River (which isn't at all dangerous) is in what Atlantic Coast state?
20. What Oklahoma metropolis sits astride the Arkansas River?
21. Itasca State Park in Minnesota is built around Lake Itasca, the source of what important river?
22. Grand Lake, Colorado, is beside a glacial lake that is the source of what major river?

Big Waters: America's Rivers // Answers

1. The Mississippi's
2. Chicago; the Chicago River has been reversed in order to keep sewage from flowing into Lake Michigan.
3. The Ohio, where the Allegheny and Monongahela Rivers converge
4. The Niagara, which has not only the falls but also a whirlpool
5. Washington, D.C.
6. Levees
7. The Hudson
8. Cincinnati
9. The Rock River
10. The Swanee
11. Philadelphia
12. New York
13. He was one-armed, which makes his strenuous explorations all the more remarkable.
14. The Tennessee Valley Authority—TVA
15. The Rio Grande
16. The Kentucky River (surprise!)
17. The Potomac
18. The fall line, where rivers form rapids and waterfalls
19. Delaware
20. Tulsa
21. The Mississippi
22. The Colorado, formerly known as the Grand River

Big Waters: America's Rivers, continued . . .

23. On what river's banks would you find Savannah, Georgia?
24. What mighty river forms the entire eastern boundary of Missouri and Arkansas?

★ Beasts and Zoos and Such

1. What sea mammal's oil was burned in colonial lamps?
2. What ring-tailed animal's name is from a Native American word meaning "he who scratches his hands"?
3. Shamu and other killer whales can be seen at what Orlando, Florida, attraction?
4. What night creatures by the thousands make their home under Austin, Texas's Congress Avenue bridge?
5. What other name is given to the sea cow, which now lives almost solely in the waters off Florida?
6. What prickly mammal is also known as a quill pig?
7. At what California national park could you see gray whales, harbor seals, and sea lions?
8. What famous dog of the movies was found in a foxhole in World War I?
9. What wild canine found throughout the South and West is also called a prairie wolf?
10. Florida is home to the key whitetail, an animal about the size of a large dog. What sort of animal is it?
11. What four-legged animals do we associate with Kentucky?
12. What famous pair of explorers sent back a live prairie dog to Thomas Jefferson?
13. If you wanted to visit a large (and free) zoo in Chicago, where would you go?
14. What type of sea creatures are often sighted off the coast of San Diego, California?
15. If you spotted a *javelina* in the Southwest, what kind of animal would you have seen?
16. Fort Bragg, California, has a March festival for watching what sort of sea creatures?

23. The Savannah River's (When in doubt, go for the most obvious answer.)
24. The Mississippi

Beasts and Zoos and Such // Answers

1. Whale's; the great industry of whaling went downhill after the discovery of petroleum.
2. The raccoon, famous for washing its food before eating
3. Sea World
4. Bats—a million, in fact
5. The manatee
6. The porcupine
7. Channel Islands
8. Rin Tin Tin
9. The coyote (which does *not* eat roadrunners)
10. A deer
11. Horses, naturally
12. Lewis and Clark; like most Americans at that time, Jefferson had never seen a prairie dog.
13. To the Lincoln Park Zoo, one of the largest free zoos in the world
14. Gray whales, making their migration from the Alaska coast to the waters off Mexico
15. The peccary, a wild piglike animal of the open spaces
16. Whales

Beasts and Zoos and Such, continued . . .

17. What name is given to the Florida park where visitors drive among free-roaming lions, ostriches, and other African animals?
18. Ruidoso, New Mexico, has a museum devoted to what useful and much loved animal?
19. If you are viewing the animals at the Audubon Park Zoo, what southern metropolis are you in?
20. What sort of creatures could you see in the Prehistoric Zoo in Ossineke, Michigan?
21. The Detroit Zoo is in what city?
22. The wild ponies of Chincoteague are found on the island of what state?
23. What type of wild animal congregates in herds at the Hardware Ranch in Logan, Utah? (Hint: antlers)
24. Waynesboro, Georgia, is known as the "_____ Capital of the World." What is it the capital of?

★ Every Bloomin' Thing

1. The Tournament of Roses is held in what southern California city?
2. What lovely blooming trees were introduced to D.C. by First Lady Helen Taft after she visited Japan?
3. On what spring holiday do many people wear carnations?
4. What rose variety, a rich purplish red, has a patriotic name?
5. What two southern states' flower is the *very* southern magnolia blossom?
6. What boutonniere flower is second in commercial value in the U.S.?
7. The Cherokee rose is the state flower of which large southern state?
8. Norfolk, Virginia, has an international festival honoring what lovely spring-blooming shrub?
9. What southwestern state has the cactus wren and the cactus blossom as state emblems?
10. The Tyler, Texas, area is the source of more than half of the U.S. supply of what popular flower?
11. What New England state's flower isn't really a flower at all, but a pinecone?

17. Lion Country Safari
18. The horse
19. New Orleans
20. Dinosaurs, of course; the park is called Dinosaur Gardens Prehistoric Zoo. (Actually, they're reproductions, not real dinosaurs.)
21. Not Detroit, but in the nearby suburb of Royal Oak
22. Virginia, on the Eastern Shore
23. Elk
24. Bird dogs; the annual Georgia Field Trials, a major hunting dog competition, is held there.

Every Bloomin' Thing // Answers

1. Pasadena
2. The cherry trees, especially noticeable near the Jefferson Memorial
3. Mother's Day; a red carnation indicates that the mother is living, a white one that she has died.
4. The American Beauty
5. Louisiana and Mississippi
6. The carnation; the rose is number one, naturally.
7. Georgia
8. The azalea
9. Arizona
10. Roses
11. Maine

Every Bloomin' Thing, continued . . .

12. San Francisco's annual Cherry Blossom Festival highlights what ethnic community?
13. What state's official flower is, appropriately, the orange blossom?
14. What flower is honored at a spring festival in Holland, Michigan?
15. What southern state changed its state flower from golden-rod to camellia because so many allergy sufferers complained?
16. The yellow rose is a symbol for what Texas city, whose name means "yellow"?
17. What Pacific state has a grape as its state flower?
18. What attractive summer flower of many colors is the center of an annual festival in Santa Cruz, California?
19. What many-colored autumn flower is the focus of a festival in Bristol, Connecticut?
20. What lovely field flower is the state flower of Texas? (Hint: margarine)
21. The town of Lompoc produces 75 percent of the world's flower seed. What state is it in?
22. San Francisco, California, has the world's largest nursery for what elegant flower? (Hint: purple)
23. What welcome spring flower is the center of a festival in Meriden, Connecticut?
24. What state's flower is, appropriately, the mayflower?
25. Lombard, Illinois, has the lovely Lilacia Park. What shrubs bloom there?
26. What major East Coast city has a Cherry Blossom Festival every April?
27. Sacramento, California, is known to flower-lovers as the "_____ Capital of the World." What flower?
28. California is the "Golden State," and its state flower is the golden _____?
29. What fruit tree blossom is popular at American weddings?
30. The *pua aloalo,* Hawaii's lovely state flower, is actually a common garden shrub known by what name?
31. The "Sunflower State" has the sunflower as the state flower. Which plains state is it?
32. Nebraska and Kentucky's state flower is (for many allergy sufferers) something to sneeze at. What yellow wildflower is it?
33. New York's flower, the rose, was voted on by what group of people?

12. The Japanese; it is one of the grandest Japanese culture festivals in the U.S.
13. Florida, naturally
14. Tulips, naturally
15. Alabama; lovely as goldenrod is, it is not appreciated by people with pollen allergies.
16. Amarillo
17. Oregon; the Oregon grape *is* a flowering plant, actually.
18. Begonias
19. Chrysanthemums; the festival is (naturally) in the fall.
20. The bluebonnet
21. California
22. Orchids; the nursery is Acres of Orchids.
23. Daffodils; over four-hundred thousand of them bloom in the area each April.
24. Massachusetts
25. Lilacs, what else?
26. Washington, D.C., home of the famous cherry trees near the Tidal Basin
27. Camellias; camellia growing is a major industry in California.
28. The golden poppy
29. Orange blossoms
30. Hibiscus
31. Kansas, which is distinctive in having the only *edible* state flower
32. Goldenrod
33. The state's schoolchildren

34. The iris was for centuries the national flower of France and is also the flower of what southern state? (Hint: country music)
35. Virginia's state tree and state flower are the same, an April-blooming species in pink and white. What?

★ Feathered Friends

1. What edible game bird did Benjamin Franklin want as the U.S. symbol?
2. Rhode Island's state bird, named for the state, can provide both eggs and meat. What is it?
3. Florida's state bird isn't the flamingo but is what much loved southern songbird?
4. The nene, a goose on the endangered species list, is the state bird of what western state?
5. Hinkley, Ohio, is the only city to celebrate the spring return of a particularly unpleasant type of bird. What is it?
6. The yellowhammer, Alabama's state bird, is what type of bird? (Hint: Woody)
7. Baraboo, Wisconsin, has a center devoted to the study of what type of endangered bird?
8. What type of wooden birds decorate the streetlights of Waupun, Wisconsin?
9. What Atlantic Coast state has a mythical chicken as its state bird?
10. What state without a seashore has the seagull as its state bird?
11. Memphis, Tennessee's famous Peabody Hotel has what sort of creatures marching daily to and from the lobby fountain?
12. What bird, the U.S.'s only native parrot, became extinct by the early 1900s?
13. What New England state has the purple lilac as its flower and the purple finch as its bird?
14. What creature of a Native American myth caused lightning and thunder? (Hint: Ford)

34. Tennessee; in the French form, it's known as the *fleur-de-lis.*
35. Dogwood

Feathered Friends // Answers

1. The turkey; Franklin knew that eagles are beautiful, but they're also noted for eating carrion and for robbing their food from other birds instead of catching their own.
2. The Rhode Island Red chicken
3. The mockingbird
4. Hawaii (which is *far* west); the nene is also known as the Hawaiian goose.
5. The buzzard; Buzzard Sunday is the first Sunday after March 15. Technically, the birds are known as turkey vultures.
6. A woodpecker; the yellowhammer is also known as a flicker.
7. Cranes—whooping cranes, to be specific; it is the International Crane Foundation.
8. Canada geese; the residents use them to welcome the many thousands of *real* Canada geese that migrate through in the spring and fall.
9. Delaware; the bird is called the blue hen chicken, and no one is quite sure just what that is.
10. Utah; gulls are water birds, not necessarily requiring *ocean* water.
11. Ducks; the duck quartet waddles in time to a John Philip Sousa march.
12. The Carolina parakeet, which was beautiful but very destructive to fruit orchards
13. New Hampshire
14. The thunderbird, naturally

Feathered Friends, continued . . .

15. What ecology-conscious twentieth-century president is buried in a bird sanctuary named for him?
16. What beloved southern songbird is the state bird of nine states?
17. What rare and graceful bird has its main winter home in Texas's Aransas Wildlife Refuge?
18. South Dakota's state bird, an Asian import, would make a tasty dinner. What is it?
19. What lake-studded northern state has the loon as its state bird?
20. What state has a state bird named for another state?
21. What majestic birds did the Pueblo tribe keep in captivity for their feathers?

★ More Big Waters: America's Rivers

1. What major river was known in the old days as "Big Muddy"? (Hint: *not* the Mississippi)
2. What eastern country was Henry Hudson seeking when he sailed up the Hudson River in 1609?
3. The world's largest land gorge is which famous one on the Colorado River?
4. What Manhattan ethnic section runs from Morningside Avenue to the Harlem River?
5. If you are floating on the Sangamon River, what midwestern state are you in?
6. The Stephen Foster Culture Center sits, appropriately enough, on what river in Florida?
7. At Columbus, Kentucky, what did Confederate soldiers stretch across the Mississippi River to halt Union gunboats?
8. What southwestern river makes a ninety-degree bend that gives Big Bend National Park its name?
9. What city sits astride the Miami River? (Hint: not Miami)
10. What famous chemical-producing city sits on the Brandywine River in Delaware?

15. Theodore Roosevelt; it's in Oyster Bay, New York.
16. The mockingbird (Happily, you aren't expected to name all nine states.)
17. The whooping crane
18. The ring-necked pheasant, which has made a new home on American prairies (and on American dinner tables)
19. Minnesota
20. Utah; the state bird is the California gull.
21. Eagles

More Big Waters: America's Rivers // Answers

1. The Missouri
2. India; he was mistaken.
3. The Grand Canyon
4. Harlem
5. Illinois; the river flows through both Decatur and Springfield, the capital.
6. The Swanee, of course; Foster's song "Old Folks at Home," also known as "Swanee River," is Florida's state song.
7. A massive chain, which is now on view at the Columbus Belmont Battlefield Park
8. The Rio Grande
9. Dayton, Ohio, believe it or not
10. Wilmington, Delaware, home of DuPont Chemical

11. What historic Texas metropolis is noted for its River Walk and its water taxis?
12. What name is given to the U-shaped lakes left behind because the Mississippi River changed its course over the years?
13. What city, Idaho's capital, is located on a river of the same name?
14. The Savannah River provides much of what state's boundary with South Carolina?
15. Boulder City, Nevada, grew up as a result of a major federal project on the Colorado River. What was it?
16. The Perdido River forms part of the border between the Florida panhandle and what state?
17. What noted western river's waters provide the irrigation for California's fertile farms?
18. What inappropriately named town in Louisiana had to be relocated four times because the Mississippi River kept drowning it?
19. Wilma Dykeman's fascinating book *The French Broad* is not about a woman, but a river. What two southeastern states is it in?
20. Virginia's Shenandoah River is the largest tributary of what major river? (Hint: D.C.)
21. The 840-mile-long Brazos River lies entirely within what huge state?
22. If you were boating on the Pearl and Yazoo Rivers, what state would you be in?

★ More Beasts and Zoos

1. What animal's hide could earn a frontier hunter as much as a hundred dollars a day?
2. What hardy desert animal was used in Texas as a supply carrier in the 1800s?
3. A hellbender is what type of American aquatic creature?
4. If you are visiting Tiger River, Sun Bear Forest, and Gorilla Tropics, what world-famous California zoo are you in?

More Big Waters: America's Rivers // Answers // continued . . .

11. San Antonio, which has developed its riverfront beautifully
12. Ox-bow lakes
13. Boise
14. Georgia's
15. The Hoover Dam
16. Alabama
17. The Colorado's
18. Waterproof; over the years the river has changed its course many times, which has proved devastating to towns and farmlands. Waterproof was *not* waterproof.
19. North Carolina and Tennessee
20. The Potomac
21. Texas
22. Mississippi

More Beasts and Zoos // Answers

1. Buffalo hides—the price being one of the key causes of the dwindling herds
2. The camel, which never was very successful in America
3. A very large (and very ugly) salamander
4. The San Diego Zoo, one of the great zoos of the world

More Beasts and Zoos, continued . . .

QUESTIONS

5. What breed of dog, named for an American city, was a cross between a bulldog and a white terrier?

6. Texas's Diablo Mountains are the last home of what horned animal of the Old West?

7. A popular St. Louis park with a petting zoo is run by what pet food company?

8. Besides horses, what slow-moving animals pulled covered wagons on the frontier?

9. If you are in the Rio Grande Zoo, what major southwestern city are you in?

10. What beasts associated with the Old West graze wild at Woolaroc in Oklahoma?

11. New York Zoological Park is better known by what name?

12. What is the only state to have a county named for an aquatic mammal?

13. If you are visiting the large zoo in Mohawk Park, what southwestern metropolis are you in?

14. What material did the early buffalo hunters use to make their huts?

15. California's lovely Catalina Island was used by the Russians for hunting what playful water animal?

16. Effigy Mounds National Monument has Native American mounds in the shapes of birds and animals, as well as in other forms. What midwestern state is it in?

17. Horse breeding is associated with what type of grass, common in Kentucky?

18. What pro-animal organization was founded in 1866 by Henry Bergh?

19. What substance was mined in Death Valley and hauled out by twenty-mule teams?

20. Hill City, South Dakota, has an animal museum named for a Jack London novel. What is it?

21. What did early buffalo hunters discover was a good use for buffalo bones?

22. What animal parts could you see on display in a San Antonio, Texas, museum?

23. Where in D.C. could you see giant pandas, lowland gorillas, and Komodo dragons?

24. What rare ten-foot mammal is found in the rivers and bays of Florida?

25. What formerly domestic animals now run wild in the Arizona ghost town of Oatman?

5. The Boston terrier

6. Bighorn sheep

7. Purina; the park is Purina Farms.

8. Oxen, which made up in endurance what they lacked in speed

9. Albuquerque, New Mexico

10. Bison (buffalo) and longhorn cattle, plus elk and other native wildlife

11. The Bronx Zoo (since it's in the Bronx)

12. Florida, which has Manatee County

13. Tulsa, Oklahoma

14. Buffalo hides—what else?

15. Otters—for their hides, of course

16. Iowa, near the town of Marquette

17. Bluegrass

18. The SPCA, Society for the Prevention of Cruelty to Animals

19. Borax (Remember the "Twenty-Mule-Team Borax" commercials?)

20. The Call of the Wild Museum

21. Fertilizer

22. Horns, along with other hunting memorabilia; they are in the Buckhorn Hall of Horns.

23. The National Zoo, of course

24. The manatee, or sea cow

25. Donkeys—or, to use the local word, burros

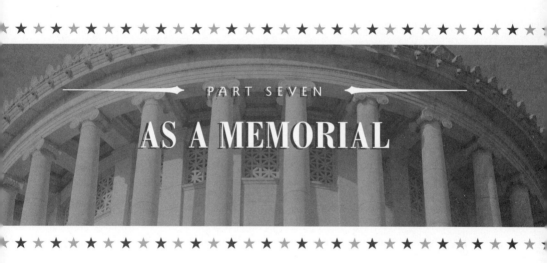

PART SEVEN

AS A MEMORIAL

★ Named in Honor of Whom?

How do we honor someone? Name something after him or her.
The name can live on in a city, a park, a museum . . . even a
hairstyle.

1. Santa Ana, California's airport is named for what star of dozens of Western films?
2. The Metrodome in Minneapolis is named for what famous Minnesota senator and presidential candidate?
3. Kentucky has a national forest named for what near-legendary frontiersman? (Hint: coonskin cap)
4. Harvard's School of Government is named for what Massachusetts-born president of the 1960s?
5. The Museum of Cavalry and Armor in Kentucky is named for what gritty World War II general?
6. The dance called the *Lindy Hop* was named after what famous American aviator?
7. What style of architecture, named for England's Hanoverian kings, was quite popular?
8. Which two states named their most populous city after Andrew Jackson?
9. Jonas Bronck, a Swedish settler, lends his name to a section of what metropolis?
10. Chicago has a world-class natural history museum named for a department store founder. Who?
11. Block Island, named for Dutch explorer Adriaen Block, is a summer resort in what New England state?
12. What state has a town that was named for Abraham Lincoln *before* he became president?
13. Cleveland, Ohio's best-known city park is named for one of the city's best-known (and richest) residents. Who?
14. The planetarium in D.C.'s National Air and Space Museum is named for what renowned German-speaking scientist?
15. What Alabama city named three of its public schools after the astronauts killed in 1967 aboard Apollo 1?
16. An island park in the Potomac River is named for which outdoors-loving president?
17. What eastern state capital was named in honor of Queen Anne of England?

Named in Honor of Whom? // Answers

1. John Wayne
2. Hubert Humphrey, senator and vice president
3. Daniel Boone
4. John F. Kennedy
5. George S. Patton
6. Charles Lindbergh
7. Georgian; George I, George II, and George III all ruled during America's early days.
8. Florida (Jacksonville) and Mississippi (Jackson)
9. New York; the section, or borough, is the Bronx.
10. Marshall Field; the museum is the Field Museum of Natural History. The chain of Marshall Field stores was acquired by Macy's in 2006.
11. Rhode Island
12. Illinois; Lincoln christened the town site with watermelon juice.
13. John D. Rockefeller, who made Cleveland the base of his lucrative Standard Oil empire
14. Albert Einstein
15. Huntsville, the "Rocket City" and NASA site; the schools were named for astronauts Virgil Grissom, Ed White, and Roger Chaffee.
16. Theodore Roosevelt
17. Annapolis, Maryland; *Annapolis* means "Anne's city."

Named in Honor of Whom? continued . . .

18. What western state has a county named for the ill-fated George Custer?
19. What Polish leader in the American Revolution has dozens of towns and counties named for him?
20. Burbank, California, was named for scientist Luther Burbank, whose specialty was what?

★ Halls of Fame

Americans like to honor the great—and sometimes the not-so-great. Somewhere, across the fifty states, is a hall of fame for everything—sports, music, dogs, tobacco spitting . . .

1. The Country Music Hall of Fame is on Music Square in what city?
2. What music hall of fame has categories of Artists, Early Influences, and Nonperformers?
3. What great American sport's hall of fame is in Cooperstown, New York?
4. The Hall of Fame for Great Americans, displaying numerous bronze busts, is in what New York City borough?
5. The gun collection in Oklahoma's Cowboy Hall of Fame is named for what motion picture gunslinger?
6. What sport's hall of fame is located (appropriately) one block from New York's Madison Square Garden?
7. Notorious for its crime rate, Miami has a hall of fame honoring what profession?
8. What state, with lots of sunshine and water, has the Water Ski Museum and Hall of Fame?
9. Abilene, Kansas, has a hall of fame for what breed of dog? (Hint: racetracks)
10. Where would you find sculpted bronze busts of famous Native Americans?
11. Hereford, Texas, has a hall of fame for what special type of cowboy?
12. What muscle-enhancing hobby has its hall of fame in York, Pennsylvania?

18. Montana, the state where Custer met his fate at Little Bighorn
19. Count Casimir Pulaski; there are Pulaskis all over the American map.
20. Botany; his impact on the cultivation of fruits and vegetables is immeasurable.

Halls of Fame // Answers

1. Nashville, Tennessee, naturally
2. The Rock and Roll Hall of Fame, begun in 1986, with its museum opening in 1995 in Cleveland
3. Baseball's
4. The Bronx; it's on the campus of Bronx Community College.
5. John Wayne
6. Boxing's
7. Law enforcement; the American Police Hall of Fame and Museum has a curious location.
8. Florida; the museum is in Polk City.
9. Greyhounds; Abilene hosts the National Greyhound Meet.
10. Oklahoma's National Hall of Fame for Famous American Indians
11. Female—cow*girls*, to be specific; it is the National Cowgirl Hall of Fame and Western Heritage Center.
12. Weight lifting; York is a major center for making weights and weight-lifting equipment.

QUESTIONS

13. Fort Lauderdale, Florida, has an international hall of fame for what watery pastime?

14. The National Mining Hall of Fame is in what mountain state?

15. What popular (and nonprofessional) sport has its hall of fame in Oklahoma City?

16. What type of person is honored with a hall of fame in Oklahoma City? (Hint: lariat)

17. If you wanted to see Elvis Presley's gold piano and Roy Acuff's yo-yo, what Nashville museum would you visit?

18. Vandalia, Ohio, has a hall of fame devoted to what type of shooting? (Hint: "Pull!")

19. King's Mills, Ohio, has a hall of fame for what college sport?

20. In what mountainous state would you find the ProRodeo Hall of Fame and American Cowboy Museum?

21. Who is the only minister honored in the Hall of Fame for Great Americans?

22. The Cartoonists' Hall of Fame is at White Plains in what northeastern state?

23. What inventor plowed into the Agricultural Hall of Fame in 1987 with his self-polishing steel plow?

✮ Grave Matters: Final Resting Places of the Famous

Graves aren't gloomy places, but (as all travelers are aware) tourist attractions. Call it silly, but we get a special feeling knowing we're actually near a famous person—or at least the mortal remains. A tomb has a way of reminding us of what the person stood for. And if you want some insights into human nature—and the American character—try reading tombstones.

1. What actor was buried in Simi Valley, California, in June 2004?

2. The bed in which George Washington died, as well as his grave, is at what Virginia site?

13. Swimming; the International Swimming Hall of Fame is a museum as well as a swim center.
14. Colorado, appropriately enough
15. Softball; the Hall of Fame and Museum also has a stadium complex.
16. Cowboys; the Cowboy Hall of Fame also contains the Rodeo Hall of Fame.
17. The Country Music Hall of Fame
18. Trapshooting
19. Football
20. Colorado; it's in Colorado Springs.
21. Colonial pastor and theologian Jonathan Edwards
22. New York
23. John Deere

Grave Matters: Final Resting Places of the Famous // Answers

1. Ronald Reagan—who had some other jobs besides acting
2. His estate, Mount Vernon

Grave Matters: Final Resting Places of the Famous, continued . . .

3. What notable achievement of Thomas Jefferson's life did he *not* mention on his tombstone?
4. Who is buried in Manhattan in Grant's Tomb?
5. What naval hero of the Revolutionary War died in France and was re-buried in the U.S. in 1905?
6. What glamorous woman, who died in March 2011, is buried in the Great Mausoleum at Forest Lawn?
7. What famous (and gloomy) poet and short-story writer is buried at First Presbyterian Church in Baltimore, Maryland?
8. What much loved western comedian's home, birthplace, and grave can be visited in Claremore, Oklahoma?
9. What honored Confederate general is buried in the chapel at Washington and Lee University?
10. What is unusual about the large bust of Abraham Lincoln by his grave?
11. What World War II and Korean War general has an imposing memorial and tomb in Norfolk, Virginia?
12. Samuel Wilson's grave is in Troy, New York. What U.S. symbol was he the original of?
13. The Tomb of the Unknown Soldier of the American Revolution is at Rome in what northeastern state?
14. The nation's twelfth president, a hero of the Mexican War, is buried in Louisville, Kentucky. Who is he?
15. When you see the letters *C.S.A.* on a tombstone, what does it mean?
16. Wisconsin Dells is, oddly, the burial site of the Confederacy's most famous spy. Who was she?

✯ Named in Honor of Whom? (Part 2)

1. What president was Washington's National Airport renamed for?
2. The University of Arkansas's school of business was named for the founder of what retail chains?
3. What beloved comedian who died in 2003 is the Burbank, California, airport named for?

3. President of the United States; he is buried at Monticello, his estate in Virginia.
4. Mrs. Grant—along with Gen. U. S. Grant, of course
5. John Paul Jones; "I have not yet begun to fight."
6. Elizabeth Taylor
7. Edgar Allan Poe
8. Will Rogers
9. Robert E. Lee; the school had originally been Washington College. The "and Lee" was added to honor Robert, who had been its president.
10. The bronze nose is shiny because so many visitors rub it.
11. Douglas MacArthur
12. "Uncle Sam"; Wilson supplied meat to American soldiers in the War of 1812. They were stamped *U.S.*, and the soldiers said it stood for "Uncle Sam."
13. New York
14. Zachary Taylor
15. The person buried there was a Confederate soldier; C.S.A. stands for the Confederate States of America.
16. The infamous Belle Boyd, who died in the city while on a lecture tour

Named in Honor of Whom? (Part 2) // Answers

1. Ronald Reagan
2. Sam Walton, founder of Wal-Mart and Sam's Club
3. Bob Hope

Named in Honor of Whom? (Part 2), continued . . .

4. Oklahoma City's airport is named for what popular cowboy comedian?
5. A Native American chief named Paduke has his name memorialized in what city?
6. Wapakoneta, Ohio, has a space museum named for what well-known astronaut?
7. Williamsburg, Virginia, was named in honor of whom?
8. What Texas metropolis is named for the first president of the Republic of Texas?
9. Brigham City, Utah, was named for what Mormon leader?
10. What state has a state park named for President Dwight Eisenhower?
11. In what state can you find Stonewall County, named for Confederate general "Stonewall" Jackson?
12. Harrisonburg, Virginia, has a large state university named for what Virginia-born president?
13. Fort Scott, Kansas, was named for one of the country's most famous soldiers of the 1800s. Who?
14. What four states were named for British rulers?
15. Roman Nose State Park was not named for a Roman but for whom?
16. What major Kentucky city on the Ohio River is named for a king of France?
17. What notorious Nevada gambling town is named for a Civil War general?
18. One of the world's best art museums in Malibu, California, is named for one of the world's richest oil men. Who?
19. Kentucky has a state park named for what great American artist famous for his paintings of birds?
20. What baseball stadium has the street address 755 Hank Aaron Drive?

★ Famous Cemeteries, Famous Occupants

1. John F. Kennedy and William Howard Taft are the only two presidents buried in what national cemetery?
2. John Ritter, Ed McMahon, and dozens of other entertainers are buried in what California cemetery?

4. Will Rogers

5. Paducah, Kentucky

6. Neil Armstrong, first man on the moon

7. William III, king of England at the time

8. Houston, named for Sam Houston

9. Brigham Young, who led the Mormons to settle the state

10. Kansas, where he grew up; the park is near Emporia.

11. Texas

12. James Madison

13. Winfield Scott, especially famed for his leadership in the Mexican War

14. Georgia (named for King George II), Virginia (named for Elizabeth I, the "Virgin Queen"), and North and South Carolina (named for King Charles II—*Carolus* in Latin)

15. Chief Henry Roman Nose, a Cheyenne Indian (who, no doubt, had a Roman nose)

16. Louisville, named for (surprise!) King Louis XVI

17. Reno, Nevada, named for Union general Jesse Reno

18. J. Paul Getty

19. John James Audubon

20. Turner Field, home of the Atlanta Braves; the "755" commemorates Hank Aaron's home run total.

Famous Cemeteries, Famous Occupants // Answers

1. Arlington, across the river from Washington

2. Forest Lawn, Hollywood Hills

QUESTIONS

3. The body of an American soldier killed during World War I in France is buried in what famous tomb in Arlington Cemetery?

4. Sleepy Hollow Cemetery has an Authors' Ridge, with the graves of Nathaniel Hawthorne, Henry David Thoreau, and Ralph Waldo Emerson. What state is it in?

5. What general and World War I hero requested to be buried in Arlington Cemetery with only an enlisted man's marker?

6. What blonde movie queen of the 1950s is buried in California's Westwood Memorial Cemetery?

7. Grove Street Cemetery, with the graves of Noah Webster, Charles Goodyear, and Eli Whitney, is in what New England college town?

8. What colorful World War II general chose to be buried among his men in a military cemetery in Luxembourg?

9. What lakeside Ohio city has the tombs of President James Garfield and millionaire John D. Rockefeller?

10. Confederate president Jefferson Davis is buried in what appropriate city?

11. Bandmaster John Philip Sousa and FBI head J. Edgar Hoover are buried in what famous D.C. cemetery?

12. In what state would you find Woodlawn Memorial Park, with the graves of Tammy Wynette, Porter Wagoner, and Jerry Reed?

13. What voice artist's tombstone is inscribed, "That's all, folks"?

14. The people in the "Unknown Plot" in Johnstown, Pennsylvania's Grandview Cemetery were the victims of what natural disaster?

15. The Tomb of the Unknown Dead of the Civil War is found in what famous federal cemetery?

16. What two Virginia-born presidents are buried in Richmond's Hollywood Cemetery? (Hint: fifth and tenth)

17. What famous author, usually associated with Missouri, is buried in Woodlawn Cemetery in Elmira, New York?

18. If you are at the Granary Burying Ground, looking at the graves of Paul Revere, Samuel Adams, and John Hancock, what historic city are you in?

3. The Tomb of the Unknown Soldier
4. Massachusetts, in the town of Concord
5. John J. Pershing
6. Marilyn Monroe; the cemetery also has such stars as Carroll O'Connor, Natalie Wood, and Peter Lorre.
7. New Haven, Connecticut, home of Yale
8. George Patton
9. Cleveland; both are in Lakeview Cemetery.
10. Richmond, Virginia (the capital of the Confederacy), in the famous Hollywood Cemetery
11. The Congressional Cemetery
12. Tennessee—Nashville, to be precise
13. Mel Blanc's; Blanc, who did voices for various Looney Tunes characters, is buried along with numerous other entertainers in the Hollywood Forever Cemetery.
14. The 1889 Johnstown flood; the 777 people in the Unknown Plot are unidentified victims.
15. Arlington, across the river from Washington
16. James Monroe, fifth president, and John Tyler, tenth president
17. Samuel Clemens, also known as Mark Twain
18. Boston, Massachusetts

★ More Grave Matters: Final Resting Places of the Famous

1. What comic who died in 2003 at age one hundred is buried at California's Mission San Fernando?
2. What entertainer is buried beside his parents at Graceland?
3. What silver-haired comic actor who died in 2010 has "Let 'er rip" on his tombstone?
4. What twentieth-century president was born, raised, and buried in Hyde Park, New York?
5. Frankfort, Kentucky, has the grave of what notable Kentucky frontiersman?
6. What two presidents (who were related) are buried in the United First Parish Church in Quincy, Massachusetts?
7. What noted political opponent of Abraham Lincoln is buried in Chicago?
8. What Virginia-born president's home and grave are at the estate of Montpelier?
9. Taos, New Mexico, has the home and grave of what noted pioneer and scout?
10. What colorful head of a Wild West show is buried in Golden, Colorado?
11. What president, nicknamed Old Hickory, is buried beside his wife, Rachel, at the Hermitage estate near Nashville?
12. Fremont, Ohio, has the grave of what president of the 1800s (who was nicknamed Rutherfraud)?
13. Which Confederate general's arm is buried at Guinea, Virginia?
14. What singer-songwriter-actor-congressman has "And the beat goes on" on his tombstone?
15. What reserved president is buried in the tiny village of Plymouth, Vermont?
16. What president of the depression era has a national historic site in Iowa City, Iowa?
17. When the body of naval hero John Paul Jones was brought to the U.S. from France, where was it appropriately buried?
18. If you wanted to see Abraham Lincoln's grave and the only home he ever owned, where would you go?

1. Bob Hope

2. Elvis Presley, of course

3. Leslie Nielsen, buried in Fort Lauderdale's Evergreen Cemetery

4. Franklin D. Roosevelt

5. Daniel Boone

6. John Adams and his son, John Quincy Adams

7. Stephen Douglas (famous for the Lincoln-Douglas debates)

8. James Madison's

9. Christopher "Kit" Carson

10. Buffalo Bill Cody

11. Andrew Jackson

12. Rutherford Hayes, the nineteenth president; his nickname came from the disputed election returns in 1876.

13. Thomas "Stonewall" Jackson's; after being wounded, Jackson's left arm was amputated, and a devoted friend gave it a prayerful burial. Jackson himself is buried in Lexington.

14. Sonny Bono, who died in 1998; "The Beat Goes On" was one of his songs.

15. Calvin Coolidge, who was born in Plymouth in 1872

16. Herbert Hoover; his birthplace, grave, and presidential library are all there.

17. At the U.S. Naval Academy

18. Springfield, Illinois

★ Named in Honor of Whom? (Part 3)

1. What style of facial hair is named for a Union general in the Civil War?
2. What southern state has a capital named for the seventh president, "Old Hickory"?
3. What explorer, with a river named for him, sailed into New York in 1609 on the *Half Moon*?
4. What state was formed from land granted by England's Charles II to a Quaker leader?
5. What major city on the Mississippi River was named for King Louis IX of France?
6. You could see *Boston 1775*, a multimedia show, in a Boston building named for a noted patriot. Who? (Hint: signature)
7. Who was Jamestown, the first successful English colony in America, named for?
8. Dutchman Adrien Van Der Donck, known as "DeJonkeer," lent his name to what New York town?
9. What Hungarian-born soldier in the Union army in the Civil War gave his name to prestigious journalism prizes?
10. Pittsburgh's museum complex is named for one of the richest men in the city's history, a name synonymous with wealth. Who?
11. What beautiful D.C. building has its three wings named for presidents Thomas Jefferson, John Adams, and James Madison?
12. Fort Worth, Texas's civic center is named for a comic usually associated with Oklahoma. Who?
13. What hyphenated Pennsylvania city is named for two members of the British Parliament who supported the colonists' side?
14. A state forest near Plymouth, Massachusetts, is named for what famous Pilgrim leader (made famous in a Longfellow poem)?
15. What oddly named Michigan city was named for a Greek fighter against the Turkish army?
16. What Quaker colonizer was cowboy comic Will Rogers named for?
17. What nickname for an Iowa resident honors the Sauk chief Black Hawk?
18. What Florida city is named for a man who was born in Tagaste, North Africa, in the year A.D. 354?
19. What president has the record of having the most towns named for him? (Hint: Old Hickory)

Named in Honor of Whom? (Part 3) // Answers

1. Sideburns, named for Ambrose Burnside, who wore them
2. Mississippi; Jackson, the capital, is named for Andrew Jackson.
3. Henry Hudson
4. Pennsylvania, named for the Quaker William Penn
5. St. Louis, Missouri; besides being a king, Louis also was a saint canonized by the Catholic church.
6. John Hancock; the John Hancock Tower has an excellent view of the city.
7. England's king, James I (the same James of the King James Version of the Bible); the name was also given to the river the colonists settled on.
8. Yonkers, now a suburb of New York City
9. Joseph Pulitzer
10. Andrew Carnegie; Carnegie is a common name for city sites in Pittsburgh.
11. The Library of Congress
12. Will Rogers
13. Wilkes-Barre
14. Miles Standish
15. Ypsilanti, named for Gen. Demetrios Ypsilanti
16. William Penn, founder of Pennsylvania; Rogers's full name was William Penn Adair Rogers.
17. Hawkeye
18. St. Augustine; he was a major Christian theologian in the late Roman Empire, famous for his *Confessions.*
19. Andrew Jackson, who just barely beats out George Washington for the honor

PART EIGHT

THE FINER THINGS: ARTISTS, AUTHORS, AND SUCH

★ Author! Author!

If you hear of Hamlet, Macbeth, *and* Romeo and Juliet, *you think of William Shakespeare. Would you be as quick to think of American authors' names if you heard the titles of some of their best-known works? Try it, and remember that they range from contemporary writers to the original colonists of the 1600s.*

1. *The Confession, The Associate, The Client, The Pelican Brief*
2. *The Purpose-Driven Life, The Purpose-Driven Church, Life's Healing Choices*
3. "The Raven," "Annabel Lee," "The Tell-Tale Heart"
4. *The Grass Is Always Greener over the Septic Tank, Motherhood: The World's Second-Oldest Profession, Aunt Erma's Cope Book*
5. *Rip Van Winkle, The Legend of Sleepy Hollow, Knickerbocker's History of New York*
6. "Because I could not stop for death," "A narrow fellow in the grass," "I felt a funeral in my brain"
7. *The World According to Garp, The Hotel New Hampshire, The Cider House Rules*
8. *Charlotte's Web, Stuart Little, Here Is New York*
9. *Little House on the Prairie, Little House in the Big Woods*
10. *The Glass Menagerie, A Streetcar Named Desire, The Rose Tattoo*
11. *It, Carrie, Pet Sematary, Misery*
12. *Poor Richard's Almanac, Autobiography, The Way to Wealth*
13. *Centennial, Hawaii, Space, Poland, Texas*
14. "To My Dear and Loving Husband," "Meditations Divine and Moral," "Epitaph on a Patriot"
15. *The Prince and the Pauper, Life on the Mississippi, The Adventures of Huckleberry Finn*
16. *Demonic, Guilty, Slander, Godless, Treason*
17. *Ethan Frome, The Age of Innocence, The House of Mirth*
18. "Stopping by Woods on a Snowy Evening," "Mending Wall," "Two Tramps in Mud Time"
19. *The Godfather, The Sicilian, Fools Die*
20. *Riders of the Purple Sage, The Spirit of the Border, West of the Pecos*

QUESTIONS

1. John Grisham, contemporary novelist
2. Rick Warren, contemporary religious writer
3. Edgar Allan Poe, poet and short-story writer (1809–1849)
4. Erma Bombeck, humorist (1927–1996)
5. Washington Irving, essayist and short-story author (1783–1859)
6. Emily Dickinson, poet (1830–1886)
7. John Irving, contemporary novelist
8. E. B. White, essayist and children's author (1899–1985)
9. Laura Ingalls Wilder, novelist (1867–1957)
10. Tennessee Williams, dramatist (1911–1983)
11. Stephen King, contemporary novelist
12. Benjamin Franklin (1706–1790)
13. James A. Michener, novelist (1907–1997)
14. Anne Bradstreet, poet (1612–1672)
15. Samuel Clemens (Mark Twain), novelist and short-story author (1835–1910)
16. Ann Coulter, contemporary political writer
17. Edith Wharton, novelist (1862–1937)
18. Robert Frost, poet (1874–1963)
19. Mario Puzo, contemporary novelist
20. Zane Grey, western novelist (1875–1939)

Author! Author! continued . . .

21. "Paul Revere's Ride," "My Lost Youth," *The Song of Hiawatha, Evangeline*
22. *The Accidental Tourist, Ladder of Years, Breathing Lessons*
23. "The Gift of the Magi," "The Ransom of Red Chief," "The Last Leaf"
24. *Walden,* "Civil Disobedience," "My Life Is like a Stroll upon the Beach"
25. *Moby Dick, Billy Budd, Typee*
26. *Lonesome Dove, Terms of Endearment, Cadillac Jack*
27. *Essays to Do Good, Magnalia Christi Americana, Political Fables*
28. *All the King's Men, Band of Angels, John Brown: The Making of a Martyr*
29. *The Lost World, Jurassic Park, Disclosure, The Andromeda Strain*
30. "Sinners in the Hands of an Angry God," *Freedom of the Will, A Treatise on Religious Affections*
31. *My Antonia, Death Comes for the Archbishop, Shadows on the Rock*
32. *Babbitt, Main Street, Dodsworth, Arrowsmith*
33. *Common Sense, The Age of Reason*
34. *The Deerslayer, The Prairie, The Last of the Mohicans*
35. "it is at moments after i have dreamed," "this is the garden, colors come and go," "humanity i love you"
36. *Our Town, The Skin of Our Death, The Matchmaker, The Bridge of San Luis Rey*
37. "Young Goodman Brown," *The Scarlet Letter, The House of the Seven Gables*
38. "Chicago," "The People, Yes," "Prayers of Steel"
39. "Self-Reliance," "Nature," "Concord Hymn"
40. *The Thin Man, The Maltese Falcon, The Dain Curse*
41. *Look Homeward Angel, The Web and the Rock, Of Time and the River*
42. *Little Women, Little Men*
43. *The Wonderful Wizard of Oz, The Patchwork Girl of Oz, Magical Monarch of Mo*

⭐ Short Reading: Newspapers and Magazines

1. William F. Buckley, who died in 2008, founded what political magazine?
2. What popular home magazine began in 1937 under the name *Fruit, Gardener, and Home*?

21. Henry Wadsworth Longfellow, poet (1807–1882)
22. Anne Tyler, contemporary novelist
23. O. Henry, short-story author (1862–1910)
24. Henry David Thoreau, poet and essayist (1817–1862)
25. Herman Melville, novelist and poet (1819–1891)
26. Larry McMurtry, contemporary novelist
27. Cotton Mather, Puritan preacher and historian (1663–1728)
28. Robert Penn Warren, novelist and poet (1905–1989)
29. Michael Crichton, novelist (1942–2008)
30. Jonathan Edwards, theologian and preacher (1703–1758)
31. Willa Cather, novelist (1873–1947)
32. Sinclair Lewis, novelist (1885–1951)
33. Thomas Paine, political essayist (1737–1809)
34. James Fenimore Cooper, novelist (1789–1851)
35. e. e. cummings, poet (1894–1962)
36. Thornton Wilder, dramatist and novelist (1897–1975)
37. Nathaniel Hawthorne, novelist and short-story writer (1804–1864)
38. Carl Sandburg, poet (1878–1967)
39. Ralph Waldo Emerson, essayist and poet (1803–1882)
40. Dashiell Hammett, mystery writer (1894–1961)
41. Thomas Wolfe, novelist (1900–1938)
42. Louisa May Alcott, novelist (1832–1888)
43. L. Frank Baum, journalist and writer (1856–1919)

Short Reading: Newspapers and Magazines // Answers

1. *National Review*
2. *Better Homes and Gardens*

3. DeWitt and Lila Wallace founded what phenomenally popular monthly magazine in 1921? (Hint: condense)

4. What popular (and colorful) monthly magazine has its own museum in Washington, D.C.?

5. What huge organization for people over fifty published *Modern Maturity* magazine?

6. *The Wall Street Journal,* one of the best-selling American newspapers, lacks what on its front page?

7. What monthly magazine founded in 1936 is famous for accepting no advertising?

8. What famous evangelist's organization publishes the magazine *Decision*?

9. What newsmagazine's first cover (in 1936) was by famed photographer Margaret Bourke-White?

10. What news weekly, published since 1933, ceased printing in 2011?

11. *Columbia* is the magazine of what fraternal order of Roman Catholic men?

12. What newsmagazine changed its "Man of the Year" honor to "Person of the Year" in 1999?

13. *Boys Life* is the official magazine of what boys' organization?

14. If you are reading a newspaper with the distinctive name *Times-Picayune,* where is the paper from?

15. The U.S.'s oldest continually published newspaper is what New England city's *Courant*?

16. The palatial estate San Simeon in California was the home of what newspaper mogul?

17. What noted publishing company, famed for its colorful food and decorating magazines, is headquartered in Menlo Park, California?

18. What is an e-zine?

19. What great American circus entrepreneur had been jailed for libel while he was a newspaper editor?

20. *The Americanization of Edward Bok,* published in 1920, is the rags-to-riches story of a magazine editor. What still-popular women's magazine did Bok edit?

21. What religious sect, with its Mother Church in Boston, publishes one of the most prestigious newspapers in America?

22. What was the significance of the magazine *Godey's Lady's Book,* first published in 1830?

3. *Reader's Digest*

4. *National Geographic*

5. The AARP—American Association of Retired Persons. The magazine is now called *AARP The Magazine.*

6. Photos

7. *Consumer Reports*

8. Billy Graham's

9. *Life*

10. *U.S. News and World Report,* which continues in an online edition; the last print edition was in December 2010.

11. The Knights of Columbus

12. *Time.* Before the change, several women had been honored as "Woman of the Year."

13. The Boy Scouts of America

14. New Orleans

15. Hartford, Connecticut's

16. William Randolph Hearst

17. Sunset Publishing, with its famous *Sunset* magazine and books

18. A magazine available on the Internet; *e-zine* comes from "electronic magazine" and is also called a webzine.

19. P. T. Barnum

20. *Ladies Home Journal*

21. The Christian Scientists, who publish *The Christian Science Monitor*

22. It was the first women's magazine.

Short Reading: Newspapers and Magazines, continued . . .

23. What housewife and humorist wrote the syndicated column "At Wit's End"?
24. What widely read conservative columnist writes for both *Newsweek* and the *Washington Post*?
25. What popular weekly magazine was launched by Walter Annenberg in 1953? (Hint: program)

★ Painters, Sculptors, and Other Artsy Types

1. What painter known for *Christina's World* and the *Helga* paintings died in 2009?
2. Thomas Kinkade, who has been dubbed "America's most-collected living artist," is known as the "Painter of" what?
3. James Whistler's 1872 painting *Arrangement in Gray and Black No. 1* is better known by what name?
4. What great painter of Americana gained fame for his *Saturday Evening Post* covers?
5. What noted painter had to go to England to get his *Birds of America* published?
6. America's largest art museum, with more than 3 million objects, is what Manhattan landmark?
7. Grant Wood's famous painting *American Gothic* shows a farm couple, with the man holding a pitchfork. What relation are the man and woman?
8. The "Gibson girl," made famous by artist Charles Dana Gibson, was what woman?
9. California's most famous cemetery has several large reproductions of famous religious paintings. What is the cemetery?
10. What redheaded comic is also famous for his paintings of clowns?
11. Florida's Ringling Museum of Art was financed with money from what type of entertainment?
12. What president's much visited statue in D.C. was sculpted by Daniel Chester French?
13. If you wanted to see the largest collection of Rembrandt paintings in America, where would you go?

23. Erma Bombeck
24. George F. Will
25. *TV Guide*

Painters, Sculptors, and Other Artsy Types // Answers

1. Andrew Wyeth
2. Light
3. "Whistler's Mother"
4. Norman Rockwell
5. John James Audubon
6. The Metropolitan Museum of Art
7. Father and daughter, according to the artist; most people assume that the two are husband and wife.
8. Gibson's wife
9. Forest Lawn, in Glendale
10. Red Skelton, who died in 1997
11. The circus; wealthy John Ringling built the museum with money from the Greatest Show on Earth.
12. Lincoln's, inside the Lincoln Memorial
13. The National Gallery of Art in D.C.

Painters, Sculptors, and Other Artsy Types, continued . . .

14. Fulton, Missouri, has a thirty-two-foot sculpture titled *Breakthrough*. What Cold War relic does it commemorate?

15. If you wanted to see a lot of paintings of dogs, what midwestern city would you visit?

16. What noted Missouri artist's home can be visited in Kansas City?

17. Sculptor Korzack Ziolkowski began work on the world's largest statue, a memorial to Sioux chief Crazy Horse. In what state?

18. What great artist is known for his more than one hundred portraits of George Washington?

19. Many limners from the colonial era are known only by the names of the families who paid them. What were they?

20. *The Wars of America,* a forty-two-figure bronze sculpture in Newark, New Jersey, was sculpted by Gutzon Borglum. What huge outdoor sculpture is he more famous for?

21. What great French sculptor's works are featured in a Philadelphia museum? (Hint: thinker)

22. What famous woman started painting because her fingers had become too stiff for embroidering?

★ Poetic Types

1. "The New Colossus," Emma Lazarus's famous poem about immigrants, is on what famous statue?

2. In a great Longfellow poem, what maiden is "the arrow-maker's daughter . . . handsomest of all the women"?

3. What title is Clement Moore's 1823 poem "A Visit from St. Nicholas" better known by?

4. What famous poet was expelled from West Point because he showed up at inspection wearing nothing but belt and gloves? (Hint: raven)

5. What great New England poet of the twentieth century published his first poems while living in England?

6. What comic baseball poem about the "Mudville Nine" was written by Ernest Thayer?

14. The Berlin Wall, which still existed when the sculpture was done

15. St. Louis; its Museum of the Dog is a center for dog-related art.

16. Thomas Hart Benton's, one of the great American artists of this century

17. South Dakota; the statue was carved from the granite of Thunderhead Mountain.

18. Gilbert Stuart

19. Portrait painters

20. Mount Rushmore, the four presidents

21. Rodin, famous for *The Thinker*

22. Grandma Moses

Poetic Types // Answers

1. The Statue of Liberty

2. Minnehaha, wife of Hiawatha in *The Song of Hiawatha*

3. "'Twas the Night before Christmas"

4. Edgar Allan Poe; the story (possibly a legend) is that he was told he had to wear belt and gloves to inspection, and so he did—and nothing else.

5. Robert Frost

6. "Casey at the Bat" ("There is no joy in Mudville / Mighty Casey has struck out.")

Poetic Types, continued . . .

QUESTIONS

7. What noted free-verse poet's home and tomb can be visited in Camden, New Jersey?

8. What noted poet's home can be visited in New Brunswick, New Jersey? (Hint: trees)

9. Remembrance Rock in Galesburg, Illinois, is the burial site of what poet noted for his *Chicago Poems* and biography of Lincoln?

10. One of America's greatest poets and essayists had his home in Concord, Massachusetts, from 1835 till 1882. Who was he?

11. Massachusetts has the Walden Pond State Reservation. What famous poet and essayist lived there in the 1800s?

12. What noted Quaker poet of the 1800s had his birthplace in Haverhill, Massachusetts?

13. What odd item did poet Joaquin Miller include in his home in Oakland, California?

14. What cockroach poet told his stories through the columns of humorist Don Marquis?

15. Poet Stephen Vincent Benét wrote *John Brown's Body*, a long narrative poem about what war?

16. The Poets' Corner in England's Westminster Abbey honors only one American, the author of *Evangeline* and "Paul Revere's Ride." Who was he?

17. What shy female poet was the "Belle of Amherst"?

18. What famous author of morbid poetry and short stories had a brief (and unsuccessful) career at the University of Virginia?

19. The Cowboy Poetry Gathering takes place in January in what western state?

20. What popular poet of the 1960s had been a deejay with a show called "Rendezvous with Rod"?

21. Historic Amherst College in Massachusetts has its library named for what popular twentieth-century New England poet?

22. What great humor poet penned such lines as "I don't mind eels / Except as meals / And the way they feel"?

23. The U.S. poet laureate is appointed by what Washington institution?

24. The great poet Vachel Lindsay committed suicide by drinking what household cleaning product?

25. Henry Wadsworth Longfellow's 1858 poem concerns the courtship of what Pilgrim leader?

26. What crusty World War II general's hobby was writing poetry?

7. Walt Whitman's, author of the famous *Leaves of Grass*
8. Joyce Kilmer's ("Poems are made by fools like me, / but only God can make a tree.")
9. Carl Sandburg
10. Ralph Waldo Emerson; the house is now a museum.
11. Henry David Thoreau, author of *Walden*
12. John Greenleaf Whittier, author of "Barefoot Boy" and other classic poems; the birthplace is now a museum.
13. His own funeral pyre; the house is a tourist site in Miller Park.
14. archy (who always wrote without capital letters, since he couldn't press the shift key on a typewriter)
15. The Civil War
16. Henry Wadsworth Longfellow
17. Emily Dickinson, who lived a quiet life in Amherst, Massachusetts, in the 1800s
18. Edgar Allan Poe
19. Nevada
20. Rod McKuen
21. Robert Frost
22. Ogden Nash, who died in 1971
23. The Library of Congress
24. Lysol
25. Miles Standish; it's *The Courtship of Miles Standish*, in which Standish loses the girl to John Alden.
26. George S. Patton's

★ More Painters, Sculptors, and Artsy Types

1. Illustrator James Montgomery Flagg gave America what patriotic symbol? (Hint: U.S.)
2. What great painter of birds had made his living as a portrait painter?
3. What classic painting of the Revolutionary War can be seen in Marblehead, Massachusetts? (Hint: fife and drum)
4. What famous painter, known for his portraits of George Washington, is buried in Boston's Central Burying Ground?
5. What artist of American small-town life has a museum in Philadelphia? (Hint: *Saturday Evening Post*)
6. James Ives and Nathaniel Currier were famous for what?
7. What type of "dangly" art was Alexander Calder famous for?
8. What mythical animals appear in the popular paintings of Arthur Davies? (Hint: horn)
9. The Brandywine River Museum in Pennsylvania pays tribute to what talented American artist family?
10. St. Petersburg, Florida, has a museum devoted to what off-the-wall Spanish artist?
11. The home of what noted painter of sea scenes can be visited in Scarborough, Maine?
12. Sculptor Jo Davison was famous for his busts of Woodrow Wilson, Will Rogers, Helen Keller, and other notables. What material did he work in?
13. What famous sculptor and painter of Old West scenes is honored with a museum in Ogdensburg, New York?
14. The Corcoran Gallery of Art in D.C. is devoted to what nation's artworks?
15. Santa Fe, New Mexico's Wheelwright Museum features the artworks of what ethnic group?
16. Salinas, California, has a unique city sculpture of a hat being tossed in the air. What, according to the artist, caused the hat to be tossed?
17. What prehistoric creatures, sculpted in steel and concrete, are in a city park in Rapid City, South Dakota?
18. What well-loved American artist (an Iowa native) has his artwork featured at Iowa State University's campus?
19. What noted sculptor died the year before finishing his colossal sculpture of four U.S. presidents?
20. What New York City artists' section is "south of Houston"?

1. Uncle Sam; he drew the original World War I "I Want You" poster, with the Uncle Sam figure modeled after himself.

2. John James Audubon

3. *Spirit of '76*, found in the town's Abbot Hall; it's by artist Archibald Willard.

4. Gilbert Stuart

5. Norman Rockwell

6. Their lithographs, the famous Currier and Ives prints

7. Mobiles

8. Unicorns

9. The Wyeths, Andrew and sons

10. Salvador Dali, famous for his surrealistic paintings

11. Winslow Homer's

12. Bronze

13. Frederic Remington

14. The U.S.'s

15. Native Americans

16. It was worn by a rodeo rider. The sculpture shows it in three stages of landing. The California Rodeo Grounds is adjacent.

17. Dinosaurs

18. Grant Wood, best known for his *American Gothic*, showing a farm couple (with the man holding a pitchfork, remember?)

19. Gutzon Borglum, who began (but did not quite finish) the Mount Rushmore memorial

20. SoHo

More Painters, Sculptors, and Artsy Types, continued . . .

21. What great American artist was elected head of the Society of *British* Artists? (Hint: mother)
22. Why did famous American painter John Singer Sargent refuse a knighthood from England's king Edward VIII?

✶ Author! Author! (Part 2)

Given the names of key titles of works by a key American author, could you name that author? Give it a try, remembering that the authors range from contemporaries to the authors of the 1600s.

1. *The Bear and the Dragon, Patriot Games, The Sum of All Fears, The Hunt for Red October*
2. *The Shadow of Your Smile, I'll Walk Alone, Daddy's Little Girl*
3. *The Cat in the Hat, Green Eggs and Ham, How the Grinch Stole Christmas*
4. *Murder in the Cathedral,* "Ash Wednesday," "The Love Song of J. Alfred Prufrock"
5. *Angels and Demons, The Lost Symbol, The Da Vinci Code*
6. *Self Matters, Love Smart, Relationship Rescue, Getting Real*
7. *As I Lay Dying, The Sound and the Fury, Sanctuary*
8. *From Bed to Worse, My Ten Years in a Quandary, The Early Worm*
9. *The Good Earth, Dragon Seed, A House Divided*
10. *Tarzan of the Apes, Princess of Mars*
11. *The March, Ragtime, Loon Lake, Welcome to Hard Times*
12. *Strange Interlude, Anna Christie, Ah Wilderness*
13. *A Farewell to Arms, The Sun Also Rises, For Whom the Bell Tolls*
14. *Farewell My Lovely, The Big Sleep, The Long Goodbye*
15. *Shogun, Noble House, Tai-pan*
16. "Only the Diamond and the Diamond's Dust"; "I Shall Forget You Presently, My Dear"; "Dirge without Music"
17. *The Great Gatsby, Tender Is the Night, The Last Tycoon*
18. *The Case of the Velvet Claws* and other Perry Mason novels

21. James Whistler
22. He claimed that, as an American citizen, it would not be proper to become "Sir John."

Author! Author! (Part 2) // Answers

1. Tom Clancy, contemporary novelist
2. Mary Higgins Clark, contemporary novelist
3. Dr. Seuss (Theodore Geisel), children's author and illustrator (1904–1991)
4. T. S. Eliot, poet, dramatist, essayist (1888–1965)
5. Dan Brown, contemporary novelist
6. Phil McGraw ("Dr. Phil"), contemporary self-help author and television personality
7. William Faulkner, novelist (1897–1962)
8. Robert Benchley, humorist (1889–1945)
9. Pearl Buck, novelist (1892–1973)
10. Edgar Rice Burroughs, novelist (1875–1950)
11. E. L. Doctorow, contemporary novelist
12. Eugene O'Neill, dramatist (1888–1953)
13. Ernest Hemingway, novelist (1899–1961)
14. Raymond Chandler, novelist (1888–1959)
15. James Clavell, novelist (1924–1994)
16. Edna St. Vincent Millay, poet (1892–1950)
17. F. Scott Fitzgerald, novelist (1896–1940)
18. Erle Stanley Gardner, mystery writer (1889–1970)

Author! Author! (Part 2), continued . . .

19. "The Lottery," *The Haunting of Hill House*, *Life among the Savages*
20. *The Oregon Trail*, *The History of the Conspiracy of Pontiac*, *The Discovery of the Great West*
21. "O Captain, My Captain"; "I Hear America Singing"; "Oneself I Sing"; "I Sing the Body Electric"
22. *The Sea Wolf*, *Call of the Wild*, *White Fang*
23. *Guys and Dolls*, *Blue Plate Special*
24. *The Heart Is a Lonely Hunter*, *Member of the Wedding*, *The Ballad of the Sad Cafe*
25. *Gone with the Wind*
26. *Everything That Rises Must Converge*, *Wise Blood*, *A Good Man Is Hard to Find*
27. "The Outcasts of Poker Flat," "Plain Language from Truth James," "The Luck of Roaring Camp"
28. *Dune*, *Dune Messiah*, *Heretics of Dune*
29. "The Chambered Nautilus," "The Deacon's Masterpiece," "Old Ironsides"
30. *The Grapes of Wrath*, *The Pearl*, *Of Mice and Men*
31. *Too Many Crooks*, *The Doorbell Rang*, and other Nero Wolfe mysteries
32. *Penrod*, *Alice Adams*, *Seventeen*
33. *My Life and Hard Times*, *Let Your Mind Alone*, "The Secret Life of Walter Mitty"
34. *I Am Charlotte Simmons*, *The Bonfire of the Vanities*, *The Painted Word*
35. *The Red Badge of Courage*, *Maggie*, *The Open Boat*
36. *Slaughterhouse Five*, *Cat's Cradle*, *Player Piano*
37. *The Martian Chronicles*, *Fahrenheit 451*, *The Illustrated Man*
38. *The Turn of the Screw*, *The Golden Bowl*, *The Ambassadors*
39. "The Congo," "The Eagle That Is Forgotten," "General William Booth Enters into Heaven"
40. *Rabbit Is Rich*, *The Centaur*, *Rabbit Run*

QUESTIONS

19. Shirley Jackson, novelist and short-story author (1919–1965)

20. Francis Parkman, historian (1823–1893)

21. Walt Whitman, poet (1819–1892)

22. Jack London, novelist (1876–1916)

23. Damon Runyon, short-story writer (1884–1946)

24. Carson McCullers, novelist (1917–1967)

25. Margaret Mitchell (1900–1949)

26. Flannery O'Connor, novelist and short-story author (1925–1964)

27. Bret Harte, short-story author (1836–1902)

28. Frank Herbert, science fiction writer (1920–1986)

29. Oliver Wendell Holmes, poet (1809–1894)

30. John Steinbeck, novelist (1902–1968)

31. Rex Stout, mystery writer (1886–1975)

32. Booth Tarkington, novelist (1869–1946)

33. James Thurber, essayist and short-story writer (1894–1961)

34. Tom Wolfe, contemporary novelist and essayist

35. Stephen Crane, novelist and short-story author (1871–1900)

36. Kurt Vonnegut, novelist (1922–2007)

37. Ray Bradbury, contemporary science fiction writer

38. Henry James, novelist (1843–1916)

39. Vachel Lindsay, poet (1879–1931)

40. John Updike, novelist (1932–2009)

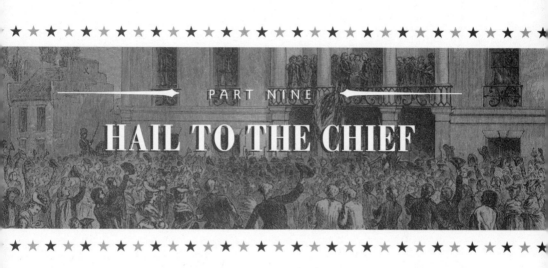

PART NINE

HAIL TO THE CHIEF

★ Presidential Trivia

America has a love-hate relationship with its chief executives—
but more love than hate. The truth is, some of our greatest
national heroes have been the presidents. Maybe it's only the
current president that people like to complain about.

1. What president did Josh Brolin portray in a 2008 film directed by Oliver Stone?
2. In Disney World's robotic Hall of Presidents, which president stands up and makes a speech?
3. What president's election gave rise to the "birther" movement?
4. Who was the only president not to live in the White House?
5. What Vermont-born president was sworn into office by his own father in his own living room?
6. What early president was the only one to serve in the House after he had been president?
7. Presidents Thomas Jefferson, James Monroe, and John Tyler had all been governors of what state?
8. What candidate ran in 1956 with the slogan "Peace, Prosperity, Progress?"
9. Which two early presidents died the same day, July 4, 1826?
10. If you took a boat tour on the *Potomac Spirit,* what famous presidential home would you see?
11. What state contributed a president to each side in the Civil War?
12. Who was president during the nation's bicentennial celebration in 1976?
13. What future U.S. president was given the nickname "Sharp Knife" by Native Americans he had subdued?
14. Thomas Jefferson was president when the U.S. bought the enormous Louisiana Territory from France. What future president negotiated the purchase?
15. Independence, Missouri, was the hometown of what twentieth-century president?
16. What Georgia port city was given as a "Christmas gift" to President Abraham Lincoln in 1864?
17. President Franklin D. Roosevelt died in 1945 at the Little White House. Where is that?

1. George W. Bush; the movie has the catchy title *W.*
2. Abraham Lincoln
3. Barack Obama, who did eventually make his U.S. birth certificate public
4. The first, George Washington
5. Calvin Coolidge, who became president after the sudden death of Warren Harding
6. John Quincy Adams, sixth president
7. Virginia
8. Dwight Eisenhower
9. John Adams, second president, and Thomas Jefferson, third president; the day was the fiftieth anniversary of the Declaration of Independence.
10. George Washington's home, Mount Vernon
11. Kentucky, which was the birthplace of both Abraham Lincoln and Jefferson Davis
12. Gerald R. Ford; Jimmy Carter beat Ford in the November 1976 election but was not sworn in until 1977.
13. Andrew Jackson
14. James Monroe
15. Harry Truman
16. Savannah; it was captured on Christmas 1864 by Union general William Sherman, who declared it was his gift to the president.
17. Warm Springs, Georgia; the Little White House was built by Roosevelt as a vacation home.

Q U E S T I O N S

18. Atlantic Beach, North Carolina, has a conservation area named for which U.S. president?

19. What tough-wooded tree lent its name to future president Andrew Jackson?

20. What honored U.S. politician was playing sandlot baseball when he learned he'd been nominated for president?

21. What future president was supreme commander of Allied forces in World War II?

22. What one-term president of the 1840s was the first to be photographed?

23. What two future presidents signed the Constitution?

24. Who was the only president who had served as an ordained minister?

25. Which two twentieth-century presidents died within a month of each other?

26. Who was the first U.S. president to refer to his D.C. home as the White House?

27. President John Tyler's plantation in Virginia was named for a place out of the Robin Hood legend. What?

28. What early president gave the shortest inaugural speech, only 134 words?

29. What five-foot-four-inch Virginia-born man was the shortest president?

30. Columbia, Tennessee, has the home of the president who masterminded the Mexican War. Who?

31. What tight-lipped U.S. president handed reporters slips of paper, stating, "I do not choose to run for president in 1928"?

32. Canton, Ohio, has the burial place of the twenty-fifth president, who was assassinated. Who was he?

33. Marion, Ohio, has the home of what man who was president in the 1920s?

34. What president's home was known as the "Texas White House" during his term in the 1960s?

35. What president (noted for serving two nonconsecutive terms) was born in Caldwell, New Jersey?

36. Composer Irving Berlin wrote the campaign song "I Like Ike" for what presidential candidate?

37. What president can you see perform "live" in Gettysburg, Pennsylvania, each summer?

38. Greeneville, Tennessee, has the home, office, and grave of what misunderstood president?

18. Theodore Roosevelt, who was an early advocate of environmentalism
19. Hickory; the tough Jackson was known as "Old Hickory."
20. Abraham Lincoln
21. Dwight Eisenhower
22. James K. Polk
23. George Washington and James Madison
24. James Garfield, twentieth president, a Disciples of Christ preacher who once baptized forty converts during a two-week evangelistic campaign
25. Harry Truman (December 26, 1972) and Lyndon Johnson (January 22, 1973); Johnson was given a state funeral, but Truman, at his wife's request, was not.
26. Theodore Roosevelt; prior to his term of office, the house had been called either the President's House or the Executive Mansion.
27. Sherwood Forest
28. George Washington
29. James Madison, fourth president
30. James K. Polk, eleventh president
31. Calvin Coolidge
32. William McKinley
33. Warren Harding, twenty-ninth president; he conducted his famous "Front Porch Campaign" from the home.
34. Lyndon Johnson's
35. Grover Cleveland; his birthplace there can be visited.
36. Dwight Eisenhower
37. Abraham Lincoln; actually, it's an actor, performing at "A. Lincoln's Place."
38. Andrew Johnson, seventeenth president, who had the unfortunate task of filling Abraham Lincoln's shoes after the Civil War

ANSWERS

39. What blind hymn writer was a lifelong friend of President Grover Cleveland?

40. The Bull Moose party, splitting from the Republicans, was founded by what grinning, bespectacled president?

★ The First Ladies

1. Who claimed her husband was the victim of a "vast right-wing conspiracy"?

2. What recent first lady was born Anne Frances Robbins but became known as Nancy Davis, a movie actress?

3. What lovely blooming trees were introduced to D.C. by First Lady Helen Taft after she visited Japan?

4. First Lady Claudia Alta Taylor was better known by what name?

5. What future first lady did not have to change her last name when she married?

6. What first lady's home can be toured in Lexington, Kentucky? (Hint: assassination)

7. What famous early first lady lived in the Todd House in Philadelphia?

8. What first lady offered her silver service for the first coins minted in the U.S.?

9. In Boone, Iowa, you can visit the birthplace of a famous first lady of the 1950s. Who?

10. A wax museum with figures of presidents and first ladies is near what famous Pennsylvania battlefield?

11. In 1890, who, at age five, met her future husband in an Independence, Missouri, Sunday school class?

12. What humbly born president of the 1860s was taught to read by his wife?

13. What famous first lady's home can be visited in Braintree, Massachusetts?

14. Who, on her first date with the future president, went to a Spike Lee movie?

15. What first lady took TV viewers on a White House tour on Valentine's Day, 1962?

QUESTIONS

39. Fanny Crosby, famous for "Blessed Assurance" and many other hymns
40. Theodore Roosevelt

The First Ladies // Answers

1. Hillary Clinton
2. Nancy Reagan
3. The cherry trees, especially noticeable around the Jefferson Memorial
4. Lady Bird Johnson, wife of Lyndon Johnson
5. Eleanor Roosevelt, who married Franklin, a cousin (So she was actually Eleanor Roosevelt Roosevelt.)
6. Mary Todd Lincoln's
7. Dolley Madison, formerly Dolley Todd
8. Martha Washington, the *first* first lady
9. Mamie Eisenhower
10. Gettysburg
11. Bess Truman, wife of Harry Truman
12. Andrew Johnson, taught by his wife, Eliza McArdle
13. Abigail Adams's; she was the wife of John Adams and mother of John Quincy Adams.
14. Michelle Obama
15. Jackie Kennedy

★ The Quotable Presidents

Did our chief executives say anything memorable? You bet-cha. Their statements—on and off the record—range from the sublime to the ridiculous. The sublime includes Lincoln's Gettysburg Address. The ridiculous includes the quote in question one.

1. According to George W. Bush, "Either you are with us, or you are with the _____."
2. What grinning, spunky president coined the phrase "Speak softly and carry a big stick"?
3. Who famously said, "I didn't inhale, and I never tried it again"?
4. What famous (and brief) speech of November 19, 1863, began, "Fourscore and seven years ago our fathers brought forth . . ."?
5. What president broke his 1964 campaign promise not to send "American boys to fight Asian wars"?
6. What president claimed to seek "peace with honor" in ending the Vietnam War?
7. What candidate ran in the 1916 presidential race with the slogan "He kept us out of war"?
8. What early vice president called the office "the most insignificant office that ever the invention of man contrived"?
9. What 330-pound president thought so little of his term that he later said, "I don't remember that I ever was president"?
10. On the eve of the depression, which presidential candidate promised "a chicken in every pot"?
11. According to President Woodrow Wilson, what war was fought "to make the world safe for democracy"?
12. Which president, who left the nation on the brink of civil war, claimed that "history will vindicate my memory"?
13. What Republican president announced on taking office in 1974, "Our long national nightmare is over"?
14. What grinning presidential candidate of the 1970s claimed, "I will never lie to you"?
15. What Republican president of the 1970s assured the nation, "I am not a crook"?

The Quotable Presidents // Answers

1. Terrorists
2. Teddy Roosevelt
3. Bill Clinton
4. Abraham Lincoln's Gettysburg Address
5. Lyndon Johnson
6. Richard Nixon
7. Woodrow Wilson, who, on being reelected, got the U.S. involved in World War I
8. John Adams, who was George Washington's vice president and, afterwards, president himself
9. William Howard Taft, twenty-seventh president
10. Herbert Hoover, who was later to regret that rash promise
11. World War I (He obviously did not foresee World War II.)
12. James Buchanan, president before Abraham Lincoln
13. Gerald Ford, who proved himself wrong when he issued a pardon to scandal-plagued Richard Nixon
14. Jimmy Carter
15. Richard Nixon

The Quotable Presidents, continued ...

16. What president wrote the inscription for Sam Houston's gravestone: "The world will take care of Houston's fame"?

17. In 1925 Calvin Coolidge said, "The business of America is" what?

18. What lanky president said, "You may fool all the people some of the time; you can even fool some of the people all the time; but you can't fool all of the people all the time"?

19. What tired president, leaving office in 1849 after watching the U.S. double in size, said, "The presidency is not a bed of roses"?

20. What D.C. building did President Benjamin Harrison refer to as "my jail"?

21. What president, never liked by liberals, appealed to what he called the "silent majority"?

22. What brassy president of the early 1900s claimed that "no president has ever enjoyed himself as much as I have enjoyed myself"?

23. What popular president of the 1800s had "Let the people rule" as his slogan?

24. What Democratic presidential candidate of the 1970s claimed he had "committed adultery in his heart" many times?

25. What future president said, during the Revolutionary War, "The united force of Europe will not be able to subdue us"?

26. Who was the first president to use the phrase "this nation under God"? (Hint: Civil War)

27. Who was given an unconditional pardon for all crimes "he committed or may have committed" by President Gerald Ford?

28. What tight-lipped president left office in 1929, stating, "It's best to get out while they still want you"?

29. What former president's last words in 1848 were, "This is the last of earth, I am content"? (Hint: son of a president)

30. What early president's last words were, "Thomas Jefferson still survives"?

31. What Democrat told reporters, "Pray for me, boys" when he became president in 1945?

16. Andrew Jackson, who had been Houston's military commander
17. Business
18. Abraham Lincoln; it is probably the best-known presidential quote of all time.
19. James K. Polk, who had administered during the Mexican War
20. The White House
21. Richard Nixon
22. Teddy Roosevelt
23. Andrew Jackson
24. Jimmy Carter
25. John Adams
26. Abraham Lincoln; the phrase is in his Gettysburg Address.
27. Richard Nixon
28. Calvin Coolidge, known as Silent Cal
29. John Quincy Adams, sixth president
30. John Adams; actually he and Jefferson died on the same day, July 4, 1826. He did not know Jefferson had died (unless he found out afterward).
31. Harry Truman

⭐ More Presidential Trivia

1. What president did Hillary Clinton call "the selected president"?
2. What Republican president was knighted by Britain's Queen Elizabeth?
3. Who received his "Slick" nickname from columnist Paul Greenberg?
4. When George Washington was inaugurated president in 1789, what city was the U.S. capital?
5. Whose death did Barack Obama announce to the United States on May 2, 2011?
6. Who has been the only U.S. president to resign from office (so far)?
7. What recent Republican president was called the "Teflon President" because scandals never seemed to stick to him?
8. What enormous statue in New York did President Grover Cleveland officially dedicate in 1886?
9. What much loved president warned, in his farewell address, against any "small, artful, enterprising minority" controlling government?
10. Nationwide TV broadcasting began in 1951 with a showing of what president's speech?
11. What Democratic president's campaign logo was a peanut with a toothy grin?
12. What outdoorsy president was the first president to ride in an automobile?
13. What president was the first that someone tried to assassinate? (Hint: hickory)
14. What Republican president was shot in the chest only two months after taking office?
15. What does the president place his left hand on while taking the oath of office?
16. President Rutherford Hayes's wife was nicknamed "Lemonade Lucy" because she refused to serve what in the White House?
17. Varina Davis was the wife of what president?
18. New Orleans's famous city square is named for (and has a statue of) a president important in the city's history. Who was he?
19. What large Asian nation was the destination of President Nixon's "journey for peace" in 1972?
20. What future first lady costarred with her husband, a future president, in a 1957 film?

More Presidential Trivia // Answers

1. George W. Bush
2. Ronald Reagan
3. Bill "Slick Willie" Clinton; Greenberg coined the name when Clinton was the governor of Arkansas.
4. New York
5. Osama bin Laden's
6. Richard Nixon, who resigned in 1974 in the wake of the Watergate scandal
7. Ronald Reagan ("Well, . . .")
8. The Statue of Liberty
9. George Washington
10. Harry Truman's; he was addressing the Japanese Peace Treaty Conference.
11. The peanut farmer, Jimmy Carter
12. Theodore Roosevelt
13. Andrew Jackson, seventh president; he proceeded to beat the man senseless with his cane.
14. Ronald Reagan, who was shot in March 1981
15. The Bible
16. Alcohol
17. Jefferson Davis, president of that *other* American nation, the Confederacy
18. Andrew Jackson, who defeated the British in the 1815 Battle of New Orleans
19. China
20. Nancy Davis, later Nancy Reagan, wife of Ronald

Q U E S T I O N S

21. At age forty-two, what man became the youngest president of the U.S.? (Hint: speak softly)

22. Presidents Rutherford Hayes, James Garfield, Benjamin Harrison, and William McKinley had all been officers during what war?

23. The University of Michigan has its library named for a graduate who became president. Who?

24. What two noted presidents' homes are near Charlottesville, Virginia?

25. Wheatland, in Lancaster, Pennsylvania, was the home of what Pennsylvania-born bachelor president?

26. Hudson, New York, has the retirement home of the eighth president, of Dutch ancestry. Who was he?

27. What very devout president of the 1860s never actually joined a church?

28. What Democratic president of the 1960s popularized the phrase "My fellow Americans"?

29. A sign reading The Buck Stops Here was found on what twentieth-century president's desk? (Hint: Missouri)

30. What president, elected in 1840, gave the longest inauguration speech and then served the shortest term?

31. The home of what swaggering twentieth-century president can be toured in Oyster Bay, New York?

32. In the 1824 presidential race, Andrew Jackson got ninety-nine electoral votes and John Quincy Adams got eighty-four. Who won?

33. What future president drafted the Treaty of Paris, ending the Revolutionary War?

34. Who is the only U.S. president never to have been elected either president or vice president?

35. What future president served as president of the Actors Guild union from 1947 until 1952?

36. What president of many terms had John Garner, Henry Wallace, and Harry Truman as vice presidents?

37. What former president held Medicare card number one? (Hint: Missouri)

38. What future president defeated Methodist evangelist Peter Cartwright in a race for congressman from Illinois?

39. "High Hopes" was the campaign song of what Democratic presidential candidate of the 1960s?

21. Theodore Roosevelt

22. The Civil War

23. Gerald R. Ford, who graduated from the school in 1935

24. Thomas Jefferson's Monticello and James Monroe's Ash Lawn

25. James Buchanan, who lived in the house from 1848 to 1868

26. Martin Van Buren; the home is a National Historic Site.

27. Abraham Lincoln, who practically knew the Bible by heart

28. Lyndon Johnson

29. Harry Truman

30. William Henry Harrison, whose speech lasted nearly two hours and whose term was thirty-two days

31. Theodore Roosevelt's; it's known as Sagamore Hill.

32. Adams; because of the closeness, the election went to the House of Representatives, which threw its support to Adams.

33. John Adams

34. Gerald Ford, who was appointed by Richard Nixon to replace Spiro Agnew

35. Ronald Reagan

36. Franklin D. Roosevelt

37. Harry Truman

38. Abraham Lincoln; curiously, at that time Cartwright was a violent opponent of slavery, while Lincoln's view was fairly moderate.

39. John F. Kennedy

More Presidential Trivia, continued ...

40. According to Herbert Hoover's campaign slogan, how many chickens would be in every American pot?

41. John Tyler was the only president elected to another nation's congress. Which nation?

42. What flamboyant president of the twentieth century had "A Hot Time in the Old Town Tonight" as his campaign song?

43. What Texas hero was a close friend of Andrew Jackson and named one of his sons for Jackson?

QUESTIONS

40. One
41. The Confederacy; Tyler was elected in 1861 but died before he ever served.
42. Theodore Roosevelt
43. Sam Houston

PART TEN

DOING IT BY THE DECADES

✭ The Babe, Billy Sunday, Etc.: The 1910s

1. In 1911 Ray Harroun was the first winner of what world-famous auto race?
2. In 1919 the Candler family sold what cola company to Atlanta banker Ernest Woodruff for $25 million?
3. In 1919 what baseball legend hit the world's longest home run (at that time), 579 feet?
4. When this girls' organization was established in 1912, Daisy Gordon became its first member. What was it?
5. What baseball-player-turned-evangelist became famous in the 1910s for his antibooze sermons?
6. What tough World War II general was an Olympic pentathlete in 1912?
7. In July 1919 what rubber company's blimp crashed in Chicago, killing thirteen people?
8. What bus company began in 1914, charging twenty-five cents for a round trip from Hibbing to Alice, Minnesota?
9. In 1910 what became the first type of aircraft to offer commercial service?
10. What metals firm was founded as the U.S. Foil Co. in 1919?
11. What world-changing waterway officially opened in 1914?
12. What lovely Caribbean islands did the U.S. purchase from Denmark in 1916?
13. What ill-fated constitutional amendment became law in 1919?
14. In 1911 Willis H. Carrier presented a paper on what subject to the American Society of Mechanical Engineers?
15. With Republicans split between Taft and Teddy Roosevelt, what Democrat was elected president in 1912?

✭ Art Deco, the Model T, Etc.: The 1920s

1. The Drive-Ur-Self car rental company, launched in 1923, is now known as what?
2. What popular (and blowable) product was invented in 1928 by Walter Diemer and marketed by his company, Fleer?

The Babe, Billy Sunday, Etc.: The 1910s // Answers

1. The Indianapolis 500
2. Coca-Cola
3. Babe Ruth
4. The Girl Scouts
5. Billy Sunday
6. George S. Patton
7. Goodyear's
8. Greyhound
9. Dirigible
10. Reynolds Aluminum, which was founded to supply tinfoil for cigarette wrappers
11. The Panama Canal
12. The Virgin Islands—St. Thomas, St. Croix, St. John
13. The Eighteenth Amendment (Prohibition), outlawing liquor in the U.S.; it was repealed in 1933.
14. Air-conditioning
15. Woodrow Wilson

Art Deco, the Model T, Etc.: The 1920s // Answers

1. Hertz
2. Bubble gum; Fleer makes the Dubble Bubble brand.

Art Deco, the Model T, Etc.: The 1920s, continued . . .

QUESTIONS

3. What silent movie star's 1926 funeral attracted over one-hundred thousand mourners, mostly women?

4. What classic car did Ford market from 1908 to 1926?

5. What popular hiking trail in the eastern U.S. opened in 1921?

6. The famous "Monkey Trial" of 1925 took place in Dayton, Tennessee. What controversial teaching was at the center of the trial?

7. In 1921 what great scientist gave a lecture at Columbia University on his theory of relativity?

8. In December 1928 what U.S. admiral established Little America in Antarctica?

9. What pilot made headlines when he landed at Le Bourget field May 21, 1927?

10. What streamlined, geometrical style popular in the 1920s is also known as *Art Moderne*?

11. What ethnic group all officially became U.S. citizens in 1924?

12. What troubled period of history began on October 29, 1929?

13. What great American event was celebrated at the 1926 World's Fair in Philadelphia?

14. What renowned female evangelist mysteriously disappeared in 1926 for thirty-seven days?

15. What manners expert published her *Etiquette: The Blue Book of Social Usage* in 1922?

16. When named chief justice in 1921, what former president was a law professor at Yale?

★ Kingfish, Kodachrome, Knute, Etc.: The 1930s

1. In 1939 Bob Kane introduced what caped crime fighter in Detective Comics No. 27?

2. "After all, tomorrow is another day" is the last line of what phenomenally popular 1939 film?

3. What pollster founded the American Institute of Public Opinion in 1935?

3. Rudolph Valentino's
4. The Model T
5. The Appalachian Trail (known as the AT to seasoned hikers)
6. Evolution; the defendant, John Scopes, was a science teacher accused of teaching evolution as fact rather than theory.
7. Albert Einstein
8. Richard E. Byrd
9. Charles Lindbergh, first person to fly solo across the Atlantic
10. Art Deco
11. Native Americans
12. The Great Depression, beginning with the stock market crash
13. The signing of the Declaration of Independence; the year was the one hundred-fiftieth anniversary, the sesquicentennial.
14. Aimee Semple McPherson, who claimed she'd been kidnapped
15. Emily Post
16. William Howard Taft

Kingfish, Kodachrome, Knute, Etc.: The 1930s // Answers

1. Batman
2. *Gone with the Wind*
3. George Gallup

Kingfish, Kodachrome, Knute, Etc.: The 1930s, continued . . .

4. What Norwegian-born football coach died in a plane crash in 1931?
5. What popular car did Ford cease marketing in 1931?
6. What new type of camera film, perfected by Leopold Maness, became available to the public in 1935?
7. What far-distant locale did Richard E. Byrd visit in 1933?
8. Millions of Americans dimmed their lights for a few moments in 1931 to remind them of the death of what inventor?
9. What ill-fated constitutional amendment was repealed in 1933?
10. Where did aviators Amelia Earhart and Fred Noonan land in 1937?
11. What famous evangelist preached the foursquare gospel from her Angelus Temple in the 1930s?
12. What still-popular cookbook by Irma Rombauer was first published in 1931?
13. What controversial southern governor was fatally shot by Dr. Carl Weiss in 1935?
14. What Nevada city's reputation as a "divorce capital" began in the 1930s?
15. What bridge, when completed over the Hudson River in 1931, was the world's longest suspension bridge?
16. In March 1933 Congress legalized beverages containing 3.2 percent of what?

★ CD, Nylons, A-Bombs, Etc.: The 1940s

1. What island city was the site of a surprise attack December 7, 1941?
2. Edwin Land invented what novel type of camera in 1947?
3. What major change in American paychecks began in July 1943?
4. What lovely blonde actress (and wife of Clark Gable) died in a plane crash in 1942?
5. What European nation landed spies on the East Coast of the U.S. in June 1942?
6. What Asian city received a fateful American bomb on August 6, 1945?
7. What enormous federal building was completed in 1943 after only sixteen months?

4. Knute Rockne, coach for Notre Dame
5. The Model A
6. Kodachrome, the first color film available to the average consumer
7. The South Pole
8. Thomas Edison, inventor of the lightbulb, among other things
9. The Eighteenth Amendment (Prohibition), outlawing liquor in the U.S. It had *not* been effective.
10. No one knows. They disappeared somewhere in the Pacific.
11. Aimee Semple McPherson
12. *The Joy of Cooking;* its revised version is still selling.
13. Huey Long, the "Kingfish"
14. Reno's, which, beginning in the 1930s, required only a six-week stay to establish the "residency" necessary for divorce
15. The George Washington Bridge
16. Alcohol

CD, Nylons, A-Bombs, Etc.: The 1940s // Answers

1. Honolulu, at Pearl Harbor
2. The Polaroid
3. Withholding of federal income tax (Alack the day!)
4. Carole Lombard
5. Germany; they were captured and executed.
6. Hiroshima, Japan
7. The Pentagon

CD, Nylons, A-Bombs, Etc.: The 1940s, continued . . .

8. What international alliance was formed by the U.S. and ten European countries in 1949?

9. Kemmons Wilson founded what worldwide hotel chain in 1945?

10. What conservative organization was named for an intelligence officer killed in China in 1945?

11. CD now stands for compact disc or certificate of deposit. What did it stand for in the 1940s?

12. What company, "like a good neighbor," became the biggest auto insurer by 1942?

13. The first stockings made of what fiber went on sale in the U.S. in 1940?

14. The first book written by this general (later a president) was *Crusade in Europe* in 1948. Who?

15. What group of Americans were forced into detention camps after the Pearl Harbor attack of 1941?

16. What baseball stadium's imposing left-field wall became "the Green Monster" after it was painted in 1947?

17. The WAVES of World War II were women in which branch of the armed services?

★ Ike, Bonzo, Interstates, Etc.: The 1950s

1. What evangelist enjoyed a burst of exposure through the aid of newspaper mogul William Randolph Hearst?

2. Henry and Richard Block founded what company in 1956?

3. What TV clown character was introduced by Larry Harmon?

4. What future president costarred with a chimpanzee in the 1952 movie *Bedtime for Bonzo*?

5. Beginning in 1955, what words were placed on all coins minted in the U.S.?

6. In 1956, what president signed a bill authorizing the construction of the interstate highway system?

7. What federal agency began publishing a "Ten Most Wanted" list?

8. What two major labor unions, with a combined membership of 15 million, merged in 1955?

8. NATO, the North Atlantic Treaty Organization
9. Holiday Inn
10. The John Birch Society
11. Civil Defense
12. State Farm
13. Nylon
14. Dwight Eisenhower
15. Japanese, including seventy-five thousand who were U.S. citizens
16. Boston's Fenway Park
17. The Navy

Ike, Bonzo, Interstates, Etc.: The 1950s // Answers

1. Billy Graham; Hearst was more attracted to Graham's anticommunist stance than to Christianity itself.
2. H & R Block, the income tax preparers
3. Bozo
4. Ronald Reagan
5. In God We Trust; they had appeared on some earlier coins, but not by federal mandate.
6. Dwight Eisenhower
7. The FBI
8. The American Federation of Labor and the Congress of Industrial Organizations—now known as AFL-CIO

9. On December 15, 1952, the Declaration of Independence was placed on permanent display in what D.C. building?
10. Author L. Ron Hubbard organized what religion in the 1950s?
11. What northeastern seaway was dedicated in 1959 by President Eisenhower and Queen Elizabeth II?
12. What now-standard type of tire was introduced in 1956?
13. What type of movie, premiering in 1952, featured a roller-coaster ride and a flight over the Rockies?
14. April 15 is the federal income tax due date. Prior to 1955, what was the due date?
15. Which president talked tough against communism but did nothing when the Soviets conquered Hungary in 1956?
16. In the 1950s, two Pennsylvania communities merged and were named for what Native American athlete?

★ Rockfests, Astronauts, Assassinations, Etc.: The 1960s

1. Where did Neil Armstrong and Edwin Aldrin set foot on July 20, 1969?
2. In 1963 Kodak introduced what camera that used a foolproof film cartridge?
3. What shocking three-word theological question appeared on a *Time* magazine cover in 1966?
4. What Republican's 1964 campaign slogan was "In your heart you know he's right"?
5. What southern governor ran for the presidency in 1968 on the American Independent ticket?
6. What politician drove his car off a bridge at Chappaquiddick Island in 1969?
7. The Beatles' final live concert of August 29, 1966, was at what California arena?

9. The National Archives
10. Scientology; Hubbard's most famous book is probably his *Dianetics*.
11. The St. Lawrence Seaway, a joint U.S.-Canada project that opened up the Great Lakes to ocean shipping
12. The tubeless tire
13. Cinerama, which used a wide, curving screen with three projectors and stereophonic sound— all very "high tech" at the time
14. March 15
15. Dwight Eisenhower
16. Jim Thorpe

Rockfests, Astronauts, Assassinations, Etc.: The 1960s // Answers

1. The moon
2. The Instamatic
3. "Is God Dead?"
4. Barry Goldwater's
5. George Wallace
6. Ted Kennedy; in the accident his secretary, Mary Jo Kopechne, was killed.
7. Candlestick Park in San Francisco

Rockfests, Astronauts, Assassinations, Etc.: The 1960s, continued . . .

8. What famous California island prison closed in 1963 and is now a museum?
9. What federal program for senior citizens began in July 1966?
10. What phenomenal pop music festival took place August 15–17, 1969?
11. What once-popular audio format went on the market in 1963?
12. In 1963, TV actor Dan Blocker opened the first of what chain of steak houses?
13. What Florida city grew astronomically after Walt Disney World began construction in the 1960s?
14. In 1963, Harvey Ball created what happy symbol?
15. What president died at Dallas's Parkland Hospital on November 22, 1963?
16. What woman's 1962 book *Silent Spring* launched the environmentalist movement?

★ Watergate, STOP-ERA, Seagulls, Etc.: The 1970s

1. In August 1974 who became the first president to resign?
2. What extremely popular 1977 disco movie was based on a magazine article, "Tribal Rites of the New Saturday Night"?
3. What third-party presidential candidate was shot and wounded at a mall by Arthur Bremer in 1972?
4. What fiction book, with bird characters, was a best-seller in 1972 and 1973?
5. According to the title of Loretta Lynn's 1976 autobiography, whose daughter is she?
6. In 1971 who published *The Vantage Point: Perspectives of the Presidency, 1963–1969*?
7. Phyllis Schlafly formed an organization in the 1970s to stop what proposed amendment?
8. What mystery disease killed twenty-nine people at a Philadelphia convention in July 1976?

8. Alcatraz, which held many notorious prisoners, including Al Capone
9. Medicare
10. Woodstock
11. Cassettes
12. Bonanza; Blocker played "Hoss" Cartwright on the long-running series *Bonanza.*
13. Orlando
14. The yellow smiley face
15. John F. Kennedy
16. Rachel Carson's; she also wrote *The Sea around Us.*

Watergate, STOP-ERA, Seagulls, Etc.: The 1970s // Answers

1. Richard Nixon
2. *Saturday Night Fever*
3. Alabama governor George Wallace
4. *Jonathan Livingston Seagull;* it was *the* best-selling fiction book in those years.
5. She's a coal miner's daughter.
6. Lyndon Johnson
7. The ERA, Equal Rights Amendment
8. Legionnaire's disease

9. What former Cabinet department became an independent federal agency in 1970? (Hint: stamps)
10. What senior citizens' activist organization was founded by Maggie Kuhn in 1970?
11. What well-known labor leader disappeared from a restaurant parking lot in 1975 and has never been found?
12. On February 5, 1974, Patty Hearst was kidnapped by what radical group?
13. Until Chet Huntley retired in 1970, who was his coanchor on the NBC news?
14. What Democratic president scored the lowest approval ratings ever, 20 percent in an August 1979 poll?
15. In 1972 what presidential candidate was supported by the organization known as CREEP?
16. What religious cult was founded by preacher Jim Jones in the 1970s?

★ LaserJets, Volcanoes, Glasnost, Etc.: The 1980s

1. What new audio format was sprung on the U.S. public in 1982?
2. What Arkansas-based retailer opened Sam's Wholesale Club chain in 1983?
3. What volcano's 1980 eruption was the first in the contiguous forty-eight states since 1921?
4. What major sports event was going on when an earthquake struck San Francisco in October 1989?
5. What fast-food chain asked people in the 1980s, "Where's the beef"?
6. What Caribbean island nation had its marxist regime deposed by U.S. troops in 1983?
7. What Ford model, introduced in the 1980s, consistently ranked as the top-selling U.S. car?
8. On April 14, 1987, nearly 120,000 people visited what branch of the Smithsonian, the one-day record for any museum?

9. The Postal Service
10. The Gray Panthers
11. Jimmy Hoffa
12. The Symbionese Liberation Army
13. David Brinkley
14. Jimmy Carter
15. Richard Nixon; CREEP was the Committee to Reelect the President.
16. The People's Temple; the group committed mass suicide in 1978.

LaserJets, Volcanoes, Glasnost, Etc.: The 1980s // Answers

1. Compact discs, better known as CDs
2. Wal-Mart
3. Mount St. Helens's
4. The World Series
5. Wendy's
6. Grenada
7. The Taurus
8. The Air and Space Museum

LaserJets, Volcanoes, Glasnost, Etc.: The 1980s, continued ...

9. What company's LaserJet printer, introduced in 1984, became the most successful product in its history? (Hint: H-P)
10. What wide-open western state was notorious in the 1980s for its five-dollar fine for speeding on interstates?
11. What Soviet leader met with Ronald Reagan at a 1985 summit conference in Switzerland?
12. What welcome item was installed in the Statue of Liberty in 1986?
13. What was given to Barney Clark during an eight-hour operation in December 1982?
14. What militant atheist received a shock in the 1980s when her son claimed to be a born-again Christian?
15. What weather phenomenon caused billions of dollars worth of damage in South Carolina in 1989?
16. What national park was renamed Denali in 1980?

★ Megamalls, Oliver North, Perot, Etc.: The 1990s

1. What evangelist was awarded the Congressional Gold Medal in 1996?
2. What nation's liberation was the object of Operation Desert Storm in 1991?
3. In November 1994 what former president revealed he had Alzheimer's disease?
4. What motion picture company opened a chain of mall stores in 1994, selling such merchandise as Roadrunner mugs and Bugs Bunny pajamas?
5. What unpopular creature did the Virginia Assembly try (and fail) to make the "state reptile" in 1994?
6. James B. Stockdale was whose vice presidential running mate in 1992?
7. What military man (later a Senate candidate) had his Iran-Contra convictions overturned in 1991?
8. What gigantic shopping center opened in 1992 at a cost of more than $650 million?
9. What Christian leader drew enormous crowds on his 1995 American tour?

9. Hewlett-Packard's
10. Montana, which was never happy with the federally imposed 55 mph speed limit
11. Mikhail Gorbachev, general secretary of the Soviet Communist Party
12. An elevator
13. An artificial heart
14. Madalyn Murray O'Hair
15. Hurricane Hugo
16. Mt. McKinley

Megamalls, Oliver North, Perot, Etc.: The 1990s // Answers

1. Billy Graham; the award was given for "enduring contributions toward faith, morality, and charity."
2. Kuwait's, which had been occupied by Iraq
3. Ronald Reagan
4. Warner Brothers, creator of the various Looney Tunes characters
5. The rattlesnake; many people objected, for obvious reasons.
6. Ross Perot's
7. Oliver North
8. The Mall of America in Minnesota
9. Pope John Paul II

10. What was unusual about the Postal Service's set of Civil War stamps issued in 1995?
11. When the federal government removed its 55 mph interstate speed limit in 1995, which western state removed *all* speed limits on interstates?
12. Michael Crichton's 1995 novel *The Lost World* was a sequel to what earlier best-seller?
13. What boxer in 1994 reclaimed his heavyweight title, which he lost twenty years earlier to Muhammad Ali?
14. What mother of a U.S. president and two senators died at age 104 in 1995?
15. In what appropriate place were the ashes of *Star Trek* creator Gene Roddenberry scattered in 1992?

★ Facebook, *American Idol,* Dubya, Etc.: The 2000s

1. What controversial former doctor died in June 2011?
2. Condoleezza Rice and Colin Powell both served in what Cabinet position under George W. Bush?
3. What movie based on a Marvel Comics character was one of the top-grossing movies of 2002?
4. In 2004 Krakow, Poland, named its city square after what U.S. president?
5. Dave Thomas, who died in 2002, founded what fast-food chain?
6. What evangelist (and son of a noted evangelist) gave the invocation at George W. Bush's inauguration?
7. What make of cars, launched by GM in 1990, was discontinued in 2010?
8. What politician gave a speech on global warming on the coldest day of 2004?
9. What encyclopedic Internet Web site was launched in 2001?
10. What beloved comic, famous for golfing with presidents, died in 2003?
11. What British statesman's bust did Barack Obama remove from the White House?

10. The stamps had words on the *back* describing the person or event portrayed on the front of each stamp.
11. Montana
12. *Jurassic Park*
13. George Foreman
14. Rose Kennedy
15. In space; they were taken aloft by the space shuttle *Columbia.*

Facebook, American Idol, Dubya, Etc.: The 2000s // Answers

1. Jack Kevorkian, the infamous "Dr. Death," who helped people commit suicide
2. Secretary of State
3. *Spider-Man*
4. Ronald Reagan, in honor of his help in ending the Cold War
5. Wendy's
6. Franklin Graham, son of Billy Graham
7. Saturn
8. Al Gore
9. Wikipedia
10. Bob Hope
11. Winston Churchill's

Facebook, *American Idol*, Dubya, Etc.: The 2000s, continued . . .

12. What "domestic diva" of TV went to prison in 2003?
13. Dick Cheney, vice president under George W. Bush, served in what Cabinet post under Bush's father?
14. What tall actor, star of TV's longest-running Western, died in June 2011?
15. What mayor was *Time* magazine's Person of the Year in 2001?
16. What pop music legend was inducted into the Rock and Roll Hall of Fame in 2001 and died in 2009?

QUESTIONS

12. Martha Stewart
13. Secretary of Defense
14. James Arness, six feet six, who for twenty years played Matt Dillon on *Gunsmoke*
15. Rudolph Giuliani, mayor of New York
16. Michael Jackson

PART ELEVEN

AMERICAN POTPOURRI

★ The American Name

*The words **America** and **American** appear in the names of thousands of organizations and businesses. But this set of questions concerns things and places for which **America** is a key part of the name, not just a convenient add-on.*

1. In a hotel with an "American plan," what do you get besides a room?
2. What cheese is the base for American cheese?
3. By what patriotic name is the common Virginia creeper vine known?
4. What midwestern state is nicknamed "Crossroads of America"?
5. American University is in what appropriate city?
6. The American Beauty is what type of flower?
7. The American saddle horse was developed in what southern state?
8. What thirty-two-story structure can be seen on Memphis, Tennessee's Mud Island?
9. What park, part of the Six Flags chain, is near Chicago, in Gurnee, Illinois?
10. What veterans' organization was founded in 1919 "to perpetuate a 100 percent Americanism"?
11. What Italian explorer is America named for?
12. What large (and rare) reptile can be found in Florida's Everglades?
13. If you are looking at the famous *American Gothic,* the painting of a midwestern farm couple, what major art museum are you in?
14. *American Notes* was a critical book by what extremely popular English novelist?
15. What is the purpose of the All-American Canal in California?
16. "The American Riviera" refers to what famous southern California beach?
17. In what northwestern state would you find American Falls?
18. Little America, abandoned in 1958, was in what far-off locale?
19. "America's most historic square mile" is the Independence National Historical Park in what city?
20. What enormous shopping center is large enough to hold seven Yankee Stadiums?
21. America's Cup is what type of race?
22. "America's Sweetheart" was what angel-faced actress of the silent movie era?

The American Name // Answers

1. All meals
2. Cheddar
3. American ivy
4. Indiana
5. Washington, D.C., naturally
6. A rose
7. Kentucky
8. The Great American Pyramid; since Memphis is named for a city in Egypt, they have to have a pyramid.
9. Six Flags Great America
10. The American Legion
11. Amerigo Vespucci, whose name in Latin is *Americus Vespucius*
12. The American crocodile (Alligators are also there, but they aren't rare at all.)
13. The Art Institute of Chicago
14. Charles Dickens; the book outraged many Americans and hurt Dickens's popularity in the U.S.
15. Irrigation; because its waters turn much of the California desert into fertile farmland, providing food for the whole U.S., the canal deserves its name.
16. Newport Beach
17. Idaho
18. Antarctica, about as far-off as you can get
19. Philadelphia
20. The Mall of America, in Minnesota
21. Yachts
22. Mary Pickford, who was still playing girls (and sometimes boys) when in her twenties

The American Name, continued . . .

23. The color-changing lizard *Anolis carolinensis* is better known as what?
24. Bombarding plutonium with neutrons produces what element?

✯ You're a Grand Old Anthem

The year 2014 is a literal "banner year," for it marks the two-hundredth anniversary of the penning of America's national anthem, a poem originally titled "The Defense of Fort McHenry" but quickly renamed "The Star-Spangled Banner." Americans hear and sing the song regularly, but just how familiar are we with the events (and the flag itself) that brought the song into being? Let's find out. . . .

1. What war was waging when the anthem was written?
2. In what East Coast city was the anthem written?
3. Francis Scott Key, the author of the anthem, was at the time a prisoner of what nation?
4. What was Key's profession?
5. The "bombs" mentioned in the first verse were in fact what?
6. An actor named Ferdinand Durang holds what distinction?
7. Key wrote the words to be sung to the old tune "To Anacreon in Heaven." Who was Anacreon?
8. Englishman John Stafford Smith, who lived from 1750 to 1836, holds what probable distinction?
9. The familiar tune of the anthem had already been used as a campaign song for which presidential candidate?
10. How many stars and stripes were on the flag when the anthem was written?
11. What distinction does Mary Pickersgill of Baltimore hold?
12. How did the original rectangular flag eventually become a square?
13. Eben Appleton donated the famous flag to what Washington museum?
14. What great American composer made an "official" arrangement of "The Star-Spangled Banner" for the U.S. army and navy bands?

23. A chameleon, specifically, the American chameleon
24. Americium

You're a Grand Old Anthem // Answers

1. The War of 1812, which (despite its name) lasted until 1815; Key wrote his poem the night of September 13–14, 1814.
2. Baltimore, where Fort McHenry is located
3. Great Britain; Key was being held on a British ship when the bombardment of Fort McHenry occurred.
4. Lawyer
5. Artillery shells, not "bombs" in the modern sense; Key literally wrote his poem by the light of the bombs and rockets.
6. Supposedly he was the first person to sing "The Star-Spangled Banner" in public, performing it often at a tavern in Baltimore.
7. A Greek poet known for his poems about wine and women
8. He was probably the composer of "To Anacreon in Heaven," the tune used for "The Star-Spangled Banner."
9. John Adams; the tune "To Anacreon in Heaven" had been used for the song "Adams and Liberty," and there is no doubt Francis Scott Key was familiar with that song.
10. Fifteen, the number of states at that time
11. She and her assistants made the flag—thirty feet by forty-two feet—that Key saw flying over Fort McHenry.
12. The Armistead family, who owned the flag for three generations, gave away snippets of it as souvenirs.
13. The Smithsonian Institution
14. John Philip Sousa

QUESTIONS

15. Under what twentieth-century president was the song officially made the U.S. national anthem?

16. What phrase associated with U.S. coins is found in the anthem's fourth stanza?

17. Who is the only singer to have had a Top 40 hit with her rendition of the anthem?

18. The flag that Key saw flying over Fort McHenry is on display in what D.C. building?

19. Over what body of water did Key see the bombs exploding?

20. What comedienne offended many people with her singing of the anthem at a 1990 baseball game?

21. What group of people is not expected to put their right hands over their hearts when the anthem is sung?

22. At what London locale was the anthem performed on September 12, 2001?

23. What religious sect does not sing the anthem nor stand while it is sung?

24. In what year's World Series was the anthem played at a sports event for the first time?

25. What silver-haired comic delivered a mangled version of the anthem in the movie *The Naked Gun*?

★ Grand Old Flags

Flags are more than just pieces of fabric. They're symbols, often highly charged with emotion. Small wonder that their design and care have been important parts of American life.

1. June 14 is what holiday?

2. What is John Philip Sousa's flag-waving march, written in 1897?

3. What familiar D.C. sight is 555 feet tall and has fifty American flags around it?

4. What southern state's flag shows a woman trampling a man?

5. What southwestern state's flag features the sun symbol of the Zia tribe on a yellow background?

6. What was added to the original U.S. flag in 1795?

15. Herbert Hoover, who signed the act of Congress into law in March 1931

16. "In God we trust." To be precise, line six of the fourth stanza is "And this be our motto, 'In God is our trust.'" The popularity of the song led to the eventual adoption of "In God we trust" as the U.S. motto.

17. Whitney Houston

18. The National Museum of American History, where it was under restoration for ten years

19. Chesapeake Bay

20. Roseanne Barr

21. Members of the military, who are expected to salute

22. Buckingham Palace, at the Changing of the Guard; the performance was to show Britain's solidarity with the United States after the 9/11 attacks.

23. Jehovah's Witnesses

24. 1918

25. Leslie Nielsen

Grand Old Flags // Answers

1. Flag Day, what else?

2. "Stars and Stripes Forever"

3. The Washington Monument

4. Virginia's; the female figure is actually an Amazon warrior woman, trampling on a tyrant. The state motto is *Sic semper tyrannis*—"Thus always to tyrants" (in other words, "Don't mess with us Virginia folks").

5. New Mexico's

6. Two new stars and stripes for the new states, Vermont and Kentucky

Grand Old Flags, continued ...

7. What state's flag was designed in 1927 by a thirteen-year-old schoolboy? (Hint: the forty-ninth state)

8. What four-word warning appeared on many colonial flags in the Revolutionary War?

9. St. Patrick's flag, a red *X* on a white field, is the flag of what Deep South state?

10. A brand new U.S. flag is flown each day over what residence?

11. Georgia's state flag has what nation's flag as part of it?

12. What is the only D.C. building where the U.S. flag is flown around the clock?

13. What is the only state that has never had a foreign flag flying over it?

14. What patriotic song's original title was "You're a Grand Old Rag"?

15. What southern state capital has been under the flags of France, England, Spain, West Florida, the Confederacy, the U.S., and the Sovereign State of Louisiana?

16. Which small eastern state has been under the flags of the Netherlands, Sweden, Britain, and the U.S.?

17. What flag—still flown, and still controversial—has thirteen white stars on a blue *X*?

18. What is the claim to fame of Baltimore seamstress Mary Pickersgill?

19. The flag of what nation flew briefly over Arizona in the 1860s?

20. By presidential proclamation, the U.S. flag flies twenty-four hours a day at what historic Maryland site?

21. What nation's flag flew over California beginning in 1821?

22. Colonial America's most famous seamstress's house can be seen in Philadelphia. Who was she?

23. What nation's flag was raised over California for the first time in 1846?

24. When draped over a casket, where should the U.S. flag's stars be?

25. On what spring holiday is the American flag supposed to fly at half-mast until noon?

26. What European nation, in 1777, was the first to officially salute the new U.S. flag?

27. The flags of Missouri and Kentucky both feature a two-part phrase. The first part is United We Stand. What is the second part?

28. What still-popular American flag was designed by Gen. Pierre G. T. Beauregard of Louisiana?

QUESTIONS

7. Alaska's

8. Don't Tread on Me—the words appeared near a rattlesnake

9. Alabama

10. The White House

11. The Confederacy's

12. The Capitol

13. Idaho

14. "You're a Grand Old Flag"; "rag" was considered a little derogatory.

15. Baton Rouge

16. Delaware

17. The Confederate battle flag

18. She made the American flag that flew over Fort McHenry when Francis Scott Key wrote "The Star-Spangled Banner."

19. The Confederate States of America, which made a few unsuccessful excursions into the Southwest

20. Fort McHenry, whose bombardment led Francis Scott Key to write "The Star-Spangled Banner"

21. Mexico's

22. Betsy Ross, maker of the first American flag

23. The U.S.'s

24. Over the body's left shoulder

25. Memorial Day

26. France, which had done everything possible to encourage American independence from England

27. Divided We Fall

28. The Confederate battle flag

⋆ Famous Firsts

1. What distinction does Rebecca Sealfon, 1997 winner of the national spelling bee, hold?
2. In 1969, Dan Evins opened the first restaurant in what "folksy" chain?
3. Who was the first American author to earn a million dollars? (Hint: outdoorsy)
4. August 16, 1999, marked the first broadcast of what popular game show?
5. What 1995 Walt Disney movie was the first entirely computer-generated film?
6. Lovastatin, which went on sale in 1987, was the first of what type of drug?
7. In 1540 the Spanish explorer Lopez de Cardemas was the first European to see what stunning sight in the future state of Arizona?
8. What popular food product was Thomas Adams the first to sell, in Jersey City in 1869? (Hint: don't swallow)
9. In May 1963, Jim Whittaker became the first American to reach what lofty spot?
10. Rev. John Mitchell of Pawhuska, Oklahoma, organized the first troop of what noted boys' organization?
11. The world's first national park was founded in Wyoming in 1872. What is it?
12. The Altair 8800, which went on sale in 1975, was the first what?
13. Lake Placid, New York, was the first U.S. site for what international event?
14. In 1909 Robert Peary was the first man to reach what far-off site?
15. Super Bowl XL in 2006 was the first to be played on what kind of turf?
16. What historic northeastern city had the nation's first daily newspaper?
17. What Hanna-Barbera character was the first animated cartoon to win an Emmy?
18. What offense was a New York cabdriver the first to be issued a ticket for in 1899?
19. What astronaut (and later U.S. senator) became the first American to orbit the earth in February 1962?
20. What southern state became, in 1836, the first state to declare Christmas as a holiday?
21. What great patriot was the U.S.'s first postmaster general?
22. What type of federal taxes were collected for the first time in 1914?

QUESTIONS

1. She was the first (but not the last) homeschooled child to win the bee.
2. Cracker Barrel
3. Jack London, author of *The Call of the Wild* and *White Fang*
4. *Who Wants to Be a Millionaire?*
5. *Toy Story*
6. Statins, which lower cholesterol
7. The Grand Canyon
8. Chewing gum (Maybe it shouldn't be considered *food* if it isn't swallowed.)
9. The top of Mount Everest
10. The Boy Scouts of America; Mitchell organized the troop in 1909.
11. Yellowstone
12. Personal computer
13. The Winter Olympics, in 1932
14. The North Pole
15. FieldTurf, which is more like natural grass than AstroTurf
16. Philadelphia
17. Huckleberry Hound
18. Speeding; he was traveling at (gasp!) 12 mph.
19. John Glenn, later a senator from Ohio
20. Alabama
21. Benjamin Franklin
22. Income taxes

Famous Firsts, continued . . .

23. In 1524 Giovanni de Verrazano was the first European to view the site of what future metropolis?

24. "The Yellow Kid," which appeared on February 16, 1896, was the first of what type of newspaper feature?

25. What electric device was first put into use at a Cleveland intersection in 1914?

26. What watchmaker sponsored the first TV commercial in 1941?

27. Oswald the Rabbit was the first animated character of what cartoon legend?

28. Alamogordo, New Mexico, was the site of the first firing of what world-changing weapon?

29. What famous four-word phrase was first used at York, Pennsylvania, in 1777?

30. What major time shift first occurred on April 24, 1932?

31. What familiar Christmas character was first drawn by cartoonist Thomas Nast?

32. What novel type of eating establishment did H. S. Thompson introduce in Chicago in 1891?

33. What gangster was the FBI's first Public Enemy Number One?

34. What new type of book, now found in most homes, was first introduced in New Haven, Connecticut, in 1878? (Hint: ring)

35. Introduced in 1950, what was America's first nationwide credit card? (Hint: eating out)

36. The first *planned* state capital city was in a Great Lake's state and named for an Italian explorer. What city and state?

37. The world's first underwater automobile tunnel, the Holland, opened in 1927 in what state?

QUESTIONS

23. New York City
24. A comic strip
25. A traffic light
26. Bulova; the commercial cost nine dollars.
27. Walt Disney
28. The atomic bomb, which was tested near the town
29. United States of America
30. Daylight Saving Time
31. Santa Claus
32. The cafeteria
33. John Dillinger
34. A telephone directory
35. Diners Club
36. Columbus, Ohio
37. New York, under the Hudson River

★ "You Can Quote Me on That"

The quotes here range from the sublime (John Paul Jones, Henry David Thoreau) to the ridiculous (Mae West, Porky Pig). If you're wondering why our beloved presidents don't appear here, it's because they're in the separate section "The Quotable Presidents" in part nine.

1. What heavyweight radio talk show host called himself the "most dangerous man in America" with "talent on loan from God"?
2. What famous document begins with these words: "When in the course of human events . . ."?
3. What fitness guru who died in 2011 said, "If it tastes good, spit it out"?
4. What inventor claimed his success was based on "hard work, based on hard thinking"?
5. What first lady did columnist William Safire call "a congenital liar" in January 1996?
6. What general, surrendering Bataan to the Japanese in World War II, vowed, "I shall return"?
7. What author of the mid-1800s said he had "experienced nature as other men are said to experience religion"?
8. "We have met the enemy and they are ours" was spoken by what notable naval commander?
9. What colonial patriot gave his famous "Give me liberty or give me death" speech in Richmond's St. John's Church?
10. What popular blonde comedienne always asked audiences, "Can we talk?"
11. The biblical phrase "Let not your heart be troubled" is the tagline of what TV political commentator?
12. What heavyweight boxing legend claimed he could "float like a butterfly, sting like a bee"?
13. What statesman, known as the Great Compromiser, often said, "I would rather be right than president"?
14. What famous document begins, "We, the people of the United States, in order to form a more perfect Union . . ."?
15. What words were always announced over the PA system at the end of an Elvis Presley concert?

1. Rush Limbaugh

2. The Declaration of Independence, penned by Thomas Jefferson

3. Jack LaLanne, who also said, "If man made it, don't eat it."

4. Thomas Edison

5. Hillary Clinton

6. Douglas MacArthur; he did.

7. Henry David Thoreau, author of *Walden*

8. Commodore Oliver Hazard Perry, who defeated a British force on Lake Erie in the War of 1812

9. Patrick Henry

10. Joan Rivers

11. Sean Hannity

12. Muhammad Ali

13. Henry Clay, who apparently was right, since he had no luck running for president

14. The Constitution; the words are from the Preamble.

15. "Elvis has left the building."

QUESTIONS

"You Can Quote Me on That," continued . . .

16. After John Wilkes Booth shot Abraham Lincoln, he yelled out the Latin phrase *Sic semper tyrannis*—"Thus ever to tyrants." What southern state's motto is this?

17. What stuttering character ended many Warner Brothers cartoons with "Th-th-th-that's all, folks"?

18. What Catholic bishop and TV personality said, "The really unforgivable sin is the denial of sin"?

19. What founder of one of the original colonies said, "Wrong is wrong, even if everyone is for it"?

20. What goofy comic ended his TV shows by saying, "Good night, and may God bless"?

21. What jumbo-nosed comic always ended his performances with "Good night, Mrs. Calabash, wherever you are"?

22. What man connected with the Bill Clinton impeachment said, "There is no excuse for perjury—never, never, never"?

23. What frontiersman, killed at the Alamo, was famous for saying, "Be sure you are right, then go ahead"?

24. What cartoon character's favorite line (as he munched a carrot) was "What's up, doc?"

25. What politically active actor said, "Political correctness is tyranny with manners"?

26. What Revolutionary War naval commander said, "I have not yet begun to fight"?

27. What famous college football coach supposedly said, "When the going gets tough, the tough get going"?

28. What wisecracking blonde movie queen of the 1930s said, "Marriage is a great institution, but I'm not ready for an institution"?

29. What founder of a famous boys' home was famous for saying, "There is no such thing as a bad boy"?

30. What revered CBS anchorman ended his broadcasts with "And that's the way it is"?

31. In 1964 what conservative presidential candidate told the Republican Convention, "Extremism in the defense of liberty is no vice"?

32. What frontier religious leader told his people, "If there's a place on this earth that nobody else wants, that's the place I am hunting for"?

16. Virginia's
17. Porky Pig
18. Fulton J. Sheen
19. William Penn, founder of Pennsylvania
20. Red Skelton
21. Jimmy Durante
22. Ken Starr
23. Davy Crockett
24. Bugs Bunny
25. Charlton Heston
26. John Paul Jones
27. Knute Rockne of Notre Dame
28. Mae West
29. Father Edward Flanagan, founder of Boys Town
30. Walter Cronkite, who died in 2009
31. Barry Goldwater
32. Brigham Young, who led the Mormons to Utah

33. What speech was Edward Everett referring to when he said, "President Lincoln has said more in a few minutes than I said in two hours. It will never be forgotten"?
34. Naval hero James Lawrence uttered the famous line "Don't give up the ship" during what war?
35. Vice President Thomas Marshall, serving under Woodrow Wilson, stated that "what this country needs is a good five-cent" what?
36. What world-famous newspaper did Adolph Ochs buy in 1896, giving it the motto "All the news that's fit to print"?
37. What legendary boxing champ was famed for entering a room and proclaiming, "I can lick any man in the house"?
38. What radio talk show host refers to America as "the greatest nation on God's green earth"?
39. According to Chief Justice John Marshall, "The power to tax involves the power to" do what?

★ Mottoes

1. In 1956, what was designated by Congress as the national motto?
2. What federal agency's motto is Fidelity, Bravery, Integrity? (Hint: note the letters)
3. What major record company had His Master's Voice as its motto?
4. Be Prepared is the official motto of what boys' organization?
5. What girls' organization, founded in 1910, has as its motto Wohelo— Work, Health, Love?
6. What U.S. service academy has Duty, Honor, Country as its motto?
7. The motto In God We Trust found on U.S. coins is also the official motto of what southern state?
8. What world-famous newspaper has the motto All the News That's Fit to Print?
9. What eastern state's motto has aroused controversy because of its political incorrectness?
10. The smallest state also has the briefest state motto, Hope. What state?

33. Lincoln's Gettysburg Address
34. The War of 1812
35. Cigar; the statement is Marshall's only claim to fame.
36. *The New York Times*
37. John L. Sullivan, the bare-knuckles Boston Strong Boy
38. Michael Medved
39. Destroy

Mottoes // Answers

1. In God We Trust, which appears on all coins
2. The FBI's
3. RCA (Remember the dog listening to the phonograph?)
4. The Boy Scouts of America
5. The Camp Fire Girls
6. The Military Academy at West Point
7. Florida
8. *The New York Times*
9. Maryland's; the motto *Fati maschii, parole femine,* was traditionally translated "Deeds are manly, words are womanly."
10. Rhode Island

Mottoes, continued . . .

11. The inspiring quote "With God all things are possible" is the motto of what midwestern state?
12. What Great Lakes state's one-word motto is Forward? (Hint: cheese)
13. What southwestern state's motto is God Enriches?
14. Labor Conquers All in what state with this motto? (Hint: oil wells)
15. Eureka is a city in—and also the state motto of—what western state?
16. What far northern state's motto is the French *L'Etoile du Nord* ("Star of the North")?
17. What Appalachian state's motto is Mountaineers Are Always Free Men?
18. A. Schwab's at 163 Beale Street has the famous motto If You Can't Find It at A. Schwab's, You Are Better Off without It. What southern metropolis is A. Schwab's in?

☆ Word and Phrase Origins

1. What world-famous architect coined the word *carport*?
2. Before *hello* was introduced into the language, what word did people use when answering the phone?
3. What sluggish, marshy outlet of a lake or river takes its name from the Choctaw word *bayuk*?
4. What term for Yankee adventurers came from the cheap luggage they carried south?
5. What term did Vice President Alben Barkley coin as shorthand for his position?
6. What famous Florida region takes its name from the Spanish word *cayos,* meaning "small islands"?
7. What American humorist, famous for his book *Autocrat of the Breakfast Table,* coined the term "mutual admiration society"?
8. What common term for stalling or hanging tough calls to mind a Civil War general?
9. Texas congressman Maury Maverick coined a term to describe meaningless government chatter. The word sounds like a turkey call. What is it?
10. What great American author took for his name a riverboat phrase meaning "water two fathoms deep"?

11. Ohio (It's from the Bible, by the way: Matthew 19:26.)

12. Wisconsin's

13. Arizona's

14. Oklahoma

15. California; *eureka* means "I have found it."

16. Minnesota's

17. West Virginia's

18. Memphis

Word and Phrase Origins // Answers

1. Frank Lloyd Wright

2. *Ahoy;* Thomas Edison coined *hello,* by the way.

3. Bayou

4. Carpetbaggers, from their cheap bags made of carpet

5. Veep; Barkley was veep from 1949 to 1953.

6. The Keys, off the tip of Florida

7. Oliver Wendell Holmes

8. Stonewalling (Remember Stonewall Jackson?)

9. Gobbledygook

10. Mark Twain, whose real name was Samuel Clemens

QUESTIONS

11. The beautiful Toccoa Falls in Georgia take their name from a Native American word meaning what?
12. What phrase did Maryland doctor Samuel Mudd contribute to our language?
13. The Articles of Confederation, adopted in 1777, was the first document to use what four words to describe the new nation?
14. The region of Acadia in Canada is the origin of the name of a group of people associated with Louisiana. Who are they?
15. The word *normalcy*, which wasn't a correct word at the time, was coined by what twentieth-century president?
16. What is the meaning of "Hoosiers," the name for Indiana residents?
17. What did the Native Americans refer to as an "iron horse"?
18. What name was given to the Sunday closing laws in the U.S.?
19. *Mesa* is a common place name in the Southwest. It is a Spanish word meaning what?
20. What autumn period took its name from the haze that resembled smoke from Native American campfires?

★ Let's Have a Contest!

Across America you could find a contest for practically everything—from beauty to running to frog jumping to chest hair. Does it mean we're a highly competitive, driven people? Or does it mean we just like to have a good time? (Isn't the answer obvious?)

1. What award is given in the Miss America contest to the contestant best liked by her peers?
2. At what famous southern speedway could you see the Mountain Dew 250 and Aaron's 499?
3. What New England city is host to a twenty-six-mile footrace each April, probably the most famous marathon in the world?
4. What type of vehicles are raced at the Little 500 in Bloomington, Indiana?
5. What national cooking contest, which began in 1949, now has a $1 million first prize?

11. Beautiful, appropriately enough
12. "My name is mud." The doctor unwittingly helped assassin John Wilkes Booth escape by treating Booth's broken leg. Mudd knew nothing of what Booth had done, but he was imprisoned nonetheless.
13. United States of America
14. The Cajuns, a word that came from *Acadians;* forced out of Canada by the English, many settled in Louisiana.
15. Warren Harding; he should have said *normality,* but since he had presidential clout, his mistake became an acceptable word.
16. No one knows.
17. A locomotive; the term came to be used by many whites also.
18. Blue laws; no one is quite sure why.
19. "Table" or "tabletop," referring to a flat-topped elevated area
20. Indian summer

Let's Have a Contest! // Answers

1. Miss Congeniality
2. The Talladega (Alabama) Superspeedway, also known as "Dega"
3. Boston, Massachusetts
4. Bicycles; if you saw the movie *Breaking Away,* you'll remember this.
5. The Pillsbury Bake-Off

Let's Have a Contest! continued . . .

6. What two contests are highlights of Tom Sawyer Days in Hannibal, Missouri?

7. In the annual Texas Water Safari, what types of motorless boats race over a 262-mile course?

8. If you attended California Calico Hullabaloo, what type of spitting contest could you enter?

9. What lofty Colorado mountain is the site of a grueling footrace every August?

10. In what heavily forested state would you be able to see the Loggerodeo?

11. If you wished to enter the Miss Crustacean contest, what New Jersey resort would you go to?

12. The Mayor's Marathon is held each June in what far northern location?

13. What appropriate name is given to the Omak, Washington, race where horses and riders race down a cliff and across a river?

14. Gilroy, California, hosts an annual cook-off for foods with what smelly vegetable?

15. What three contests comprise the IronMan Triathlon?

16. Akron, Ohio, is the site for what motorless race for kids?

17. The Great American Duck Race takes place in a state not noted for abundance of water. What southwestern state is it?

18. If you wanted to watch the Golden Girl of the Old West contest, where would you go?

19. Nashville's annual Swine Ball is held in conjunction with what type of cook-off?

20. What airy form of transportation is the focus of an annual race in Indianola, Iowa?

21. Imperial Beach, California, hosts an annual competition for what "gritty" constructions?

22. What California city hosts an international auto race on its downtown streets?

23. What famous horse race—part of the Triple Crown—is run at Pimlico in Baltimore?

24. What men-only contest started by Carnival cruise line is now a feature of every cruise ship?

25. If you wanted to test your lungs in the Conch Shell Blowing Contest, what Florida island would you go to?

6. The fence-painting contest and the frog-jumping contest (both inspired by incidents from Mark Twain's books)
7. Canoes
8. Tobacco spitting
9. Pike's Peak; the Pike's Peak Marathon is not for the timid.
10. Washington; it combines logging contests with rodeos and is held in Sedro Woolley.
11. Ocean City; the contest is held every August.
12. Anchorage, Alaska
13. The Stampede and Suicide Race, held in August
14. Garlic; the cook-off is part of the annual Gilroy Garlic Festival.
15. Swimming, biking, and running
16. The All-American Soap Box Derby, held every August
17. New Mexico; the race also has contests for Duck Queen, Darling Duckling, and Best-Dressed Duck.
18. Pecos, Texas; it's part of the annual West of the Pecos Rodeo.
19. Barbecue
20. Hot-air balloons; the town also has a balloon museum.
21. Sandcastles; it's the U.S. Open Sandcastle Competition.
22. Long Beach, which hosts the Toyota Grand Prix every April
23. The Preakness
24. The Mr. Hairy Chest contest
25. Key West

Let's Have a Contest! continued . . .

26. What type of small buildings are raced in Mountain Home, Arkansas, during the annual Bean Days?
27. What type of (distinctively country) music competition is held in Nashville each June?
28. In what western state could you watch a Kinetic Sculpture Race?

★ More Famous Firsts

1. In 1987 what Republican president submitted the first *trillion*-dollar budget to Congress?
2. What city in 1996 became the first southern city to host the Olympics?
3. What new ride did George Ferris introduce at the 1893 World's Fair in Chicago?
4. What cartoon cat was the first animated creature to be transmitted on TV?
5. Who first placed his (very large) signature on the Declaration of Independence?
6. In 1951 parties were first held to sell what line of plastic housewares?
7. What classic book for kids was the first novel ever completed on a type-writer? (Hint: whitewashing a fence)
8. "A. Mutt," America's first daily comic strip, evolved into what strip with two men in its title?
9. In 1890 murderer William Kemmler became the first man to be executed by what method?
10. What twentieth-century president was the first to be born in a hospital? (Hint: peanuts)
11. What place was Alan Shepard the first American to visit in May 1961?
12. What railroad line, the nation's first, was started at Baltimore, Maryland?
13. What event began a world-changing communications revolution in America on August 20, 1920?
14. Astronaut Ed White became the first American astronaut to do what?
15. The first theme park built around a country music theme was what?
16. Which of the thirteen colonies was the first to authorize its representa-tives to vote for separating from Britain?

26. Outhouses (on wheels, naturally)
27. The Grand Masters Fiddlers Convention
28. California (where else?); it's held in Eureka.

More Famous Firsts // Answers

1. Ronald Reagan
2. Atlanta, Georgia
3. The Ferris wheel, of course
4. Felix the Cat
5. John Hancock, president of the Continental Congress at the time
6. Tupperware
7. Mark Twain's *Tom Sawyer*
8. "Mutt and Jeff"; the original "A. Mutt" premiered in 1907.
9. Electrocution; this occurred in New York's Auburn Prison.
10. Jimmy Carter
11. Space
12. The famous Baltimore & Ohio
13. The first commercial radio broadcast
14. Walk in space
15. Opryland in (of course) Nashville, Tennessee
16. North Carolina

More Famous Firsts, continued...

17. Who was the first president born in the twentieth century? (Hint: assassination)
18. What Confederate state was the first to reenter the Union after the Civil War ended?
19. The first use of artificial rain to fight a forest fire was in 1947 near Concord in this "Granite State." What state?
20. In 1928, who became the first woman to fly across the Atlantic?
21. In 1939 who became the first British monarch to visit the U.S.?
22. On July 4, 1831, "America" was first sung at what historic city's Park Street Church at the foot of Beacon Hill?
23. Who was the first president whose parents survived him?
24. What great artist was just twenty-two when he illustrated his first *Saturday Evening Post* cover in 1916?
25. During the War of 1812, who became the first president to face enemy gunfire while in office?
26. In 1835 who became the first (and only) president to pay off the national debt?
27. Virginia Dare, the first English child born in America, was born in what state?
28. What explorer, who has a mountain named for him, led the first American group into Colorado?
29. The world's first commercial airline service was established in 1914 between what two Florida cities?
30. Chapel Hill, North Carolina, had the first state college in America. What college?
31. America's first written constitution, signed in 1620 aboard a ship, was drawn up by what group?
32. What aviation feat did C. P. Rodgers accomplish in 1911?
33. The House of Burgesses, the New World's first representative assembly, met in what colony in 1619?
34. What was significant about the 1927 Al Jolson film *The Jazz Singer*?
35. The first English settlement in America was named for what famous English soldier and author?
36. A 1903 trip from New York to California was the first coast-to-coast trip made in what form of transportation?

17. John F. Kennedy, born in 1917
18. Tennessee
19. New Hampshire
20. Amelia Earhart
21. George VI
22. Boston
23. John F. Kennedy, who died young because of being assassinated
24. Norman Rockwell
25. James Madison
26. Andrew Jackson (Ah, how times have changed.)
27. The future North Carolina; her parents were part of the famous "Lost Colony" that disappeared without a trace in the 1580s.
28. Zebulon Pike, for whom Pike's Peak is named
29. Tampa and St. Petersburg, which are only a few miles apart; the service was called the "flying boat."
30. The University of North Carolina
31. The Pilgrims, who signed the Mayflower Compact before going ashore
32. The first transcontinental flight (with numerous stops—no nonstops in those days)
33. Virginia, at the Jamestown colony
34. It was the first talking movie—or part-talking, anyway. The landmark film (which is partly silent) marked the end of the silent movie era.
35. Sir Walter Raleigh, famous at the court of Queen Elizabeth I; Fort Raleigh, on the North Carolina coast, was named for him.
36. Automobile; the trip lasted from May 23 to August 1.

PART TWELVE

TEN QUESTIONS
(ABOUT EACH STATE)

★ The Heart of Dixie, Alabama

1. The famous Iron Bowl, first held in 1893, is between which two renowned college football teams?
2. What polluted steel town had the nickname Pittsburgh of the South?
3. Cloudmont, an Alabama ski resort, seems too far south for snow. Why is there snow there so often?
4. What city is considered the birthplace of the U.S. space program?
5. What port city has a Mardi Gras second only to the one in New Orleans?
6. What pioneering country music star has a memorial in Montgomery? (Hint: cheatin' heart)
7. Talladega has a hall of fame for what sport?
8. In what noted college town could you drive on Paul W. Bryant Drive?
9. Tuskegee University is connected with which noted black scientist?
10. How did the town of Haleyville react when the state seceded from the Union in 1861?

★ The Last Frontier, Alaska

1. What boom began at Bonanza Creek in 1897?
2. The Diomede Islands off Alaska are divided between the U.S. and what nation?
3. The state song, "Alaska, My Alaska," uses the tune from what familiar Christmas song?
4. The name of the state sport might remind you of cornmeal. What is the sport?
5. Capt. Vitus Bering, visiting Alaska in 1740, claimed it for what nation?
6. What well-loved cowboy comic died in a plane crash in Alaska in 1935?
7. What playful sea animal was almost wiped out by Russian fur traders in the 1700s?
8. Purchased for the U.S. in 1867 by Secretary of State William Seward, Alaska was called Seward's Folly. What nation was it purchased from?
9. You can visit the Last Chance Mining Museum in what capital of the Last Frontier?
10. Practically no trees grow in this 1,100-mile-long island chain, but there are grasses and flowers. What islands?

The Heart of Dixie, Alabama // Answers

1. Alabama and Auburn; the name *Iron Bowl* stems from its original location at Legion Field in Birmingham, center of the steel industry. Since 2000, the Bowl is held at Auburn in odd-numbered years, Alabama in even-numbered years.
2. Birmingham, which, like Pittsburgh, is now a very pretty, clean, and breathable city
3. The Cloudmont snow is manufactured.
4. Huntsville, home of NASA's Space Flight Center and home to rocket scientist Wernher von Braun
5. Mobile, which, like New Orleans, has a rich French heritage
6. The legendary Hank Williams
7. Auto racing; the International Motorsports Hall of Fame is next to the renowned Talladega Superspeedway.
8. Tuscaloosa, home of the University of Alabama, where Paul "Bear" Bryant coached football for many years
9. George Washington Carver, who helped develop peanut and sweet potato products
10. The citizens voted to secede from the state.

The Last Frontier, Alaska // Answers

1. The Klondike Gold Rush
2. Russia
3. "O Christmas Tree," also known as "O Tannenbaum"
4. "Mushing"—that is, dogsled racing
5. Russia, the nation that Alaska is closest to
6. Will Rogers
7. The sea otter
8. Russia
9. Juneau
10. The Aleutians

★ The Grand Canyon State, Arizona

1. The University of Phoenix Stadium is host to what football bowl game?
2. The Native Americans who first led Spanish explorers to the Grand Canyon belonged to what tribe?
3. What beautiful spot has served as the most popular background scenery in western movies?
4. Lake Havasu City has what enormous structure, brought over from London?
5. What large, extinct creatures could you see in animated form in the Mesa Southwest Museum?
6. What weather phenomenon waters the green fields of cotton, melons, and lettuce near Phoenix?
7. Known as the Jewel of the Desert, the Biltmore Hotel is in what major city?
8. The beautiful sandstone fort in Pipe Spring National Monument was built by what religious group?
9. What animals can you ride into the Grand Canyon?
10. Why does the town of Bisbee not have mail delivered to people's homes?

★ The Land of Opportunity, Arkansas

1. What national park centers around 143-degree water?
2. What 1848 event in California changed Fort Smith, Arkansas, into a boomtown?
3. What is Hope famous for?
4. Eureka Springs has a museum devoted to figurines of what water creatures?
5. Governor Winthrop Rockefeller founded a museum devoted to one of his favorite hobbies. What?
6. Mountain View is host to what popular music contest?
7. What type of structures are raced in Mountain Home's annual Bean Days?
8. Rogers has a museum devoted to what type of weapon for children?
9. What town claims that it saw the first fighting of the Civil War?
10. What crucial metal originates in the state of Arkansas?

The Grand Canyon State, Arizona // Answers

1. The Fiesta Bowl
2. Hopi
3. The stunning Monument Valley (Where would John Wayne have been without it?)
4. London Bridge, center of the twenty-one-acre English Village; the bridge was brought over in 1968.
5. Dinosaurs
6. None does. The farming is all done by irrigation.
7. Phoenix
8. The Mormons; it was a guardhouse for families protecting the church's cattle herds.
9. Mules; horses ride *around* the canyon, but not into it.
10. The town's streets are too steep even for mail carriers.

The Land of Opportunity, Arkansas // Answers

1. Hot Springs; this is the temperature of the water from the park's forty-seven springs.
2. The discovery of gold, leading to the gold rush; Fort Smith became a favorite starting place for wagons heading west.
3. Its annual Watermelon Festival, with a competition for the biggest; one winner weighed 260 pounds.
4. Frogs; it is the Frog Fantasies collection.
5. Cars; the Museum of Automobiles in Morrilton has many cars from Rockefeller's own large personal collection.
6. The Arkansas State Fiddler's Contest, held in September
7. Outhouses (on wheels, of course)
8. Air guns—that is, BB guns and pellet guns; the museum is run by the Daisy company, maker of such guns.
9. Pine Bluff; several days before Charleston's Fort Sumter was fired on (the official beginning of the war), Pine Bluff locals fired on a federal gunboat and confiscated its supplies.
10. Aluminum, made from the bauxite ore that is common in Arkansas

★ The Golden State, California

1. What famous mail service had its western end in California?
2. Beverly Hills is entirely surrounded by what metropolis?
3. What popular attraction lies on eighty acres in Anaheim?
4. Grizzly Peak towers above what college town?
5. California's highest and lowest points are only eighty miles apart. What are they?
6. Big Sur on the coast is home to what awesome trees?
7. What pro baseball team plays its home games in Anaheim Stadium?
8. Calexico sits across the border from what Mexican city?
9. Telescope Peak, eleven thousand feet high, towers above what low-lying site?
10. What island paradise was developed by chewing-gum dollars?

★ The Centennial State, Colorado

1. Why is Colorado the Centennial State?
2. "Bolder Boulder," held in Boulder, is what type of event?
3. Pike's Peak towers over what major city?
4. What federal military school has an eye-catching modern campus in Colorado Springs?
5. What sport did Norwegian Carl Howelsen bring to Steamboat Springs in 1913?
6. What substance covers the dome of Colorado's capitol?
7. What moneymaking operation is found in Denver?
8. What city receives thousands of valentine cards each year?
9. What sports commission has its headquarters in Colorado Springs?
10. What famous lawman was sheriff of Trinidad, Colorado?

★ The Constitution State, Connecticut

1. What familiar Revolutionary War song is the state song? (Hint: macaroni)
2. What noted dictionary maker's birthplace can be visited in Hartford?

The Golden State, California // Answers

1. The Pony Express, ending at Sacramento
2. Los Angeles
3. Disneyland
4. Berkeley, home of the main campus of the University of California
5. Death Valley (282 feet *below* sea level) and Mount Whitney (14,494 feet)
6. Redwoods
7. The Angels
8. Mexicali (Notice any similarity of names?)
9. Death Valley, which is mostly *below* sea level
10. Catalina Island, developed by the Wrigley Company

The Centennial State, Colorado // Answers

1. It became a state in 1876, the country's centennial.
2. A foot race
3. Colorado Springs
4. The U.S. Air Force Academy
5. Skiing; since then the town has become "Ski Town U.S.A."
6. Gold from the Colorado mines
7. The U.S. Mint—literally a moneymaking place
8. Loveland; people mail them there, hoping to get them remailed with the city's postmark.
9. The U.S. Olympic Committee
10. Bat Masterson

The Constitution State, Connecticut // Answers

1. "Yankee Doodle"
2. Noah Webster's

The Constitution State, Connecticut, continued . . .

3. Bristol has a museum for what colorful fairground rides?
4. What important naval items are based at Groton?
5. What major white-collar industry is associated with Hartford?
6. What pro hockey team plays its home games at the Hartford Civic Center?
7. What very old Bible could you see in Yale University's Rare Book Library?
8. What historic river flows through the center of Connecticut?
9. What boring household items are made very interesting in a Bristol museum?
10. What's the distinction of the Lake Compounce Festival Park in Connecticut?

✫ The First State, Delaware

1. Why does Delaware call itself the First State?
2. What tree connected with Christmas is the state tree?
3. What tiny colorful bug is the state's official insect?
4. Why is Rehoboth Beach called the "Summer Capital"?
5. What noted chemical company do we associate with Wilmington, Delaware?
6. Delaware has the fewest counties of any state. How many?
7. Treasures of the Sea in Georgetown displays what type of item from the ocean bottom?
8. The Zwaanendael Museum in Lewes honors what ethnic group?
9. The famous DuPont family of Delaware got their start by producing what product?
10. The Delmarva Peninsula is divided among Delaware and what two other states?

3. Carousels; it's the New England Carousel Museum.
4. Submarines
5. Insurance; many companies are headquartered there.
6. The Whalers
7. The Gutenberg Bible, the oldest printed Bible
8. The Connecticut, appropriately enough
9. Locks; the Lock Museum of America displays many interesting antique locks.
10. It's the nation's oldest continuously operating amusement park.

The First State, Delaware // Answers

1. It was the first state to ratify the U.S. Constitution (Dec. 7, 1787).
2. Holly—American holly, to be specific
3. The ladybug, one of the few insects people actually seem to like
4. Because of the many D.C. residents who vacation there
5. DuPont
6. Three; Rhode Island, a smaller state, has five.
7. Coins and jewels taken from sunken ships
8. The Dutch, who were early settlers of the state
9. Gunpowder
10. Maryland and Virginia; DELaware, MARyland, and VirginiA yield Delmarva.

★ The Sunshine State, Florida

1. What popular tourist attraction opened in 1971?
2. What (as if you couldn't guess) is Florida's chief industry?
3. What city is only ninety miles from Havana, Cuba?
4. What Spanish explorer who visited the state is commemorated by two county names?
5. What city is Florida's "Speed Beach"?
6. To ride the Incredible Hulk and the Dragon Challenge roller coasters, where would you go?
7. In terms of area, the nation's largest city is what metropolis?
8. What county is named for a large (and rare) sea mammal?
9. What city hosted the Cigar Bowl for small-college football teams?
10. What warm, sunny city is named for a cold, cloudy city in Russia?

★ The Peach State, Georgia

1. What world-famous novel (which made a world-famous movie) is set in Georgia in the 1860s?
2. What famous hiking trail has its southern end in Georgia?
3. What valuable item caused a rush to Dahlonega in 1828?
4. What is the most commonly used street name in Atlanta?
5. What historic city has twenty-two park-like "squares" that delight tourists?
6. Warm Springs has the Little White House. What president built this as a vacation home?
7. What Civil War general led a destructive march through Georgia in 1864?
8. What two famous English preachers are connected with colonial Georgia?
9. Augusta is the site of what famous golf tournament?
10. What sports arena is often called "The Ted"?

The Sunshine State, Florida // Answers

1. Walt Disney World, of course
2. Tourism—surprise!
3. Key West
4. Hernando DeSoto; believe it or not, Florida has a Hernando County and a DeSoto County.
5. Daytona Beach, where several speed records were set during the early days of the automobile
6. Universal's Islands of Adventure, Orlando
7. Jacksonville; the city is so large because its city limits are the same as those of its surrounding county, Duval.
8. Manatee
9. Tampa, which for a time was known for making cigars; the Cigar Bowl was held from 1946 to 1954.
10. St. Petersburg

The Peach State, Georgia // Answers

1. *Gone with the Wind*, of course
2. The Appalachian Trail
3. Gold; it was America's first gold rush.
4. Peachtree; there are over thirty-five variations of the name—Peachtree Street, Peachtree Circle, Peachtree Memorial Drive, etc.
5. Savannah
6. Franklin D. Roosevelt, who died there
7. Union general William Tecumseh Sherman—not one of the most beloved men in Georgia history
8. John and Charles Wesley, the founders of the Methodist movement in the 1700s
9. The Masters, held in April
10. Turner Field in Atlanta, named for media mogul Ted Turner; the Atlanta Braves have played there since 1997.

★ The Aloha State, Hawaii

1. What notorious attack occurred at 7:55 A.M. on December 7, 1941?
2. Besides pineapple, what is the state's chief farm product?
3. What ethnic group outnumbers white residents in the state?
4. What popular 1970s TV series always ended with the words "Book 'em"?
5. Liliuokalani, Hawaii's last queen, wrote what popular song?
6. What business (as if you couldn't guess) is the state's prime moneymaker?
7. The nene, the state bird, is what sort of bird?
8. Hawaii is the only state to grow what drinkable crop?
9. In 1901 who founded the Hawaiian Pineapple Company?
10. The Big Island, Hawaii, has volcanic sands of what distinctive color?

★ The Gem State, Idaho

1. What (as if you couldn't guess) is Idaho's chief farm product?
2. Why is Idaho the Gem State?
3. What beautiful valley is Idaho's main year-round recreation area?
4. What city takes its name from the French *les bois* ("the woods")?
5. What kind of races are held at Idaho's annual Oktubberfest?
6. What town shares its name with a formerly communist nation's capital?
7. What kind of sculpting is featured in Sun Valley's Winterfest?
8. The famous River of No Return goes by the name of a fish. What?
9. What ancient vehicles are raced at the fairgrounds in Jerome?
10. What valuable mineral would you find in the gravel of Idaho City?

★ Land of Lincoln, Illinois

1. Scarface was what notorious Italian gangster of Chicago?
2. What worldwide fast-food chain has its headquarters in the posh suburb of Oak Brook? (Hint: arch)

The Aloha State, Hawaii // Answers

1. The Japanese attack on Pearl Harbor
2. Sugarcane
3. Asians, mostly Japanese; it is the only state in which white residents are not the majority.
4. *Hawaii Five-O*
5. "Aloha Oe"
6. Tourism, naturally
7. A goose
8. Coffee
9. James Dole (as in Dole Pineapple)
10. Black

The Gem State, Idaho // Answers

1. Potatoes
2. Its name means "gem of the mountains."
3. Sun Valley
4. Boise, the capital
5. Tub races, what else?
6. Moscow
7. Snow sculpting
8. Salmon
9. Chariots
10. Gold

Land of Lincoln, Illinois // Answers

1. Al Capone
2. McDonald's

Land of Lincoln, Illinois, continued . . .

3. What president is buried in Oak Ridge Cemetery in Springfield?
4. If you are riding the CTA's "L" trains, where are you?
5. What religious group's temple ruins can be seen in Nauvoo?
6. Wheaton College's museum of evangelism is named for what evangelist?
7. North Michigan Avenue, a key Chicago shopping area, has what nickname?
8. If you are watching the Power play in Chicago, what sport are you watching?
9. Galena has the home of what Civil War general and (later) president?
10. Chicago Zoological Park is not in Chicago but in what suburb?

✭ The Hoosier State, Indiana

1. What notable auto race was first held in 1911?
2. What type of vehicles race in the Little 500 in Bloomington?
3. What well-known state college is in West Lafayette?
4. Berne is named for the capital of Switzerland. What sort of people settled the town?
5. Holiday World amusement park is found in a town with an appropriate name. What?
6. South Bend is home to what world-famous Catholic college?
7. Valparaiso has an annual festival devoted to what munchable item?
8. Two Indiana residents, both with the same last name, became president. Who were they?
9. What holiday weekend is the Indianapolis 500 held?
10. The Squire Boone Caverns in Indiana were discovered by what famous frontiersman?

3. Abraham Lincoln, naturally
4. Chicago; the Chicago Transit Authority (CTA) trains serve as both elevated transit (the "L") and as subway transit depending on what part of the city they're in.
5. The Mormons's
6. Billy Graham; Graham is a Wheaton College alumnus.
7. The Magnificent Mile
8. Soccer (indoor soccer to be exact)
9. Ulysses S. Grant, eighteenth president
10. Brookfield; it's usually just called the Brookfield Zoo.

The Hoosier State, Indiana // Answers

1. The Indianapolis 500
2. Bicycles; the race was featured in the movie *Breaking Away*.
3. Purdue, home of the Boilermakers
4. Swiss—to be specific, Swiss Mennonites who were fleeing religious persecution in their homeland
5. Santa Claus
6. The University of Notre Dame
7. Popcorn; the Popcorn Festival is held in mid-September.
8. William Henry Harrison, ninth president, one-time governor of the Indiana Territory, and his grandson Benjamin Harrison, twenty-third president
9. Memorial Day
10. Daniel Boone, who happened to have a brother named Squire

★ The Hawkeye State, Iowa

1. WHO radio in Des Moines launched the public career of what future president?
2. What noted washer and dryer manufacturer has its home in Newton?
3. What Western movie hero was born in Winterset in 1907?
4. What county is noted for its covered bridges? (Hint: Eastwood)
5. The Dutch town of Pella has a spring festival honoring what flower?
6. What revolutionary invention had its birth at Iowa State University in the 1930s? (Hint: chip)
7. Iowa, which has no coast, has a town with what oceanic name?
8. What Wild West character's home can be visited in Bettendorf?
9. The Pufferbilly Days in Boone focus on what form of transportation?
10. The National Rivers Hall of Fame is in what riverside town?

★ The Sunflower State, Kansas

1. What familiar cowboy song is the state song? (Hint: buffalo)
2. What famous cow town was the hometown of Dwight Eisenhower?
3. What is the most notorious building in Leavenworth?
4. What antibooze crusader's home can be visited in Medicine Lodge?
5. What adorable rodent has a state park named for it in Norton?
6. The Boot Hill Museum is in what legendary town?
7. What city is the country's largest producer of aircraft?
8. The annual Huff 'n' Puff Rally in Topeka involves what form of recreation?
9. What antislavery radical has a memorial in Osawatomie?
10. McPherson has a June festival honoring what Celtic instrument?

★ The Bluegrass State, Kentucky

1. What world-famous race is the Run for the Roses?
2. What noted country singer was born a coal miner's daughter?
3. What metal do we associate with Fort Knox?

The Hawkeye State, Iowa // Answers

1. Ronald Reagan, who was a sportscaster at WHO
2. Maytag
3. John Wayne; his birthplace there can be toured.
4. Madison County; this was true long before *The Bridges of Madison County* became a popular book and movie.
5. Tulips, what else?
6. The electronic digital computer, built by John Atanasoff
7. Atlantic
8. Buffalo Bill Cody's; the home features (surprise!) buffalo.
9. Railways
10. Dubuque, which is on the Mississippi River

The Sunflower State, Kansas // Answers

1. "Home on the Range"
2. Abilene
3. The federal penitentiary, naturally
4. The famous (or infamous) Carry Nation, known for chopping up saloons with a hatchet
5. The prairie dog
6. Dodge City, of course
7. Wichita
8. Hot-air ballooning
9. John Brown; in the 1856 Battle of Osawatomie, five of his followers were killed. He was often referred to as Osawatomie Brown.
10. Bagpipes (Those with sensitive ears, take note.)

The Bluegrass State, Kentucky // Answers

1. The Kentucky Derby, held in Louisville
2. Loretta Lynn, from Butcher Hollow, Kentucky
3. Gold, naturally; the U.S. Bullion Depository is there.

The Bluegrass State, Kentucky, continued . . .

4. In Bowling Green what popular American sports cars are manufactured?
5. What president's boyhood home is found near Hodgenville? (Hint: log cabin)
6. What noted fast-food entrepreneur is buried in Louisville's Cave Hill Cemetery?
7. What famous racetrack is located at 700 Central Avenue in Louisville?
8. What well-known boys' organization has a museum in Murray?
9. Old Fort Boonesborough was named for what pioneer?
10. What county was named for the ruling family of France in the 1700s?

★ The Pelican State, Louisiana

1. What football match is played in the Superdome on New Year's Day?
2. What season, celebrated riotously in New Orleans, runs from January 6 to Shrove Tuesday?
3. Gumbo is a food associated with what style of cooking?
4. If you are having dinner in the Big Easy, where are you?
5. What French emperor sold the Louisiana Territory to the U.S. in 1803?
6. A crawdad, a popular ingredient in Louisiana cooking, is what sort of creature?
7. What name is given to New Orleans's picturesque old section?
8. What town calls itself the "Capital of French Louisiana"?
9. Southern Louisiana has a pine forest area called the Ozone Belt. Where did it get this name?
10. What colorful Louisiana politician of the 1930s had the nickname Kingfish?

★ The Pine Tree State, Maine

1. What edible sea creature is celebrated at an annual festival in Rockland, Maine?
2. What stunning national park is found on Mount Desert Island?

The Bluegrass State, Kentucky // Answers // continued . . .

4. Corvettes
5. Abraham Lincoln's; the cabin is not his actual home but a replica.
6. Harlan B. Sanders of Kentucky Fried Chicken fame
7. Churchill Downs, famed for the Kentucky Derby
8. The Boy Scouts; the National Scouting Museum is on the campus of Murray State University.
9. Daniel Boone; the present fort is a replica of the one Boone built in 1775.
10. Bourbon, which has lent its name to a famous Kentucky product

The Pelican State, Louisiana // Answers

1. The Sugar Bowl
2. Carnival, which climaxes on Shrove Tuesday—also better known as Mardi Gras
3. Cajun, native to Louisiana but now popular worldwide
4. New Orleans; its nickname refers to the laid-back lifestyle of the city.
5. Napoleon, of course
6. A crayfish, a small lobsterlike crustacean; in the South they're usually called crawfish or crawdads.
7. The French Quarter, also known by the French name *Vieux Carré*
8. Lafayette, which is the center of the state's distinctive Cajun district
9. The thick forests supposedly improve the quality of the air.
10. Huey Long, who was assassinated in 1935

The Pine Tree State, Maine // Answers

1. Lobsters, at the Maine Lobster Festival
2. Acadia

QUESTIONS

The Pine Tree State, Maine, continued . . .

3. How did the Calendar Islands get their name?
4. Bangor has a thirty-one-foot statue of what legendary lumberjack?
5. Maine's northernmost city is named for what hoofed animal of cold areas?
6. Kennebunkport gained fame as the summer home of what recent president?
7. What exactly is the Headlight in Portland?
8. What Viking explorer is thought to have landed on Monhegan Island around the year 1000?
9. What famed mail-order clothing firm has its headquarters in Freeport?
10. What noise would you hear in the Thunder Hole in Acadia National Park?

✶ The Old Line State, Maryland

1. What baseball legend's birthplace is a museum in Baltimore?
2. What jet, often in the news, has its home at Andrews Air Force Base?
3. What famous federal college is in Annapolis?
4. What horse race dominates Baltimore life each May?
5. What pro baseball team plays its home games at Camden Yards?
6. What familiar Christmas tune is the state song sung to?
7. Smith Island was named for what famous English pioneer?
8. What archaic pastime is the state sport of Maryland?
9. What famous boundary line was established in 1767?
10. What great naval hero is buried in the chapel of the U.S. Naval Academy?

✶ The Bay State, Massachusetts

1. What famous rock on the Massachusetts coast weighs seven tons?
2. If you are walking the Freedom Trail, what historic city are you touring?
3. What Pilgrim leader became, in 1631, the first elected official in America?

3. There are (supposedly) 365 of them.
4. Paul Bunyan
5. Caribou
6. George Bush
7. A lighthouse, built in 1791
8. Leif Eriksson, son of Erik the Red
9. L. L. Bean, known especially for its sportswear
10. The roar of ocean waves crashing against granite rocks

The Old Line State, Maryland // Answers

1. Babe Ruth's
2. *Air Force One*, the presidential plane
3. The U.S. Naval Academy
4. The Preakness
5. The Baltimore Orioles
6. "O Christmas Tree" (also known as "O Tannenbaum"); "Maryland, My Maryland" was written for this tune.
7. John Smith (of Pocahontas fame)
8. Jousting, a holdover from medieval times
9. The Mason-Dixon line, drawn as the boundary between Maryland and Pennsylvania
10. John Paul Jones, famous for saying, "I have not yet begun to fight."

The Bay State, Massachusetts // Answers

1. Plymouth Rock, site of the Pilgrims' landing
2. Boston, of course
3. John Winthrop, elected governor of the Massachusetts colony

4. What noted woman poet's home can be visited in Amherst?
5. What Massachusetts-born president was the first with a middle name?
6. What lovely tree, almost destroyed by disease, is the state tree?
7. Who, in April 1775, set out on a historic ride from his house at 19 North Square in Boston?
8. Where do the Boston Red Sox play their home games?
9. Massachusetts Hall, built in 1720, is the oldest building on what historic college campus?
10. What well-known fruit was developed in Concord in 1848?

★ The Wolverine State, Michigan

1. A Frenchman named Cadillac founded what city?
2. Grand Rapids has a museum devoted to which Republican president?
3. What is the only Great Lake that does *not* touch Michigan?
4. How did Detroit get the nickname Motown?
5. Battle Creek Sanitarium was the birthplace of what familiar breakfast food?
6. Dearborn has a museum devoted to what noted auto king?
7. On what holiday does Detroit hold its famous Santa Claus Parade?
8. Where can you walk on "singing sand"?
9. What ethnic group established the town of Holland?
10. What major political party was founded in Jackson in 1854?

★ The North Star State, Minnesota

1. What colossal shopping center is in Bloomington, Minnesota?
2. Minnesota Mining and Manufacturing is better known by what corporate name?
3. What mythical lumberjack had his home in the logging camps of Minnesota?

4. Emily Dickinson's; the house, where she was born and died, was built in 1813. She was some-times called "the belle of Amherst."
5. John Quincy Adams (This is fortunate, since it helps distinguish him from his father, President John Adams.)
6. The elm
7. Paul Revere
8. Fenway Park
9. Harvard
10. The Concord grape, of course

The Wolverine State, Michigan // Answers

1. Detroit, of course
2. Gerald Ford, a Michigan man
3. Lake Ontario
4. It's a short form of "Motor Town." Detroit was, and is, an auto center.
5. Corn flakes
6. Henry Ford, born in Dearborn in 1863
7. Thanksgiving Day
8. On the beaches at Grand Haven, where the sand emits a peculiar whistle when walked on
9. Dutch, of course
10. The Republicans

The North Star State, Minnesota // Answers

1. The famous Mall of America, with more than four hundred stores and restaurants
2. 3M
3. Paul Bunyan

ANSWERS

The North Star State, Minnesota, continued . . .

4. What football team plays home games in the Hubert Humphrey Metrodome?
5. Who participates in the John Beargrease Marathon?
6. What popular singer and movie star has a museum in Grand Rapids? (Hint: Oz)
7. What peas-and-corn company do you associate with Le Sueur, Minnesota?
8. What national park is named for early French explorers of the region?
9. What famous hospital would you find in Rochester?
10. What wild-voiced water bird is the state bird?

★ The Magnolia State, Mississippi

1. What world-famous rock-and-roller was born in Tupelo?
2. What Gulf Coast city is the site of the Seafood Industry Museum?
3. Greenwood has a museum devoted to which important southern crop?
4. What state shares the Gulf Islands National Seashore with Mississippi?
5. Meridian has a museum devoted to the Father of Country Music. Who was he?
6. What riverside town was the Gibraltar of the Confederacy?
7. What Nobel Prize–winning author's home is Rowan Oak in Oxford?
8. Which river is the "singing river"?
9. The historic road known as the Natchez Trace connected Natchez, Mississippi, with what Tennessee city?
10. If you are in the Great Mississippi River Balloon Race, where are you?

★ The Show Me State, Missouri

1. St. Louis's tallest structure is not an office or residence but a metal semi-circle. What is it?
2. What Missouri town is often called Nashville West?

4. The Minnesota Vikings
5. Sled dogs
6. Judy Garland; the town also has a Judy Garland Festival each June.
7. Green Giant, which was founded there
8. Voyageurs National Park
9. The Mayo Clinic
10. The loon

The Magnolia State, Mississippi // Answers

1. Elvis Presley, of course
2. Biloxi
3. Cotton; the Cottonlandia Museum is a popular tourist attraction.
4. Florida
5. Jimmie Rodgers, known as "The Singing Brakeman"
6. Vicksburg, which withstood a long, hard siege by Gen. Ulysses S. Grant
7. William Faulkner's
8. The Pascagoula River, which makes a weird sound on summer and fall evenings; according to legend, it is the sound of an Indian tribe that committed mass suicide by jumping into the river.
9. Nashville
10. Natchez, Mississippi, during the festival known as the Natchez Pilgrimage

The Show Me State, Missouri // Answers

1. The Gateway Arch, 630 feet tall, on the riverfront
2. Branson, with its cluster of country music showplaces

The Show Me State, Missouri, continued . . .

3. What greeting card company is Kansas City's most famous corporation?
4. What sports-minded religious organization is headquartered in Kansas City?
5. What noted author's home could you visit in Hannibal?
6. St. Joseph was the eastern end of what famous mail service?
7. What city was, in 1904, the first U.S. site of the summer Olympics?
8. What name do most Missourians call their state capital?
9. Where would you find a museum devoted to Confederate guerrillas?
10. What type of item is featured in Memoryville USA?

★ Big Sky Country, Montana

1. Whose last stand is reenacted at the Little Big Horn Days in Hardin?
2. What did Montana do with freeway speed limits in 1995?
3. In what national park can you enjoy a snowball fight in midsummer?
4. What metal—appropriate for the state—covers the capitol dome in Helena?
5. In the Governor's Cup Race each February, what sort of runners participate?
6. What kind of people train at Montana's Smokejumper Center?
7. What material is the Top of the World Bar carved from?
8. What great American river has its source in Three Forks?
9. What Native American practice is commemorated at Buffalo Jump State Monument?
10. In what once lawless town can you visit the notorious Robbers' Roost?

★ The Cornhusker State, Nebraska

1. What tree-planting holiday was first observed on April 10, 1872, in Nebraska?
2. The college baseball World Series is held in what city?
3. Lincoln, Nebraska, has the hall of fame for what trivial pastime?

The Show Me State, Missouri // Answers // continued . . .

3. Hallmark
4. The Fellowship of Christian Athletes
5. Mark Twain's
6. The Pony Express
7. St. Louis
8. "Jeff City," short for the real name, Jefferson City
9. The town of Nevada, which has the Bushwhacker Museum; Nevada was a center of the bush-whackers' operation.
10. Antique cars

Big Sky Country, Montana // Answers

1. George Custer's
2. Removed them completely; on interstate highways, motorists are simply advised to drive "safely."
3. Glacier National Park
4. Copper, a key product in the state
5. Sled dogs
6. Airborne firefighters, who are trained in parachuting
7. Snow; the bar is in a snowbank atop eleven-thousand-foot Beartooth Pass.
8. The Missouri, formed at the confluence of the Gallatin, Jefferson, and Madison Rivers
9. Driving bison over cliffs
10. Virginia City, which, in its heyday, had 190 murders in seven months; it is now restored as a tourist town.

The Cornhusker State, Nebraska // Answers

1. Arbor Day
2. Omaha
3. Trivia

The Cornhusker State, Nebraska, continued . . .

4. You can ride a wagon train in Bridgeport, Nebraska, that travels on what famous western trail?
5. What renowned author of frontier novels has a museum in Hastings?
6. How does Nebraska's legislature differ radically from other states'?
7. What famous presidential candidate of the early 1900s was first elected to Congress from Nebraska?
8. What president's statue is on the capitol grounds in Lincoln?
9. North Platte was hometown of what noted Wild West showman?
10. What president of the 1970s was born in Omaha?

★ The Silver State, Nevada

1. The tallest building in Las Vegas is (naturally) what type of building?
2. Not surprisingly, what is Nevada's state metal?
3. What resort lake on Nevada's border takes its name from a Washo tribe word for "big water"?
4. Boulder City is the only Nevada town where what activity is *not* legal?
5. The state capital was named for what famous frontiersman?
6. Who (or what) owns 90 percent of Nevada's land?
7. It is "gambling" in the rest of the U.S., but what is it in Nevada?
8. Nevada's first non–Native American settlement was made by what religious group?
9. What is distinctive about the rodeo held every July in Fallon?
10. What chilly natural phenomenon can be found in Great Basin National Park?

★ The Granite State, New Hampshire

1. What appropriate name is given to the mountain range that includes Mount Washington, Mount Adams, and Mount Jackson?
2. The Connecticut River separates New Hampshire from what state?

4. The Oregon Trail
5. Willa Cather, author of *Death Comes for the Archbishop, My Antonia,* and other classics
6. It is unicameral—that is, it has one house instead of two.
7. William Jennings Bryan, the "Great Commoner"
8. Abraham Lincoln's (did anyone miss this?)
9. Buffalo Bill Cody; his ranch in the town can be visited.
10. Gerald Ford

The Silver State, Nevada // Answers

1. A hotel-casino
2. Silver; Nevada is the Silver State.
3. Lake Tahoe
4. Gambling
5. Kit Carson
6. The federal government
7. "Gaming"
8. The Mormons
9. It is the All Indian Rodeo.
10. A glacier

The Granite State, New Hampshire // Answers

1. The Presidential Range
2. Vermont

QUESTIONS

The Granite State, New Hampshire, continued . . .

3. What great American play is set in fictional Grover's Corners, New Hampshire?
4. What Ivy League college, founded as a Native American school, is found in Hanover?
5. They are called mountain "passes" in most places, but in New Hampshire they're called what?
6. What colony was New Hampshire part of from 1623 to 1679?
7. What great New England poet's farm can be visited in Derry?
8. What warmhearted movie with Henry Fonda and Katharine Hepburn was filmed on Squam Lake?
9. What makes the state so important in presidential election years?
10. What man born in New Hampshire in 1804 was known as "Handsome Frank"?

⋆ The Garden State, New Jersey

1. What beach resort do we associate with the Miss America pageant?
2. In 1893 what inventor established a motion picture lot at his lab in West Orange?
3. What famous river crossing is reenacted at Trenton every Christmas?
4. Though Trenton is the capital, Drumthwacket, the governor's home, is in what college town?
5. What popular seaside candy was introduced at Asbury Park?
6. For two months in 1784 what city was the temporary capital of the U.S.?
7. What sports field did Alexander Cartwright lay out for the first time in 1846 in Hoboken?
8. What agency for helping the blind become mobile is headquartered in Morristown?
9. Pepperidge Farm breads, Prego sauces, and V8 juice are marketed by what famous soup company headquartered in New Jersey?
10. What city has a similar name as a province of Canada?

3. *Our Town,* by Thornton Wilder
4. Dartmouth
5. Notches
6. Massachusetts; in 1679 it became a separate colony.
7. Robert Frost's
8. *On Golden Pond*
9. It holds the first primaries in the nation.
10. Franklin Pierce, American president

The Garden State, New Jersey // Answers

1. Atlantic City, although since 2006 the pageant has been held in Las Vegas
2. Thomas Edison
3. George Washington crossing the Delaware
4. Princeton
5. Saltwater taffy
6. Trenton
7. A baseball field
8. The Seeing Eye
9. Campbell
10. New Brunswick, Canada; and Brunswick, Georgia

★ Land of Enchantment, New Mexico

1. What is the state bird (even though it doesn't go "beep-beep")?
2. What big city is seat of Bernalillo County, New Mexico's most populous?
3. The Old Spanish Trail ran from Los Angeles to what city?
4. The state has the nation's highest percentage of what ethnic group?
5. The famous Philmont Ranch is operated by what boys' association?
6. What famous cavern was once named Bat Cave?
7. One of the state's most visited sites has a name meaning "beans." What is it?
8. What are the main items on display at the Million Dollar Museum?
9. The majestic waterfall near Carlsbad is named for what famous chief?
10. The College of Santa Fe has its theatre center named for what gracious red-haired movie queen of the 1940s?

★ The Empire State, New York

1. What city has been called City of Brotherly Shove?
2. If you are riding the *Maid of the Mist* boat, where are you?
3. What New York street was originally a cow path running through the "bouweries" (farms)?
4. What redheaded TV comedienne hailed from Jamestown?
5. What implement of execution was first used in Auburn Prison in 1890?
6. What household product is associated with Corning, New York?
7. What New York City transport used to be called "the world's greatest five-cent ride"?
8. What persecuted French religious group founded the town of New Palz?
9. What game began in America when John Reid formed the St. Andrews Club in Yonkers in 1888?
10. What enormous statue arrived in New York in 214 packing cases in June 1885? (Hint: torch)

QUESTIONS

Land of Enchantment, New Mexico // Answers

1. The roadrunner
2. Albuquerque
3. Santa Fe, capital of New Mexico
4. Native Americans; they are 9 percent of the state population.
5. The Boy Scouts; it is their largest camp in the U.S.
6. Carlsbad Caverns, which (like many caves) is a home for bats
7. The fascinating Frijoles Canyon; *frijole* is Spanish for "bean."
8. Dolls and dollhouses, oddly enough
9. Sitting Bull
10. Greer Garson, famous for *Mrs. Miniver* and other films

The Empire State, New York // Answers

1. New York City, what else?
2. Niagara Falls
3. Broadway
4. Lucille Ball
5. The electric chair
6. Glass, naturally
7. The Staten Island ferry
8. The Huguenots, Protestants who were expelled from France in the 1600s
9. Golf, which had been brought over (naturally) from Scotland
10. The Statue of Liberty

★ The Tar Heel State, North Carolina

1. What two great Americans have a memorial at Kill Devil Hills?
2. What (now controversial) plant is North Carolina's chief crop?
3. What is the distinction of Virginia Dare, born on Roanoke Island in 1587?
4. What college town is known as the City of Medicine?
5. What slang expression comes from the name of Buncombe County?
6. What awesome 250-room chateau was built in Asheville by the Vanderbilts?
7. Bath was the occasional home of what infamous pirate?
8. What famous event took place in 1590 on Roanoke Island?
9. *Horn in the West* is an outdoor drama telling the tale of what famous American backwoodsman?
10. What part of the state is the Graveyard of the Atlantic?

★ The Sioux State, North Dakota

1. What large, edible flower is a key crop in North Dakota?
2. Who receives all the state's profits from gambling?
3. What tree, almost destroyed by disease, is the state tree?
4. Bismarck, the capital, was named for the chancellor of Germany. Why?
5. What author of best-selling westerns was a North Dakota man?
6. The annual Norsk Hostfest honors what immigrant group?
7. The Fork Union Trading Post commemorates what frontier trade?
8. What ill-fated army man was the commander of Fort Abraham Lincoln?
9. Fargo has a museum devoted to what baseball legend?
10. What lovely garden sits astride the U.S.-Canada border?

★ The Buckeye State, Ohio

1. Canton, Ohio, has the Hall of Fame of what major sport?
2. Ohio has what vegetable juice as its state drink?

QUESTIONS

The Tar Heel State, North Carolina // Answers

1. Aviation pioneers Orville and Wilbur Wright, who did their first flights nearby
2. Tobacco
3. She was the first English child born in America.
4. Durham, home to Duke University's famous medical school and hospital
5. The word *bunkum*, meaning "nonsense"
6. The Biltmore estate, now open to tourists
7. Edward Teach, better known as Blackbeard; when not plundering in the Caribbean, Teach lived in Bath.
8. The mysterious disappearance of the English colony established there in 1587; this was the famous "Lost Colony."
9. Daniel Boone; appropriately, the drama is held at Boone, North Carolina.
10. The islands known as the Outer Banks; numerous ships have been wrecked in the treacherous waters nearby.

The Sioux State, North Dakota // Answers

1. Sunflowers, a source of both seeds and oil
2. Nonprofit and charitable organizations
3. The American elm, almost wiped out by Dutch elm disease
4. Locals hoped to attract German investment in railroads passing through the area.
5. Louis L'Amour
6. The Norwegians
7. The fur trade
8. George Custer; it was his last command before he went to his "last stand" at Little Bighorn.
9. Roger Maris; Fargo was his hometown.
10. The International Peace Garden, a 2,300-acre landscaped park; the U.S. part is in North Dakota.

The Buckeye State, Ohio // Answers

1. Pro football
2. Tomato juice (It could have had a V8!)

ANSWERS

3. Ohio's shoreline stretches 262 miles along what Great Lake?
4. What bar soap that floats was invented in Cincinnati?
5. Ohio State University and the state capitol are both in what city?
6. Cleveland is the site of what music museum, opened in 1995?
7. A replica of whose bicycle shop is in Dayton's Carillon Park?
8. Rubber companies Goodrich, Goodyear, Firestone, and General Tire are all in what city?
9. What pleasant city once had the nickname Porkopolis?
10. Evangelist Charles Finney was president of what prestigious Ohio college?

★ The Sooner State, Oklahoma

1. What was the original name for the territory that became Oklahoma?
2. What universally loved comic was known as Oklahoma's Favorite Son?
3. What evangelist founded a university, named for himself, in 1963?
4. What hearty American dish is featured in a Tulsa cook-off every September?
5. What hulking frontier beast is the state animal?
6. Berwyn changed its name to honor what cowboy actor and singer?
7. Fort Sill has the burial place of what infamous Apache leader?
8. What country singer made Muskogee world-famous with his "Okie from Muskogee"?
9. Okmulgee is the world center for what type of nut? (Hint: pies)
10. Shawnee was the hometown of what world-famous Native American athlete?

★ The Beaver State, Oregon

1. What famous lake occupies the base of a volcano?
2. What commodity first attracted settlers to Oregon?
3. What major city was founded by Methodist missionary Jason Lee?

3. Erie
4. Ivory, invented by Procter & Gamble
5. Columbus
6. The Rock and Roll Hall of Fame
7. The Wright brothers; they were pedalers before they were fliers.
8. Akron
9. Cincinnati, once well known as a pork-packing center
10. Oberlin; Finney, the Billy Graham of his day, served as president of the college from 1851 until 1866.

The Sooner State, Oklahoma // Answers

1. The Indian Territory
2. Will Rogers
3. Oral Roberts; it is in Tulsa.
4. Chili, naturally
5. The buffalo, or bison, naturally
6. Gene Autry; the town is now Autry.
7. Geronimo, who died at the fort
8. Merle Haggard
9. Pecans; over 5 million pounds are harvested annually, and there is a Pecan Festival every June.
10. Jim Thorpe, football player and Olympic medalist

The Beaver State, Oregon // Answers

1. Crater Lake; the volcano was known as Mount Mazano.
2. Furs
3. Salem, the capital

The Beaver State, Oregon, continued . . .

4. What town is named for an early fur trade entrepreneur?
5. What foreign power fired upon Fort Stevens in 1942?
6. What remarkable piece of metal was found in 1913 by George Armstrong?
7. What popular seasonal flower is a key product of Brookings? (Hint: eggs)
8. Depoe Bay claims it is the world capital for watching what sea creatures?
9. The lovely Fleet of Flowers Ceremony on the coast honors what people?
10. What sea creatures could you see in the caverns near Florence?

★ The Keystone State, Pennsylvania

1. Flight 93 National Memorial commemorates what dramatic event?
2. What all-American sport was first played professionally at Latrobe in 1895?
3. What glowing bug is the state insect?
4. What emblems did the Pennsylvania Dutch paint on barns to ward off evil spirits?
5. About half of all Pennsylvanians live in what two cities' metro areas?
6. In 1859, what natural resource was struck sixty-nine feet below Titusville?
7. Moravians seeking religious freedom founded what biblically named town?
8. What film star saw a museum opened in his honor in 1995 in his hometown of Indiana? (Hint: it's a wonderful life)
9. What globe-trotting evangelist's statue is on the campus of the University of Pennsylvania?
10. Who claimed that the new colony would be a "holy experiment"?

★ Little Rhody, Rhode Island

1. The (domestic) state bird is named for the state. What is it?
2. What colonial pastor established Providence as "a shelter for persons distressed in conscience"?
3. What Ivy League school was named for a donor who contributed $5,000?

4. Astoria, named for John Jacob Astor
5. Japan; firing from a submarine, the Japanese were the first nation to fire upon the forty-eight states since the War of 1812.
6. The Armstrong Gold Nugget, weighing more than eighty ounces
7. Easter lilies
8. Whales, fairly common in that area
9. Those who have lost their lives at sea
10. Sea lions

The Keystone State, Pennsylvania // Answers

1. The crash of United Airlines flight 93 on September 11, 2001; the passengers on the hijacked plane prevented the hijackers from hitting their intended target, although sadly everyone on the plane died.
2. Football
3. The firefly (one of the rare insects that people actually like)
4. Hex signs
5. Philadelphia's and Pittsburgh's
6. Petroleum, the first oil strike in America
7. Bethlehem, founded in 1741
8. Jimmy Stewart
9. George Whitefield, an Englishman who preached to huge crowds on both sides of the Atlantic in the colonial era; Benjamin Franklin, who helped establish the university, was an admirer of Whitefield.
10. The colony's Quaker founder, William Penn, who wanted religious freedom—a noted change from Europe in that era

Little Rhody, Rhode Island // Answers

1. The Rhode Island red, a breed of chicken
2. Roger Williams, who advocated religious liberty in the new settlement; he had been booted out of Massachusetts for his religious views.
3. Brown University (In 1804, when he gave the gift, $5,000 went further than it now does.)

Little Rhody, Rhode Island, continued . . .

4. What is the full official name of the state?
5. The smallest state has the shortest state motto, only four letters. What?
6. What kind of fruit is a Rhode Island Greening?
7. What seaport became *the* summer place for the rich after the Civil War?
8. The first church of what denomination was founded in the state? (Hint: water)
9. Narragansett holds a *winter* competition for what unlikely water sport?
10. What Christian group's three-hundred-year-old church could you visit in Newport?

⋆ The Palmetto State, South Carolina

1. What resort town is the state's most popular beach area?
2. The state bird, named for the state itself, is what?
3. What war began with the firing on Fort Sumter in April 1861?
4. What all-male college became the center of a national controversy in 1995?
5. What three-hundred-year-old city was the first city in the U.S. to have a chamber of commerce?
6. Who was the state named for?
7. What industrial town is the Textile Center of the World?
8. Parris Island is training ground for which branch of the U.S. military?
9. What conservative Christian college bills itself as the "world's most unusual university"?
10. What plant, used to make a blue dye, was a major crop for many decades?

⋆ The Coyote State, South Dakota

1. What enormous sculpture did Gutzon Borglum begin in 1927?
2. What (formerly) wild town was home to such characters as Wild Bill Hickok and Calamity Jane?
3. What edible game bird, imported from Asia, is the state bird?

QUESTIONS

4. The State of Rhode Island and Providence Plantations
5. The word *Hope*
6. An apple
7. Newport, with its palatial "cottages"
8. Baptist, founded in 1638
9. Surfing; the New England Surfing Championship is held in February.
10. The Quakers, or Friends; their meeting house dates to 1699.

The Palmetto State, South Carolina // Answers

1. Myrtle Beach
2. The Carolina wren
3. The Civil War, of course; the fort is on an island near Charleston.
4. The Citadel, the state military college in Charleston; the controversy concerned the admission of a female student to the all-male school.
5. Charleston
6. King Charles II of England, ruler when the colony was founded in 1663 (The name *Charles* in Latin is *Carolus*.)
7. Greenville
8. The marines; their recruit depot has been on the island since 1915.
9. Bob Jones University, in Greenville
10. Indigo; modern chemical dyes have made indigo obsolete.

The Coyote State, South Dakota // Answers

1. The four presidents sculpture at Mount Rushmore
2. Deadwood
3. The ring-necked pheasant

The Coyote State, South Dakota, continued . . .

4. What future national park was discovered because it whistled?
5. How did Mobridge get its name?
6. Whose faces would you see on a six-thousand-foot mountain in the Black Hills?
7. What state was admitted to the Union the same day as South Dakota?
8. What huge building, done in Byzantine architecture, is decorated with colored corn?
9. Near Mt. Rushmore is a wax museum honoring what group of men?
10. The town of Lead was actually a center for mining what?

★ The Volunteer State, Tennessee

1. What breed of horse do we associate with Tennessee?
2. What famous home is in Memphis at 3797 Elvis Presley Boulevard?
3. The 1982 World's Fair "Energy Turns the World" was held in what mountain city?
4. What "leisure" crop is the leading cash crop of Tennessee?
5. What large city is situated on picturesque Lookout Mountain?
6. Gatlinburg is the "Gateway to" what famous national park?
7. In 1977 Congress officially designated what city as Home of the Blues?
8. In 1776, Tennessee became a county of what eastern state?
9. What large denomination has many of its national offices in Nashville?
10. What present-day radio show began in 1925 as the "WSM Barn Dance"?

★ The Lone Star State, Texas

1. Texas, known as a friendly place, has what one-word state motto?
2. What hero served as Tennessee governor in the 1820s and Texas governor in the 1850s?
3. What leader, born in 1793, has been called the Father of Texas?
4. Former Texas Ranger John Reid became what masked Western hero?

4. Wind Cave in South Dakota; the cave, which blows air in or out, was first noticed in 1881 because settlers heard the whistling sound.
5. A contraction of "bridge on the Missouri," or, even shorter, "Mo. bridge"
6. Four presidents'—Washington, Jefferson, Lincoln, and Theodore Roosevelt; this is Mount Rushmore.
7. North Dakota, naturally; both were admitted in 1889.
8. The Corn Palace, one of America's unique buildings
9. U.S. presidents, of course; the Parade of Presidents also has other historical figures.
10. Gold

The Volunteer State, Tennessee // Answers

1. The Tennessee Walking Horse, of course
2. Presley's home, Graceland
3. Knoxville, which still has the Sunsphere from the fair
4. Tobacco
5. Chattanooga
6. The Great Smoky Mountains
7. Memphis
8. North Carolina; the entire area at that time was Washington County. The state became independent in 1796.
9. The Southern Baptists
10. The Grand Ole Opry

The Lone Star State, Texas // Answers

1. Friendship
2. Sam Houston
3. Stephen Austin
4. The Lone Ranger

5. Beginning in 1821, what nation did Texas belong to?
6. What pro baseball team plays in Arlington Stadium?
7. Austin has a museum devoted to what short-story author, known for his "twist" endings?
8. Aside from Hawaii cities, the nation's southernmost city is what?
9. What were the citizens of Corsicana drilling for when they struck oil in 1894?
10. What Texas town is named for a breed of cattle?

★ The Beehive State, Utah

1. What enormous Utah church has 375 people in its choir?
2. What religious leader had more than twenty-five wives?
3. What lake is so salty that only one species of shrimp lives in it?
4. The Beehive State has what appropriate one-word state motto?
5. What communication system arrived in Salt Lake City in 1860?
6. What national park is named for rock domes that resemble the U.S. Capitol?
7. What distinctive color are the windswept sand dunes near Kanab?
8. What kind of material is sculpted in Park City's annual sculpture contest?
9. What bird is honored in a monument in Salt Lake City?
10. The Bonneville Salt Flats are used for what type of sport?

★ The Green Mountain State, Vermont

1. What laid-back president was born on the Fourth of July in Plymouth, Vermont?
2. What wild (and edible) grass is the state flower of Vermont?
3. The Connecticut River separates Vermont from what state?
4. Rutland has a museum devoted to what popular New England sweet?

QUESTIONS

5. Mexico, which had just won independence from Spain
6. The Texas Rangers
7. O. Henry
8. Brownsville, Texas
9. Water (Call it serendipity.)
10. Hereford

The Beehive State, Utah // Answers

1. The Mormon Tabernacle in Salt Lake City
2. Brigham Young, leader of the Mormons in Utah
3. The Great Salt Lake
4. "Industry"
5. The Pony Express
6. Capitol Reef, in Utah
7. Pink; they can be seen at Coral Pink Sand Dunes State Park.
8. Snow
9. The seagull, the state bird; gulls saved the crops from crickets in 1848.
10. Auto racing; some of the world's fastest cars race against the clock on the Flats, hoping to set new speed records.

The Green Mountain State, Vermont // Answers

1. Calvin Coolidge, born in 1872 in a store that is still operating
2. Red clover (edible for *animals* anyway)
3. New Hampshire (You didn't think it was Connecticut, did you?)
4. Maple syrup and sugar; Rutland has the New England Maple Museum.

QUESTIONS

The Green Mountain State, Vermont, continued . . .

5. The small town of St. Albans was raided by what nation's soldiers in 1864?
6. In Waterbury you can tour the plant of what popular ice-cream company?
7. What short-lived nation came into being on July 8, 1777?
8. What Revolutionary War band was headquartered in Bennington?
9. In Arlington you can see hundreds of magazine covers by what famed American artist?
10. The 260-mile Long Trail winds through what picturesque mountains?

★ The Old Dominion, Virginia

1. What enormous geometrically shaped federal building is in Arlington?
2. By the 1630s the Virginia Company exported 1.5 million pounds per year of what crop?
3. The FBI academy is in what oddly named Virginia town?
4. What glamorous actress was for a time married to Senator John Warner?
5. What Virginia-born president designed the capitol building in Richmond?
6. Why is Virginia called Mother of Presidents?
7. What queen of England was Virginia named for?
8. Liberty University was founded by what noted TV preacher?
9. The world's largest textile mill, Dan River, is found in what city?
10. The late-summer festival in Virginia Beach is named for what ancient sea god?

★ The Evergreen State, Washington

1. What destructive volcano made headlines in 1980?
2. What national park has the wettest climate in the forty-eight contiguous states?
3. According to the song, the bluest skies you've ever seen are in what city?
4. Gonzaga University has the Crosby Center, named for what famous singing alumnus?

5. The Confederacy's; they robbed the town's banks and fled to Canada with $200,000.
6. Ben & Jerry's; free samples are given.
7. The Republic of Vermont, which existed until Vermont officially joined the U.S. in 1791
8. The Green Mountain Boys, led by Ethan Allen
9. Norman Rockwell, famous for his *Saturday Evening Post* covers
10. The Green Mountains

The Old Dominion, Virginia // Answers

1. The Pentagon
2. Tobacco
3. Quantico
4. Elizabeth Taylor
5. Thomas Jefferson, third president
6. Eight U.S. presidents were born there. No other state has produced so many.
7. Elizabeth I, the unmarried and supposedly *virgin* queen; she was ruling when England's first attempts at settlement in America were made.
8. Jerry Falwell
9. Danville, which is on (surprise!) the Dan River
10. Neptune

The Evergreen State, Washington // Answers

1. Mount St. Helens
2. Olympic, averaging about 134 inches of precipitation per year
3. Seattle
4. Bing Crosby, of course; the center has a Crosbyana Room with Bing's Academy Award, gold records, and other memorabilia.

ANSWERS

QUESTIONS

The Evergreen State, Washington, continued . . .

5. What oddly named city is called "the city they liked so much they named it twice"?
6. The Ski to Sea Festival involves what forms of racing?
7. What city's George Washington Park is named for a black man?
8. What mighty river of the Northwest is tamed by the Grand Coulee Dam?
9. What bland vegetable is the center of a festival in Pullman?
10. What man-made project turned dry areas of Washington State into rich farmland?

☆ The Mountain State, West Virginia

1. What notorious feud began in 1882 with the murder of Ellison Hatfield?
2. What summer holiday was first observed in West Virginia in 1908?
3. What much loved Confederate general was born in Clarksburg in 1824?
4. What town was the target of a raid by antislavery radical John Brown in 1859?
5. What was the state's proposed name when it seceded from Virginia in 1861?
6. White Sulphur Springs has a spring festival honoring what pesky garden weed?
7. What was the attraction of visitors to Berkeley Springs?
8. In what unusual quarters is the Youth Museum of Beckley?
9. What valuable energy source was discovered here in 1742?
10. What key city lies on the Kanawha River?

☆ The Badger State, Wisconsin

1. As America's Dairyland, Wisconsin has what state domestic animal?
2. What metropolis has the Pabst Mansion, Pabst Theatre, and Pabst Brewery?
3. How did the Apostle Islands get their name?
4. What city has a lovely French name meaning "clear water"?
5. What noted clothing manufacturer is headquartered in Oshkosh?

The Evergreen State, Washington // Answers // continued . . .

5. Walla Walla; the name is Indian and means "many waters."
6. Skiing, running, canoeing, biking, and sailboating
7. Centralia, Washington's; the park is named not for the first president but for a former slave with the same name. He went west and founded Centralia.
8. The Columbia
9. Lentils; the National Lentil Festival is held in September.
10. The Grand Coulee Dam, which allows the waters of the wild Columbia River to serve the useful purpose of irrigation

The Mountain State, West Virginia // Answers

1. The Hatfield-McCoy feud, which lasted eight years
2. Father's Day, which was not officially a national holiday until 1972
3. Thomas "Stonewall" Jackson; at the time of his birth, Clarksburg was still in Virginia; West Virginia was not a separate state.
4. Harpers Ferry; Brown's gang intended to raid the federal arsenal and then arm the slaves, which would lead to a slave revolt.
5. Kanawha, the name of a major river in the area
6. The dandelion (which is a weed or flower or vegetable, depending on your point of view)
7. The mineral springs, with their supposed healing powers
8. Four railroad boxcars
9. Coal, long a mainstay of the economy
10. The capital, Charleston

The Badger State, Wisconsin // Answers

1. The cow (surprise!)
2. Milwaukee, which is famous for producing . . .
3. Their early discoverers thought there were twelve of them.
4. Eau Claire
5. OshKosh B'gosh (what else?)

The Badger State, Wisconsin, continued . . .

6. What kind of creatures are the focus of the Honey Acres Museum?
7. If you are riding in an amphibious vehicle called a Dells Duck, where are you?
8. Monroe is known as the center of what cheese-making industry?
9. What pro football team plays some of its exhibition games in Milwaukee?
10. What city sits on a narrow piece of land between Lake Monona and Lake Mendota?

★ The Cowboy State, Wyoming

1. What famous geyser erupts every seventy-four minutes?
2. What "hole" in Wyoming is one of America's main ski resorts?
3. What spirited animal is on Wyoming license plates?
4. What eye-catching landmark looks like a giant tree stump, eight hundred feet high?
5. Why is Independence Rock called the Register of the Desert?
6. What very western form of transportation has its own museum in Lusk?
7. The world's largest mineral hot springs are found where?
8. The world's largest geyser basin is in what national park?
9. What distinctive type of ranch was first established in 1904?
10. What is distinctive about the Rocky Mountain Rodeo in Rock Springs?

★ A Capital City, D.C.

1. What memorial to an Asian war was dedicated in July 1995?
2. What Asian country donated the two giant pandas in the National Zoo?
3. What president's memorial, with thirty-six Greek columns, has its back to the Potomac River?
4. What name is given to the freeway that wraps around D.C.?
5. What curious geometrical shape is the Hirschhorn Museum?
6. The FBI building in D.C. is named for what longtime FBI director?

6. Bees, of course; the museum is devoted to bee-keeping and honey production.
7. In Wisconsin Dells; the Ducks provide land-and-water tours of the Wisconsin River.
8. Swiss cheese
9. The Green Bay Packers
10. The capital, Madison

The Cowboy State, Wyoming // Answers

1. Old Faithful, in Yellowstone; the 74 is an average; the geyser has varied from 30 to 120 minutes between eruptions.
2. Jackson Hole
3. A bucking horse
4. The Devil's Tower National Monument
5. It has been inscribed with more than fifty thousand pioneer names.
6. The stagecoach
7. At the appropriately named town of Thermopolis
8. Yellowstone, famed for the Old Faithful geyser
9. A dude ranch—for weekend cowboys and others
10. It is an all-girl rodeo. The rodeo also includes a goat-tying competition.

A Capital City, D.C. // Answers

1. The Korean War Memorial
2. China
3. Abraham Lincoln's
4. The Capital Beltway, usually just called the Beltway
5. A cylinder; the building aroused controversy when it opened in 1974.
6. J. Edgar Hoover

A Capital City, D.C., continued . . .

7. In what museum could you see the Wright brothers' plane and the *Apollo 11* command module?
8. If you wished to see the Declaration of Independence and the original Constitution, where would you go?
9. Where could you see the First Ladies Collection?
10. What war saw the burning of most of D.C.'s public buildings?

QUESTIONS

7. The National Air and Space Museum
8. To the National Archives
9. The National Museum of American History
10. The War of 1812

PART THIRTEEN

THINGS OF THE SPIRIT

✯ The Bible in America

Many of America's early settlers were Europeans fleeing religious persecution. Not surprisingly, the Bible had (and still has) a massive influence on American life.

1. What popular horror novelist began publishing biblical novels in 2005?
2. What recent president said, "The Bible is pretty good about keeping your ego in check"?
3. What Bible version was the best-selling nonfiction book of 1972 and 1973? (Hint: alive)
4. What biblical epic starring Charlton Heston was the top movie moneymaker of the 1950s?
5. What organization founded in 1898 is famous for placing Bibles in hotel rooms?
6. What dictionary maker published a "corrected" King James Version in which he pointed out words that had changed in meaning since the first publication of the KJV?
7. What American president published an edition of the Gospels that left out all the miracles?
8. What religious group famous for door-to-door evangelism publishes the New World version of the Bible?
9. What president during the 1800s said that reading the Bible was "the best cure for the blues"?
10. William Murray, author of *My Life without God,* was the son of what anti-Bible crusader?
11. What version of the Bible did the Pilgrims bring with them in the 1620s?
12. In what Pennsylvania city could you see the Dead Sea, the Jordan River, and the Sea of Galilee?
13. What phenomenally popular translation was published in 1978?
14. Which religious sect uses the Bible and a book titled *Science and Health, with Key to the Scriptures?*
15. What was the first book printed in America? (No, not the Bible, but you're on the right track.)
16. What famous movie director directed three lush epics about biblical subjects?
17. What state capital city named for a biblical character was originally named Pig's Eye?

1. Anne Rice, author of a series of vampire novels; in 2005, she published *Christ the Lord: Out of Egypt,* and in 2008, *Christ the Lord: The Road to Cana.*
2. George W. Bush
3. *The Living Bible,* a paraphrase by Kenneth Taylor and published by Tyndale House
4. *The Ten Commandments;* Heston played Moses.
5. The Gideons
6. Noah Webster, who published his "corrected" Bible in 1833
7. Thomas Jefferson
8. The Jehovah's Witnesses
9. Abraham Lincoln
10. Madalyn Murray O'Hair, who played a key role in the Supreme Court decision banning Bible reading in public schools; interestingly, her son William became a Christian.
11. The *Geneva Bible,* a translation made in 1560; though the King James Version was published in 1611, it was not yet popular when the Pilgrims came to America.
12. Pittsburgh; they're in the Rodef Shalom Biblical Botanical Garden.
13. The New International Version
14. Christian Science, founded in America by Mary Baker Eddy
15. *The Bay Psalm Book,* published in Massachusetts in the 1600s; it consisted of rhyming paraphrases of the Psalms.
16. Cecil B. DeMille, who directed *The Ten Commandments, Samson and Delilah,* and *The King of Kings*
17. Saint Paul

The Bible in America, continued...

18. If you wanted to see a 1456 Gutenberg Bible in Washington, D.C., where would you go?
19. The year 2011 was the four hundredth anniversary of what significant event?
20. What world-renowned evangelist (and former shoe salesman) founded a famous Bible college in Chicago?
21. What breakfast cereal originally had the biblical name Elijah's Manna?
22. What Revolutionary War hero wrote a book denying that the Bible is the Word of God?
23. In what year was the first English Bible published in America?
24. Who were the "Bible communists"?
25. What Bible passage was ordered removed from Kentucky public school classrooms after the 1980 Supreme Court decision *Stone v. Graham*?
26. What leader of a Christian sect deduced (wrongly) from the Bible that the Second Coming of Jesus would occur in 1844?
27. Which state was planned by its founders to be a "Bible commonwealth"?
28. Which original Supreme Court justice helped support the American Bible Society in its early days?
29. Which great statesman defended the Bible's authority in the famous Scopes evolution trial in 1925?
30. In the years before the Civil War, what Bible passages did the abolition-ists use to prove slavery was unchristian?
31. What is the claim to fame (biblically speaking) of New York commis-sioner of education James Edward Allen?
32. What 1984 law gave public school students the right to hold religious meetings and study the Bible in schools—*after* class hours?
33. What organization, famous for distributing free or inexpensive Bibles, was founded in 1816?
34. In 1881 the Hare family of Philadelphia published the *Christian Spiritual Bible*. What strange teaching, popular today, was behind this version?
35. What Bible passage was behind the Salem, Massachusetts, witch trials in the 1600s?
36. What was the distinction of *The New England Primer*, the first children's spelling book published in America?
37. The first American Bible in a European language was not in English but in what language?

18. The Library of Congress
19. The 1611 publication of the King James Version, the most popular English version
20. D. L. Moody, founder of the Moody Bible Institute
21. Post Toasties
22. Ethan Allen, leader of the famous band the Green Mountain Boys from Vermont; Allen wrote a book, published in 1784, titled *Reason the Only Oracle of Man.* In it he discussed his religious beliefs, among which was his belief that human reason made a divinely revealed Bible unnecessary.
23. 1777—significantly, the year after the Declaration of Independence was signed
24. They are better known as the Oneida Community, founded in Oneida, New York, in 1848 by John Humphrey Noyes. The commune's practices were highly questionable (to put it mildly), as they practiced communal marriage and various other deeds that put them outside the mainstream of Christianity.
25. The Ten Commandments; the 1980 decision was that the state of Kentucky (and, thus, any state) could not mandate the posting of the Ten Commandments in public schools.
26. William Miller, founder of the Seventh-day Adventists
27. Massachusetts; the original Puritan settlers in the 1600s wanted the colony to order itself according to biblical principles.
28. John Jay, who is also famous as one of the authors of *The Federalist Papers*
29. William Jennings Bryan, who had served as secretary of state under Woodrow Wilson
30. None; the Bible does not directly condemn slavery—a fact that slave-holding Christians in the South were much aware of.
31. Allen (who died in 1971) ordered the removal of the Ten Commandments from New York schools.
32. The Equal Access Law
33. The American Bible Society
34. Reincarnation; people living at that time often referred to it as the "reincarnation Bible."
35. Exodus 22:18: "Thou shalt not suffer a witch to live." This is not, by the way, the only Bible passage to condemn sorcery and the occult.
36. It taught the letters of the alphabet by linking each letter to a biblical person or idea. For example, the entry for *A* reads "In Adam's fall / We sinned all." The *Z* entry reads "Zacchaeus he / Did climb the tree / Our Lord to see." (Quite a difference from "*A* is for apple, *B* is for boy, *C* is for . . .")
37. German, published in Pennsylvania in 1740, when all English-language Bibles were still required to be printed in England

The Bible in America, continued . . .

38. Hiram Bingham, a missionary from Vermont, translated the Bible for what islands (which later became a state)?
39. What organization, with its headquarters in Yankee territory, supplied Bibles for Confederate soldiers?
40. What Old Testament book influenced Abraham Lincoln to issue the Emancipation Proclamation, freeing all slaves?

⋆ Churches, Cathedrals, Chapels, Shrines

Churches are places to worship God. They're also used for weddings, funerals . . . sometimes even political meetings. People argue about whether America is a "Christian nation," but one thing's for sure: churches have played a key role in our heritage.

1. Whose sermons are broadcast from the enormous Lakewood Church in Houston?
2. Which California church is longer than a football field and composed of more than ten thousand panes of glass?
3. What Christian denomination, famous for helping the poor, claims that the open air is "our greatest cathedral"?
4. What historic southern city was known as the "Holy City" because of the many church spires on the city skyline?
5. The beautiful cathedral in New Orleans's Jackson Square is named for a king of France. Who?
6. The First Presbyterian Church in Springfield, Illinois, has a pew used by what famous political family?
7. New York Avenue Presbyterian Church in D.C. was pastored by one of America's best-known twentieth-century preachers. Who?
8. What ballistic souvenir does St. Paul's church in Norfolk, Virginia, keep from the Revolutionary War?
9. The Shrine of the Sun in Colorado Springs is a memorial to what lovable cowboy entertainer?

38. The Hawaiian Islands; he published the Hawaiian translation in 1839.
39. The American Bible Society, headquartered in New York; there was also, in the Civil War years, a Confederate Bible Society.
40. Exodus, with its story of the Hebrew slaves being freed from Egypt; Lincoln claimed to be especially influenced by Exodus 6:5: "I [God] have also heard the groaning of the children of Israel, whom the Egyptians keep in bondage; and I have remembered my covenant."

Churches, Cathedrals, Chapels, Shrines // Answers

1. Joel Osteen
2. The Crystal Cathedral, founded by pastor Robert Schuller
3. The Salvation Army
4. Charleston, South Carolina
5. Louis—as in Louisiana; the king, Louis IX, is also recognized as a saint by the Catholic church, and the cathedral is known as St. Louis Cathedral. It is probably one of the most photographed churches in America.
6. The Abraham Lincoln family, who attended the church until Lincoln moved to Washington
7. Peter Marshall, subject of the book and movie *A Man Called Peter*
8. A British cannonball, embedded in the church's wall
9. Will Rogers

Churches, Cathedrals, Chapels, Shrines, continued . . .

10. If you are attending a French-language service in the historic Huguenot Church, where are you?

11. Historic Christ Episcopal Church had George Washington, Betsy Ross, and Benjamin Franklin among its worshipers. In what Pennsylvania city is it?

12. The lovely St. Matthew's Cathedral in D.C. was the site of what assassinated president's funeral?

13. What phenomenal shopping center in Minnesota has had more than five thousand weddings (as of mid-2011) inside it?

14. Thomas Road Baptist Church in Lynchburg, Virginia, was long pastored by what noted TV preacher?

15. The Shrine of the Immaculate Conception, the largest Catholic church in the U.S., is in what city?

16. The beautiful Gothic chapel at the University of Pittsburgh was named for a local food manufacturer. Who? (Hint: ketchup)

17. The National Shrine of St. Dymphna in Ohio is a memorial to people with what sort of illness?

18. The oldest Methodist church in the U.S. is St. George's in what historic northeastern city?

19. Washington, D.C.'s enormous National City Christian Church is of what denomination?

20. Charleston, South Carolina's famous St. Michael's Episcopal Church is a noted landmark in the city. Its famous steeple was painted black during the Civil War. Why?

21. Cincinnati has an oddly named Roman Catholic cathedral. What disciple of Jesus does it honor?

22. The oldest cathedral in the U.S. is the Basilica of the Assumption in what eastern city? (Hint: orioles)

23. Built in the 1600s, the San Miguel Mission is the oldest church still in use in the U.S. Where is it?

24. In what beautiful Wyoming park can you see the log Chapel of the Transfiguration?

25. The historic Gloria Dei church, Philadelphia's oldest church, was of what denomination?

26. What Episcopal church in D.C. is known as the "Church of the Presidents"?

27. The largest Quaker church in the world is in what historically Quaker city?

10. Charleston, South Carolina; the beautiful old church now uses English in the services also.
11. Philadelphia
12. John F. Kennedy's
13. The Mall of America, which has its own Chapel of Love
14. Jerry Falwell
15. Washington, D.C.
16. Heinz, maker of ketchup, tomato sauce, etc.
17. Mental; St. Dymphna is the patron saint of people with mental or nervous disorders.
18. Philadelphia; it was founded in 1769.
19. The Disciples of Christ
20. Residents were afraid the highly visible steeple would make an easy target for Yankee cannons.
21. Peter; the church is called St. Peter in Chains Cathedral, referring to Peter's imprisonment (Acts 12).
22. Baltimore, Maryland
23. Santa Fe, New Mexico
24. Grand Teton
25. Lutheran; it is known as the Old Swedes church.
26. St. John's Church; many presidents have attended services there.
27. Philadelphia; actually, Quakers don't have churches—they have "meeting houses." This one is the Arch Street Meeting House.

Churches, Cathedrals, Chapels, Shrines, continued . . .

28. What famed Catholic cathedral, which can seat 2,400, is at Fifth Avenue and Fiftieth Street in New York?

29. The Chapel in the Hills in South Dakota is modeled on the churches of what nation?

30. The Boal Mansion in Pennsylvania has a four-hundred-year-old chapel that belonged to what famous explorer?

31. The Chapel of the Presidents in D.C. is in what denomination's National Church?

32. The Washington Memorial Chapel can be found at what famous Pennsylvania site?

33. Seaman's Bethel is a "Whaleman's Chapel" built like a ship. In what historic whaling port is it?

34. What huge Manhattan church, under construction since 1892, will be the world's largest Gothic building when completed?

35. New York Avenue Presbyterian Church in D.C. has a marker on the pew of a famous president who attended there. Who?

36. D.C.'s beautiful Cathedral Church of St. Peter and St. Paul is better known by what name?

37. What unpleasant news did Confederate president Jefferson Davis receive while worshiping at Richmond's St. Paul's Church?

38. What multisite suburban Chicago church was first in the world to install enormous LED video screens in the sanctuary?

★ Religious Notables

1. What megachurch pastor did *Newsweek* dub one of the "15 People Who Make America Great" in 2006?

2. Who, on April 20, 2008, drew a crowd of sixty thousand to Yankee Stadium?

3. What pizza millionaire founded a Christian university in Florida?

4. Evangelist Charles Finney, known as the "Father of Modern Revivalism," also served as president of what elite college?

5. What American colonizer had been kicked out of England's Oxford University for his nonconformist religious views?

28. St. Patrick's

29. Norway; the Lutheran church is a replica of a Norwegian stave church.

30. Christopher Columbus; it was dismantled and brought to the U.S. in 1909. It has several items that belonged to Columbus.

31. Presbyterian

32. Valley Forge; the chapel has Pews of the Patriots.

33. New Bedford, Massachusetts

34. St. John the Divine, an Episcopal cathedral

35. Abraham Lincoln, who attended—but never actually joined—the church

36. The National Cathedral

37. News that he must evacuate Richmond, due to the approach of Union troops; in effect, the message was, "The war's over, Mr. President."

38. Willow Creek Community Church; the church's main site in South Barrington, Illinois, seats more than seven thousand people and has high-definition, fourteen feet by twenty-four feet LED screens.

Religious Notables // Answers

1. Rick Warren, pastor of Saddleback Church in southern California

2. Pope Benedict XVI

3. Tom Monaghan, founder of Domino's as well as Ave Maria University in Naples; Monaghan's religious convictions led some groups to boycott Domino's. He sold the company in 1998 for $1 billion.

4. Oberlin, in Ohio

5. William Penn, later a leader of the Quakers and founder of Pennsylvania

Religious Notables, continued . . .

QUESTIONS

6. What politician, an ordained Baptist minister, plays with a band called Capitol Offense?

7. What religious revival of the 1730s and 1740s had theologian Jonathan Edwards as one of its key movers?

8. What pro baseball player left the game in 1890 and became one of the world's greatest evangelists?

9. What upbeat minister sold millions of copies of *The Power of Positive Thinking*?

10. What Chicago shoe salesman became a world-famous evangelist in the 1870s?

11. What televangelist, college founder, and political activist died in May 2007?

12. The Christian Coalition was founded in 1989 by what televangelist?

13. What dynamic author and speaker broadcasts the program *Enjoying Everyday Life*?

14. Bill Bright, who died in 2003, founded what organization for college students?

15. T. D. Jakes pastors what huge nondenominational church in Dallas?

16. What department store founder, who originally called his stores Golden Rule stores, was noted for his charitable giving to religious groups?

17. What evangelist opened the "City of Faith" medical complex in Tulsa, Oklahoma?

18. What colony was founded in the 1600s because Swedish king Gustavus Adolphus wanted to convert Native Americans to Christianity?

19. The Grand Ole Opry's original home, the Ryman Auditorium, was originally built for what purpose?

20. In 1740 evangelist George Whitefield attracted a crowd of thirty thousand people in what New England city?

21. What televangelist has broadcast *Life Today* for many years?

22. What sad fate befell frontier missionary Marcus Whitman, who helped settle Washington State?

23. Kenneth Taylor, who died in 2005, penned America's best-selling nonfiction book of 1972 and 1973. What was it?

24. Who paid a visit to Billy Graham at his North Carolina home on April 25, 2010?

25. John Wimber, who died in 1997, was the founder of what large network of charismatic churches?

6. Mike Huckabee, former governor of Arkansas
7. The Great Awakening, which swept through all the colonies, particularly New England
8. Billy Sunday
9. Norman Vincent Peale
10. D. L. Moody, who founded Chicago's Moody Bible Institute
11. Jerry Falwell
12. Pat Robertson
13. Joyce Meyer
14. Campus Crusade for Christ
15. The Potter's House
16. J. C. Penney, a minister's son and very devout man
17. Oral Roberts
18. Delaware, which later came under English control
19. Preaching; Ryman, a riverboat manufacturer, constructed a suitable auditorium for Sam Jones, his favorite evangelist.
20. Boston; Whitefield was one of the most acclaimed preachers in the Great Awakening.
21. James Robison
22. He and his wife were killed by Native Americans.
23. *The Living Bible*
24. Barack Obama
25. The Vineyard Fellowship

PART FOURTEEN

AMERICA MONTH BY MONTH

★ January

1. What British leader did George W. Bush award the Presidential Medal of Freedom to in January 2009?
2. David Nelson, who died in January 2011, was the son of what famous sit-com couple of the 1950s?
3. What pastor of a large California church delivered the invocation at the January 2009 inauguration of Barack Obama?
4. Former pro wrestler Jesse Ventura was sworn in as governor of what state in January 1999?
5. In January 2002, which three nations did George W. Bush call the "axis of evil"?
6. What great American artist died in January 2009? (Hint: *Christina's World*)
7. At the January 2002 American Music Awards, what pop idol was dubbed Artist of the Century?
8. What popular political novel published in January 1996 was written by "Anonymous"?
9. What state became the first to ban smoking in restaurants in January 1998?
10. What presidential hopeful said in January 2008, "You campaign in poetry; you govern in prose"?
11. What fitness guru died at age ninety-six in January 2011?
12. What high-profile political wife said in January 2010, "My children are sane"?
13. J. D. Salinger, who died in January 2010, authored what popular novel about a disillusioned teen?
14. Don Budge, who was killed in a car accident in January 2000, was a star in what sport?
15. What baseball legend admitted in January 2010 that in his heyday he had used steroids?
16. What Web site launched in January 1994 was first called David and Jerry's Guide to the World Wide Web?
17. What head of a popular fast-food chain died in January 2002?

1. Tony Blair, former British prime minister
2. Ozzie and Harriet
3. Rick Warren, pastor of Saddleback Church
4. Minnesota
5. Iran, Iraq, and North Korea
6. Andrew Wyeth
7. Michael Jackson
8. *Primary Colors;* it was later revealed that columnist Joe Klein had written it.
9. California
10. Hillary Clinton
11. Jack LaLanne
12. Michelle Obama, on being asked what she was proudest of in her children
13. *The Catcher in the Rye,* published in 1951
14. Tennis
15. Mark McGwire
16. Yahoo!
17. Dave Thomas, founder of Wendy's

★ February

1. What aide to Barack Obama was elected mayor of Chicago in February 2011?
2. FBI agent Robert Hanssen was arrested in February 2001 for spying for what country?
3. What computer mogul took a pie in the face in February 1998 in Belgium?
4. In February 2011, a computer beat two humans on what TV game show?
5. Washington National Airport received what new name in February 1998?
6. What *Looney Tunes* animator died in February 2002 at age eighty-nine?
7. Actor Fess Parker, who died in February 2010, was famous for portraying what two frontiersmen on TV?
8. What "outlaw" country music legend died in February 2002?
9. What controversial woman was dropped as a Jenny Craig weight-loss spokesperson in February 2000?
10. What beloved, deep-voiced radio broadcaster died in February 2009? (Hint: the rest of the story)
11. What scandal-plagued athlete sold his Heisman Trophy for $230,000 in February 1999?
12. In February 2002, what Bush Cabinet member performed a gospel song he had written at an evangelical seminary?
13. What NASCAR racer died in the final lap of the Daytona 500 in February 2001?
14. What popular (and controversial) movie opened, appropriately, on Ash Wednesday, February 25, 2004?
15. What popular Internet video site was launched in February 2005?
16. What "neighborly" host of a long-running children's TV show died in February 2003?

1. Rahm Emanuel, who had been Obama's chief of staff
2. The former Soviet Union; Hanssen was given a life sentence.
3. Bill Gates of Microsoft
4. *Jeopardy;* the IBM computer was named Watson.
5. Ronald Reagan Airport
6. Chuck Jones
7. Davy Crockett and Daniel Boone
8. Waylon Jennings
9. Monica Lewinsky; many TV stations refused to run the ads she appeared in.
10. Paul Harvey
11. O. J. Simpson
12. John Ashcroft, attorney general
13. Dale Earnhardt
14. *The Passion of the Christ,* directed by Mel Gibson
15. YouTube
16. Fred Rogers, better known as "Mister Rogers"

★ March

1. What actress known for her beauty (and many marriages) died at age seventy-nine in March 2011?
2. On March 3, 1999, Barbara Walters's interview of what woman drew 70 million viewers?
3. Actor Peter Graves, who died in March 2010, was best known for his role on what TV series that premiered in 1966?
4. What new product did the Apple company unveil in March 2011?
5. What politician testified before Congress in March 2007 about a "planetary emergency"?
6. Geraldine Ferraro, who died in March 2011, held what political distinction?
7. What was the distinction of "Do," who died March 26, 1997?
8. When Rielle Hunter said in March 2010, "The home was wrecked already," what politician's home was she speaking of?
9. What pop music legend told Michelle Obama in March 2010 that he was her husband's "number one fan"?
10. What boxing champ, imprisoned for three years on a moral charge, was released March 25, 1995?
11. What brief but famous video did George Holliday record on March 3, 1991?
12. What theme park opened in Carlsbad, California, in March 1999? (Hint: toys)
13. Country music star Julius Kuczynski, who died in March 2000, was better known by what "little" name?
14. What animated movie about a young Viking finding an unusual pet was released in March 2010?
15. *Let Freedom Ring*, a book about terrorism released in March 2004, is by what TV host?
16. What beloved TV comic of the 1950s died in March 2002 at age ninety-three?
17. TV icon Art Linkletter, who died in March 2010, is remembered for hosting what show?
18. What football player (and sportscaster and actor) died in March 2010?

1. Elizabeth Taylor
2. Monica Lewinsky
3. *Mission: Impossible*
4. The iPad 2
5. Al Gore
6. She was the first woman to run for the office of vice president (1988).
7. "Do" (born Marshall Applewhite) and his cult, known as Heaven's Gate, committed mass suicide.
8. John Edwards; Hunter was his mistress and was accused of being a home wrecker.
9. Stevie Wonder
10. Mike Tyson, who went on to fight again
11. The police beating of Rodney King
12. Legoland
13. Pee Wee King
14. *How to Train Your Dragon*
15. Sean Hannity
16. Milton Berle
17. *Kids Say the Darndest Things*
18. Merlin Olsen

★ April

1. In April 2009, Barack Obama caused controversy when he bowed to what monarch?
2. What Mexican food chain announced on April 1, 1996, that it had purchased the Liberty Bell?
3. What silver-haired actor, famed for his role in a nighttime soap opera, died in April 2010?
4. In April 2009, General Motors announced it was closing which division?
5. What religious leader drew a crowd of 47,000 in Washington in April 2008?
6. What Virginia college was the scene of a bloody shooting on April 16, 2007?
7. What automaker, based in Japan, was very much in the news in April 2010?
8. What outspoken radio broadcaster caused a ruckus in April 2007 due to his remarks about certain female athletes? (Hint: cowboy hat)
9. What controversial movie director asked in April 2008, "How did George Bush go from being an alcoholic bum to the most powerful figure in the world?"
10. What did Eric Harris and Dylan Klebold infamously do on April 20, 1999?
11. What leading man and hero of ancient movie epics died in April 2008?
12. What action movie based on Greek mythology was released in April 2010?
13. What controversial—and immensely popular—novel dealing with alternative biblical history was published in April 2003?
14. Complete the title of this TV game show that premiered in April 2001: *The _____ Link.*
15. The documentary movie *Expelled,* released in April 2008, deals with what ongoing religious controversy?
16. In April 2002, George W. Bush called for a ban on what controversial scientific activity?
17. What eighty-year-old former astronaut was cut from the TV show *Dancing with the Stars* in April 2010?
18. Evangelist David Wilkerson, who died in April 2011, was best known for what book?

1. The king of Saudi Arabia
2. Taco Bell; it was an April Fool's joke.
3. John Forsythe
4. Pontiac
5. Pope Benedict XVI
6. Virginia Tech, where a student killed thirty-two others before committing suicide
7. Toyota, thanks to recalls of some popular models
8. Don Imus
9. Oliver Stone
10. They killed a teacher and twelve fellow students in the Columbine High School massacre.
11. Charlton Heston
12. *Clash of the Titans*
13. *The Da Vinci Code*
14. *Weakest*
15. Evolution
16. Human cloning
17. Buzz Aldrin
18. *The Cross and the Switchblade*

★ May

1. In May 2002, who became the first president (or ex-president) to visit Communist Cuba?
2. What soap opera actress finally won an Emmy in May 1999—after nineteen nominations?
3. What golfing legend died in May 2002 at age eighty-nine?
4. What enemy's death did Barack Obama announce on May 1, 2011?
5. Who stated in May 2008 that he had quit playing golf because it seemed inappropriate while war was going on?
6. What sitcom set in Seattle aired its final episode on May 13, 2004?
7. What child star of the 1930s died in May 2011?
8. What reality TV show premiered on May 31, 2000? (Hint: tribes)
9. What heavy-breathing movie villain appeared on the cover of *Time* on May 9, 2005?
10. What long-running sitcom ended in May 1998 with the four main characters sent to jail?
11. What legendary singer-actor died in May 1998? (Hint: blue eyes)
12. In May 2011 it was announced that San Francisco residents would vote on banning what common surgical procedure? (Hint: baby boys)
13. What sultry star of 1980s TV said in May 2010, "Television has become predictable, vulgar, and nasty"?
14. What much-discussed "little blue pill" came on the market in May 1998?
15. What comic said in May 2008 that Hillary Clinton admired the Iranians because they stoned adulterers?
16. What multimillionaire movie director said in May 2007 that *Spider-Man 3* was just "a silly movie"?
17. What diminutive star of a popular 1980s sitcom died in May 2010?
18. What baseball legend, known as "Killer" because of his power hitting, died in May 2011?

★ June

1. In June 2000, what much-discussed child was sent back to Cuba?
2. What criminal, notorious for his bombing of a federal building, was executed in June 2001?

1. Jimmy Carter
2. Susan Lucci of *All My Children*
3. Sam Snead
4. Osama bin Laden
5. George W. Bush
6. *Frasier*
7. Jackie Cooper, who appeared in *The Champ, Treasure Island,* and other classics
8. *Survivor*
9. Darth Vader, of *Star Wars* fame
10. *Seinfeld*
11. Frank Sinatra
12. Circumcision
13. Joan Collins
14. Viagra
15. Jay Leno
16. George Lucas, creator of the *Star Wars* brand
17. Gary Coleman
18. Harmon Killebrew, also known as "Hammerin' Harmon"

1. Elian Gonzalez
2. Timothy McVeigh, perpetrator of the Oklahoma City bombing

QUESTIONS

3. What horror movie was released, appropriately, on 6-6-06?
4. What new Cabinet department did George W. Bush propose in June 2002?
5. What advice columnist, born Esther Lederer, died in June 2002?
6. In June 2001, what make of car (named for a colony) was discontinued?
7. On June 15, 2007, what silver-haired man did his last stint on a long-running game show?
8. In June 2010, Robert Byrd, the longest-serving U.S. senator, died. What state did he represent?
9. What 1960s music legend was given an honorary doctor of music degree in June 2004?
10. What Oscar-winning actress announced in June 2011 that she was home-schooling her children?
11. Edward Whitacre Jr., who said in June 2009, "I don't know anything about cars," had been named head of what corporation?
12. What Oscar-winning actress was arrested for drugs in June 2008 and claimed, "I was researching a part"?
13. What glamorous TV star and "poster girl" of the 1970s died of cancer in June 2009?
14. Jeff MacNelly, who died in June 2000, created what comic strip about a newspaper run by birds?
15. Robert Trent Jones, who died in June 2000, was famous for designing what?
16. What homespun singer and businessman died in June 2010? (Hint: sausage)
17. What was launched in June 2003 to give people some relief from telemarketers?

★ July

1. What New York landmark reopened its "crown" to visitors on July 4, 2009?
2. What son of a famous political family died in a plane crash in July 1999?
3. What millionaire became the first person to circle the world by balloon, solo, in July 2002?

3. *The Omen*, with its references to the Antichrist and the number 666
4. The Department of Homeland Security
5. Ann Landers
6. Plymouth
7. Bob Barker, host of *The Price Is Right*
8. West Virginia
9. Bob Dylan; the degree was awarded by Scotland's University of St. Andrews.
10. Angelina Jolie
11. General Motors
12. Tatum O'Neal
13. Farrah Fawcett
14. "Shoe"
15. Golf courses
16. Jimmy Dean
17. The National Do Not Call Registry

July // Answers

1. The Statue of Liberty, whose "crown" (viewing deck) had closed after the 9/11 attacks
2. John F. Kennedy Jr.
3. Steve Fossett

July, continued . . .

4. What venerable CBS news anchorman died in July 2009? (Hint: "That's the way it is.")
5. What author, best known for her horror novels, announced on July 29, 2010, "Today I quit being a Christian"?
6. What satellite radio network was launched on July 1, 2002?
7. What baseball legend died in July 2002—and was cryogenically frozen?
8. What singer performed at Shea Stadium in July 2008, the last event before it was demolished?
9. What beloved comedian died at age one hundred in July 2003? (Hint: ski slope nose)
10. What Internet retailer, originally named "Cadabra," was launched in July 1995?
11. In July 1995, the Walt Disney Company acquired what TV network for $19 billion?
12. What political commentator and press secretary for George W. Bush died of colon cancer in July 2008?
13. What pop singer (with no last name) said in July 2010, "The Internet's completely over"?
14. Who was dermatologist Arnold Klein referring to in July 2009 when he said, "No matter what Michael wanted, someone would give it"?
15. What "grumpy old" comic actor died July 1, 2000? (Hint: *Odd Couple*)
16. What Internet music service shut down in July 2001 following a court order?
17. What five-and-dime store chain shut down in July 1997, after being in business 120 years?
18. What rhythmic reality TV show debuted on the Fox network in July 2005?

★ August

1. Who broke Hank Aaron's home run record in August 2007?
2. The sunken submarine *H. L. Hunley,* raised from the ocean floor in August 2000, had belonged to what nation?
3. What long-term senator from a famous family died in August 2009?

4. Walter Cronkite
5. Anne Rice, who a few years earlier had announced she had become a Christian and would write novels about Jesus
6. Sirius
7. Ted Williams
8. Billy Joel
9. Bob Hope
10. Amazon; it was decided that "Cadabra" sounded too much like "cadaver."
11. ABC
12. Tony Snow
13. Prince (Actually, he *does* have a last name, but he doesn't use it professionally.)
14. Michael Jackson
15. Walter Matthau
16. Napster
17. The F. W. Woolworth Company
18. *So You Think You Can Dance?*

August // Answers

1. Barry Bonds
2. The Confederate States of America
3. Ted Kennedy

4. What natural disaster caused major devastation in August 2005?

5. What New York landmark reopened to visitors in August 2004?

6. The Restoring Honor rally in August 2010, hosted by broadcaster Glenn Beck, was held at what D.C. landmark? (Hint: muscles)

7. What actor-turned-politician gave a speech to the Republican convention in August 2004?

8. What politician was asked in August 2008 how many houses he owned— a question he could not answer?

9. What murderer of a pop music legend asked for parole in August 2008?

10. Ted Stevens, who died in a plane crash in August 2010, was a longtime senator from what state?

11. What one-contestant TV quiz show premiered in August 1999? (Hint: "Is that your *final* answer?")

12. Eunice Shriver, founder of the Special Olympics, died in August 2009. What political notable was her brother?

13. In August 2008, what swimmer broke Mark Spitz's record of seven Olympic gold medals?

14. What country music singer and actor died in August 2008? (Hint: cannonball)

15. Merv Griffin, who died in August 2007, created what two still-running TV game shows?

16. Don Hewitt, who died in August 2009, was the longtime producer of what Sunday night TV program?

17. Which two long-standing airlines announced their merger in August 2010?

18. What pop singer's death in 2009 was ruled a homicide by drug overdose in August 2010?

QUESTIONS

★ September

1. What historic baseball stadium held its last home game on September 21, 2008?

2. William Rosenberg, who died in September 2002, founded what food chain? (Hint: coffee)

4. Hurricane Katrina
5. The Statue of Liberty, which had closed after the 9/11 attacks; the "crown," however, did not reopen until 2009.
6. The Lincoln Memorial
7. Arnold Schwarzenegger
8. Presidential candidate John McCain, who owned seven houses
9. Mark Chapman, who had killed John Lennon; parole was denied.
10. Alaska
11. *Who Wants to Be a Millionaire?*
12. John F. Kennedy—and also Robert Kennedy and Ted Kennedy
13. Michael Phelps, who won eight
14. Jerry Reed
15. *Jeopardy* and *Wheel of Fortune*
16. *60 Minutes*
17. United and Continental
18. Michael Jackson's

September // Answers

1. Yankee Stadium—or, to be precise, the *old* Yankee Stadium, which was demolished in 2009, the year the new Yankee Stadium opened
2. Dunkin' Donuts

3. What much-used Web site was founded by Larry Page and his partners in September 1998?

4. In September 2009, what soap opera ended after airing for more than seven decades?

5. What Internet service provider, which once dominated the market, announced in September 2007 that it was becoming an advertising business?

6. What megachurch pastor and author accompanied George W. Bush on a visit to areas hit by Hurricane Katrina in September 2005?

7. What automaker introduced the first American-made hybrid vehicle in September 2004?

8. A September 2010 *Time* cover showed what large animal in a teacup?

9. What political leader lamented in September 2010, "They talk about me like a dog"?

10. What best-selling novel, set in Japan, was published in September 1997?

11. What controversial figure of the Vietnam War said in September 2009, "Not a day goes by that I do not feel remorse"?

12. Who said, in September 2008, "You can put lipstick on a pig, but it's still a pig"?

13. What group was Rudy Giuliani addressing in September 2007 when he answered a cell phone call from his wife? (Hint: bang)

14. What brassy political commentator was shown sticking his tongue out on the September 28, 2009, issue of *Time*?

15. What popular Dan Brown novel, published in September 2009, deals with the Freemasons?

16. What football legend died at age sixty-nine in September 2002?

17. What man associated with the impeachment of Bill Clinton became president of Baylor University in September 2010?

18. What environmental disaster was finally "sealed" in September 2010? (Hint: gulf)

3. Google

4. *The Guiding Light;* its seventy-two-year run included both TV and radio.

5. AOL (America Online)

6. T. D. Jakes, pastor of The Potter's House church in Dallas

7. Ford, which introduced the Escape SUV

8. An elephant; the cover story was about the Tea Party movement, and the elephant represented Republicans.

9. Barack Obama; "They" referred to Republicans.

10. *Memoirs of a Geisha* by Arthur Golden

11. William Calley, apologizing for the 1968 My Lai massacre

12. Barack Obama; many thought he was referring to candidate Sarah Palin.

13. The National Rifle Association

14. Glenn Beck; the cover story was titled "Mad Man."

15. *The Lost Symbol*

16. Johnny Unitas

17. Ken Starr

18. The BP oil spill in the Gulf of Mexico

★ October

1. What city and its metro area were terrorized by two snipers in October 2002?

2. In October 2007, what comic began hosting the long-running *The Price Is Right*?

3. What seventy-seven-year-old senator became, in October 1998, the oldest man in space?

4. Barbara Billingsley, who died in October 2010, was the adorable mom on what 1950s sitcom?

5. What Christian men's group drew thousands to D.C. with its Stand in the Gap rally in October 1997?

6. What multimillionaire said in October 2010, "If your culture doesn't like geeks, you're in real trouble"?

7. What much-criticized announcement was made on October 3, 2005, involving Harriet Miers?

8. Congress passed the Copyright Extension Act in October 1998. What singer-songwriter-congressman is it named for?

9. What movie about the origins of Facebook was released in October 2010?

10. The best-selling book *Culture Warrior*, published in October 2007, is by what TV political commentator? (Hint: No spin)

11. Tom Bosley, who died in October 2010, played the lovable dad in what sitcom set in the 1950s?

12. The popular book *Your Best Life Now*, published in October 2004, is by Joel Osteen, pastor of what huge church in Houston?

13. Steve Allen, who died October 31, 2000, was the first host of what late-night show?

14. What Internet money transfer Web site was purchased by eBay in October 2002?

15. Operation Enduring Freedom, launched in October 2001, refers to America's military involvement in what country?

16. What uniquely designed church in the Los Angeles area filed for bankruptcy in October 2010?

1. Washington, D.C.
2. Drew Carey
3. John Glenn, who was an astronaut before his Senate days
4. *Leave It to Beaver*
5. Promise Keepers
6. Bill Gates of Microsoft
7. George W. Bush announced her nomination to the Supreme Court. A ruckus ensued, and later that month the nomination was withdrawn.
8. Sonny Bono, one of the act's sponsors; he died shortly before it was passed.
9. *The Social Network*
10. Bill O'Reilly
11. *Happy Days*
12. Lakewood Church
13. *The Tonight Show*
14. PayPal
15. Afghanistan
16. The Crystal Cathedral

★ November

1. What notorious sniper was executed in November 2009?
2. In November 2004, Ken Jennings ended his amazing winning streak on what TV game show?
3. What Texas army base was the site of a shooting spree on November 5, 2009?
4. What state became notorious for its "hanging chads" in November 2000?
5. On a November 1998 *60 Minutes* segment, who ran a videotape of himself giving a man a lethal injection?
6. According to a November 2008 poll, what radio talk show host was said to be the most trusted news personality in America?
7. What political figure said, in a November 1995 press conference, "We all know the leopard can't change his stripes"?
8. The best-selling book *Decision Points*, published in November 2010, was by what ex-president?
9. What did Bobbi McCaughey of Iowa produce on November 19, 1997?
10. Who was Barack Obama addressing in November 2009 when he said, "I urge you to choose Chicago"?
11. What action movie legend said in November 2007, "War is natural. Peace is an accident"?
12. What Chicago Bears Hall of Famer died at age forty-five in November 1999?
13. What Bush Cabinet member stepped down in November 2006, saying, "I have benefitted greatly from criticism, and at no time have I suffered a lack"?
14. What forty-five-year-old, in November 1994, became the oldest man to win a boxing title?
15. What best-selling autobiography, published in November 2010, was written by an author who died in 1910? (Hint: bushy mustache)
16. In November 2002, Nancy Pelosi became the first woman to hold what federal office?
17. What Green Party presidential candidate drew 2.7 percent of the popular vote in November 2000?

1. John Allen Muhammad, one of the two snipers who targeted the D.C. area in 2002
2. *Jeopardy;* Jennings won seventy-four consecutive games.
3. Fort Hood
4. Florida, where numerous ballots were improperly punched, delaying the outcome of the presidential election
5. Jack Kevorkian, "Dr. Death," who was afterward charged with and convicted of homicide
6. Rush Limbaugh
7. Al Gore
8. George W. Bush
9. Septuplets
10. The International Olympic Committee; Obama tried unsuccessfully to lobby for Chicago as the site of the 2016 Olympics.
11. Sylvester Stallone
12. Walter Payton
13. Donald Rumsfeld
14. George Foreman, who knocked out heavyweight champion Michael Moorer in the tenth round
15. Mark Twain
16. Speaker of the House of Representatives
17. Ralph Nader

★ December

1. What former football player and actor was sent to Nevada's Lovelock prison in December 2008?
2. What TV evangelist (and university founder) died in December 2009?
3. What venerable department store chain announced its closing in December 2000?
4. What territory did the United States relinquish control of on December 31, 1999?
5. Umar Abdulmutallab was arrested on December 25, 2009, for concealing explosives in what location?
6. What movie comedy, set in the Depression South and based on Homer's *Odyssey,* premiered in December 2000?
7. What sports legend took a leave from his game in December 2009 in the wake of extramarital scandals?
8. What longtime enemy of the United States was executed by hanging on December 30, 2006?
9. Rod Blagojevich, arrested for federal corruption charges in December 2008, was governor of what state?
10. What baby-faced Internet millionaire was *Time* magazine's Person of the Year in December 2010?
11. What sobering but inspiring Steven Spielberg movie was released in December 1993?
12. Who shared with Bill Clinton the title "Men of the Year" on the December 28, 1998, cover of *Time?*
13. What foreign automaker's name was added to the Sun Bowl in December 2010?
14. What soul singer died on Christmas Day 2006? (Hint: Godfather)
15. What Western movie, a remake of a John Wayne classic, opened in December 2010?
16. Clayton Moore, who died in December 1999, was remembered for playing what masked Western hero?
17. What zany comic strip with a biblical name was launched in December 2001?
18. What movie director famous for his *Pink Panther* movies died in December 2010?

QUESTIONS

1. O. J. Simpson, who was sentenced to thirty-three years for robbery, kidnapping, and other felonies
2. Oral Roberts
3. Montgomery Ward (or "Monkey Ward," as it was colloquially known)
4. The Panama Canal
5. His underwear; his attempt to blow up Northwest Airlines Flight 253 failed, fortunately.
6. *O Brother, Where Art Thou?*
7. Tiger Woods
8. Saddam Hussein
9. Illinois
10. Mark Zuckerberg, founder of Facebook
11. *Schindler's List*
12. Special prosecutor Ken Starr
13. Hyundai
14. James Brown
15. *True Grit*
16. The Lone Ranger
17. "Pearls before Swine," by Stephan Pastis
18. Blake Edwards, husband of Julie Andrews